ENGLISH

STAREVIEW

WRITING FOR THE
COMPREHENSIVE TEST

Author:
Anne Coen McCabe

Editors:
Wayne Garnsey
Paul Stich
Judith Shuback – *Associate Editor*

N & N Publishing Company, Inc.
18 Montgomery Street   Middletown, New York 10940

www.nandnpublishing.com   email: nn4text@warwick.net
(800) NN4 TEXT

Dedication

Dedicated to Bill McCabe and Sister Grace Florian McInerney, each of whom taught me English and showed me how to teach effectively.

Special Credits

Thanks to my many colleagues who have contributed their knowledge, skills, and years of experience to making education vibrant.

Sincere thanks to these educators
for their assistance in the preparation of this manuscript:

Kathleen Corbett
Siobhan McCabe
William McCabe
Mary Joyce Michael
Barbara Searle

Reference

Top-rate references are most important to consistency in word use. We are grateful to the authors, editors, contributors, and publishers of this excellent resource: **The American Heritage Dictionary**© for fundamental definitions and appropriate word usage [available on CD-ROM through SoftKey Multimedia Inc, Cambridge, MA].

The grammatical conventions used in this *STAReview* are representative of those used on state Comprehensive Tests in English, specifically NYS.

© Copyright 2004
N & N Publishing Company, Inc.
18 Montgomery Street   Middletown, New York 10940
www.nandnpublishing.com   (800) NN4 TEXT   email: NN4TEXT@warwick.com

Paperback Edition: ISBN # 0-935487 81 6
1 2 3 4 5 6 7 8 9 0 BMP 2010 2009 2008 2007 2006 2005 2004

Printed in the United States of America, BookMart Press, NJ
SAN # 216 - 4221

TABLE OF CONTENTS

INTRODUCTION

This is a book about writing in its many facets. Although reading, writing, speaking, and listening are all forms of communication, writing is special. Writing is a skill which will provide constant enjoyment as does reading. Writing requires you to be more precise than speech, and writing has a permanence which speech and listening lack. Finally, writing provides you with the opportunity to craft your product in a way speech rarely does.

The aspects of writing which this book will explore will take you from the basic tools of language, through the steps of the writing process, to the honing of the writing piece as art, to the obligations which writing places upon the writer, and finally to the execution of writing in such a skilled manner that writing on this level will ensure your certification as a competent practitioner of the medium.

Writing is another way to activate the self. As such, it will always have elements of challenge in the task, frustration in the attempt at execution, and remarkable joy at success. Value writing as a way to enhance your understanding of others and yourself. Use this book to help you write better. The first section of the book involves the tedium of rules. However, these rules are necessary if all the speakers of the language are to increase the probability of clear communication. The second section provides the emerging writer with a process that will increase focus and ease the burden of seeking a path from task to product. The third section stresses the unique style of each writer and suggests ways of perfecting this style. The fourth section stresses the implicit agreement that all writers must respect: the need to truthfully address and incorporate the ideas of others. Finally, the book puts you in the driver's seat and steers you toward the completion of state certification as a competent writer.

Read, write, listen, speak, enjoy the language and the chance to communicate. Enjoy this book and make it work for you. May all the goodness and joy of life that writing may help you secure be yours.

• • • • • • • • • • • • • • • • • • •

MEANING OF THE ☆

Stars ☆ are reminders of important material, identifiers of special procedures or methods, or perhaps "hints" to help put you on the "right path."

Stars ☆ also give the student additional information making total understanding better.

UNIT ONE
TOOLS OF WRITING

The first thing to understand is that there are eight essential types of words. They are called the eight **parts of speech** and they are classifications of words based on how they are used in sentences. The next section will review key ideas about verbs, nouns, pronouns, adjectives, adverbs, prepositions, conjunctions, and interjections.

CHAPTER ONE: VERBS – THE ACTION WORDS

If you were creating a new language, you would need certain jobs to be done. You would need words to show action and ways of existing; these are the English verbs. Writing relies on words doing jobs. The key jobs express existence and activity. The words which express a way of existing and action are called **verbs**. Verbs are the only words which can act as **simple predicates** – those words which convey the central action or way of existing of a noun or pronoun.

A verb can be **conjugated** – put into a pattern showing how it changes spelling as it accompanies the first, second, and third person singular and plural pronouns. It is important to recognize verbs because you need to recognize predicates.

Verbs can indicate:	
Tense	time
Number	singular or plural
Person	who or what experiences the action as evidenced by **first person** (the speaker), **second person** (the one spoken to), or **third person** (the one spoken about)
Mood	one of three attitudes is conveyed about the action: **indicative** (stating), **imperative** (commanding or requesting), or **subjunctive** (speculation of some sort)
Voice	informs as to whether the subject is doing (**active voice**) or receiving the predicate action (**passive voice**)

The verb "to be" is a key **linking verb** – a verb that expresses a way of being (to be), a way of relating to the senses (to see), or a way of indicating a condition rather than an activity (to become). Here are some other commonly used verbs which are often linking verbs:

appear	feel	look	smell	stay
become	grow	remain	sound	taste
		seem		

Get used to seeing the verb "to be" in all its forms so that you can always recognize it as a verb. The **infinitive form** is the "to" form of the verb (such as "to be").

When conjugated in the **present tense**, the verb relates <u>action which is happening now</u> (e.g., "He sneezes."), something habitual (e.g., "He works for that company also."), and discussion of plots in literary discussions (e.g., "The wolf eats the grandmother and waits for Red to come.").

Present Tense		
<u>Singular</u>		<u>Plural</u>
I **am**	1st person	we **are**
you **are**	2nd person	you **are**
he **is** she **is** it **is**	3rd person	they **are**

Conjugating a verb in the **past tense** allows you to express <u>action(s) occurring earlier than now</u>.

Past Tense		
<u>Singular</u>		<u>Plural</u>
I **was**	1st person	we **were**
you **were**	2nd person	you **were**
he **was** she **was** it **was**	3rd person	they **were**

Conjugating a verb in the **future tense** <u>allows you to speak of events yet to come</u>.

Future Tense		
<u>Singular</u>		<u>Plural</u>
I **will be**	1st person	we **will be**
you **will be**	2nd person	you **will be**
he **will be** she **will be** it **will be**	3rd person	they **will be**

There are three more tenses in English.

The **present perfect tense** allows you to express an action or way of existing that <u>began in the past and continues to the present</u>. It is conjugated by using the **past participle** – the part of the verb that shows the past with the word "has" (singular) or "have" (plural).

Present Perfect Tense		
<u>Singular</u>		<u>Plural</u>
I **have been**	1st person	we **have been**
you **have been**	2nd person	you **have been**
he **has been** she **has been** it **has been**	3rd person	they **have been**

The **past perfect tense** allows you to express an action or a way of existing that <u>occurred before another past action</u> (e.g., "She had studied, so she did well on the test."). When conjugated, the past perfect tense combines the form showing the past tense of the verb and the word "had" (the past tense of "to have").

Past Perfect Tense		
<u>Singular</u>		<u>Plural</u>
I **had been**	1st person	we **had been**
you **had been**	2nd person	you **had been**
he **had been** she **had been** it **had been**	3rd person	they **had been**

Future Perfect Tense		
<u>Singular</u>		<u>Plural</u>
I **shall have been**	1st person	we **shall have been**
you **will have been**	2nd person	you **will have been**
he **will have been** she **will have been** it **will have been**	3rd person	they **will have been**

The **future perfect tense** allows you to express an action or way of existing that <u>will be finished before a certain time in the future</u>. It is conjugated by using the word "shall" for the first person ("will" to indicate the second and third persons) and by adding "have" plus the past participle.

Note that the proper construction is "will have," "should have," "would have," and "could have." (These are sometimes contracted to be "should've," "would've," and "could've.")

EXERCISE 1A - TENSE

Directions: For each item, choose the proper tense of the verb "to be."

Example: By my next birthday, I will have been working here three years.

1   He had _____ my friend first and then I met Paul, and we all have _____ friends ever since.

2   Last year, I _____ the winner of the contest.

3   We _____ ___ the only people at the prom next week who know how to dance well.

4   They _____ here now, but tomorrow they _____ ___ in Vermont at the state fair.

5   He __ the instructor now; many years ago in grammar school he ____ _____ a student of judo and last year in college he____ merely an assistant to the instructor.

As you can see, the verb "to be" is highly **inflected** (changes its spelling often) as it moves through the tenses. The reason is that "to be" is an **irregular** verb. These verbs are sometimes called "strong verbs." They trace their intense inflection back to the early roots of the English language. Irregular verbs can present a problem for both new and experienced speakers of English.

On the pages that follow is a list of some commonly used irregular verbs with which you need to be familiar. A good way to memorize them is to make a short sentence using each form (e.g., "Today I eat. Yesterday I ate. By last week I had eaten all the candy in the house.") The infinitive form is first, so you can be clear as to the verb with which you are working.

Infinitive	Present	Past	Past Participle (uses some form of the verb "to have")
to be	am	was	been
to bear	bear	bore	borne
to beat	beat	beat	beaten
to become	become	became	become
to begin	begin	began	begun
to bend	bend	bent	bent
to bet	bet	bet	bet
to bite	bite	bit	bitten
to bleed	bleed	bled	bled
to blow	blow	blew	blown
to break	break	broke	broken
to breed	breed	bred	bred
to bring	bring	brought	brought
to build	build	built	built
to burst	burst	burst	burst
to buy	buy	bought	bought
to catch	catch	caught	caught
to choose	choose	chose	chosen
to creep	creep	crept	crept
to cut	cut	cut	cut
to dig	dig	dug	dug
to dive	dive	dived (or dove)	dived
to do	do	did	done
to draw	draw	drew	drawn
to drink	drink	drank	drunk
to drive	drive	drove	driven
to eat	eat	ate	eaten
to fall	fall	fell	fallen
to feed	feed	fed	fed
to feel	feel	felt	felt
to fight	fight	fought	fought
to find	find	found	found
to fit	fit	fit	fit
to flee	flee	fled	fled
to fly	fly	flew	flown
to forget	forget	forgot	forgotten
to forgive	forgive	forgave	forgiven
to freeze	freeze	froze	frozen
to get	get	got	gotten
to give	give	gave	given
to go	go	went	gone
to grind	grind	ground	ground
to grow	grow	grew	grown

Infinitive	Present	Past	Past Participle (uses some form of the verb "to have")
to hang	hang	hung	hung (used with things)
to hang	hang	hanged	hanged (used with people)
to have	have	had	had
to hear	hear	heard	heard
to hit	hit	hit	hit
to hold	hold	held	held
to hurt	hurt	hurt	hurt
to keep	keep	kept	kept
to know	know	knew	known
to lay	lay	laid	laid (to place)
to lead	lead	led	led
to leave	leave	left	left
to lend	lend	lent	lent
to leap	leap	leapt	leapt
to let	let	let	let
to lie	lie	lay	lain (to recline)
to lose	lose	lost	lost
to make	make	made	made
to mean	mean	meant	meant
to meet	meet	met	met
to pay	pay	paid	paid
to put	put	put	put
to quit	quit	quit	quit
to read	read	read	read
to ride	ride	rode	ridden
to ring	ring	rang	rung
to rise	rise	rose	risen
to run	run	ran	run
to say	say	said	said
to see	see	saw	seen
to sell	sell	sold	sold
to send	send	sent	sent
to set	set	set	set
to shake	shake	shook	shaken
to shed	shed	shed	shed
to shine	shine	shone (or shined)	shone (or shined)
to shoot	shoot	shot	shot
to shut	shut	shut	shut
to sing	sing	sang	sung
to sink	sink	sank (or sunk)	sunk
to sit	sit	sat	sat
to slay	slay	slew	slain
to sleep	sleep	slept	slept

Infinitive	Present	Past	Past Participle (uses some form of the verb "to have")
to slide	slide	slid	slid
to slit	slit	slit	slit
to speak	speak	spoke	spoken
to speed	speed	sped	sped
to spend	spend	spent	spent
to spin	spin	spun	spun
to spread	spread	spread	spread
to spring	spring	sprang (or sprung)	sprung
to stand	stand	stood	stood
to steal	steal	stole	stolen
to stink	stink	stank (or stunk)	stunk
to strike	strike	struck	struck
to strive	strive	strove (or strived)	striven (or strived)
to swear	swear	swore	sworn
to sweep	sweep	swept	swept
to swim	swim	swam	swum
to swing	swing	swung	swung
to take	take	took	taken
to teach	teach	taught	taught
to tear	tear	tore	torn
to tell	tell	told	told
to think	think	thought	thought
to throw	throw	threw	thrown
to thrust	thrust	thrust	thrust
to understand	understand	understood	understood
to wake	wake	woke	woken
to wear	wear	wore	worn
to weave	weave	wove	woven
to win	win	won	won
to wind	wind	wound	wound
to write	write	wrote	written

Some spelling irregularities of certain verbs which adhere to the same spelling rule as nouns ending in "y" should be reviewed. This is the rule: if a singular noun ends in "y" and the "y" is preceded by a consonant, change the "y" to an "i" and add "es." Some verbs also change their infinitive "y" to an "i" and add "es" when the "y" is preceded by a consonant. Verbs in the third person singular – present tense become the following in the past tense:

"to cry" becomes "he cried"
"to fry" becomes "he fried"
"to pry" becomes "he pried"
"to try" becomes "he tried"

Now see if you can actually use these irregular verbs in the proper form in sentences.

EXERCISE 1B – VERB FORM

Directions: For each item, place the proper form of the verb in the blank. Be sure to spell the form appropriately.

Example: I <u>spoke</u> (to speak) too soon.

1 I _____ (to help) my mother often, but today I shall _____ (to flee) the city and spend some time relaxing with my friends.

2 I _____ (to hear) the news about the accident from my friend, so I _____ (to leave) the party.

3 He _____ (to shake) his fist at me, yet I had _____ (to do) nothing to annoy him.

4 I _____ (to lose) my shoe in that mud, and the muck was so deep that the shoe _____ (to sink) and was completely covered.

5 I _____ (to quit) that job because the boss _____ (to accuse) me of stealing from the company.

6 After you have _____ (to feed) the cat, _____ (to slide) the key under the door.

7 He _____ (to try) to be funny, but I have never _____ (to understand) his silly jokes.

8 When was that poem about war _____ (to write)?

9 Tanya _____ (to wind) up that music box too tightly; I think she _____ (to break) it.

10 He _____ (to swing) at that pitch, but I think he should have _____ (to hold) the bat still and waited for the next ball.

11 I _____ (to choose) my lab partner already, but I don't know when Bill will _____ (to choose) his lab partner.

12 After the bell had _____ (to ring), she _____ (to teach) the class how to lead the band, and I _____ (to lead) it first.

13 I _____ (to meet) him at that party when he_____ (to pry) open that bottle with his grandfather's false teeth.

14 She has been _____ (to bite) by a dog.

15 Will you _____ (to read) that book to the toddler so that I can put away the toys that he has _____ (to take) out and left on the floor?

16 He _____ (to leap) up and _____ (to run) for the door as soon as she opened it.

17 After the knight _____ (to slay) the dragon, he _____ (to hide) under the dragon's tail until the evil ogress left.

18 I had _____ (to forgive) him for his insults, but he still _____ (to fight) with me anyway.

19 You would have _____ (to pay) for that work when they gave you a bill.

20 He _____ (to bring) the disc he had _____ (to buy) last week.

Reminder: In English the sign of the third person singular is almost always "s." This "s" in the third person singular applies even for irregular verbs. However, the "s" does not show up in the third person plural.

Example: "to walk"

singular	plural
I walk	we walk
you walk	you walk
he walk<u>s</u>	they walk
she walk<u>s</u>	
it walk<u>s</u>	

Example: "to try"

singular	plural
I try	we try
you try	you try
he trie<u>s</u>	they try
she trie<u>s</u>	
it trie<u>s</u>	

This is a strange idea for English because "s" is almost always a sign of plural when it is added to a noun.

The most important fact to remember about verbs is that they are the most lively action words of the language. Verbs speak of happening and existing. Good writing uses vivid verbs which clearly picture an activity. When presented with a writing task, you will choose words to form your word picture. Verbs will help you think more clearly and write with greater power.

CHAPTER TWO:
NOUNS AND PRONOUNS – THE NAMERS
NOUNS: THE MAIN NAMERS

If you were creating a language, after deciding on words that would indicate existence and activity, you would probably need words which name. In English, there are two parts of speech which name: nouns and pronouns.

Nouns are words which name people, places, things, and ideas. **Pronouns** are words which take the place of nouns, so they too are words which name. If you select your nouns with great care, you should make a clearer picture.

Take some time to review some basic rules about using nouns.

1   **Proper nouns**, which name particular persons, places, things, and ideas, must be capitalized. **Common nouns**, which name other than particular people, places, things, and ideas, are not capitalized unless they begin sentences, are in titles, or are the first entries in formal outlines.
Example: My friend John (proper noun) is a man (common noun).

The capitalization of some nouns causes a great deal of confusion.

a   Do not capitalize "mother," "father," "sister," "brother," "grandfather," or "grandmother" unless you could appropriately substitute the name of your relative in the sentence.
Examples: My mother is a nurse. / May I use the car, Mother?

b   Do not capitalize the name "elementary school," "high school, middle school," "college," or "university" unless it is part of the full name being given.
Example: I went to high school at Oceanside High School.

c   Do not capitalize "freshman (men)," "sophomore," "junior," or "senior."

d Do not capitalize the compass directions unless they refer to an area of the country.
Example: I went south on Main Street to begin my trip to the South.

e Capitalize all languages, but do not capitalize general subjects.
Example: I like all languages, but I love English.

2 The **possessive**, ownership form, of nouns is indicated by an apostrophe.

a Use an apostrophe followed by an "s" to form the possessive of singular nouns not ending in "s."
Examples: Adelle's dress is very stylish. / One hour's work pays little.

b Use just an apostrophe after the "s" of a singular noun ending in "s" in order to avoid an unpleasant "s" sound.
Example: Moses' friend was very faithful to him.

c For plural forms of nouns, write the plural form (regular or irregular) and add an " 's" unless the plural ends in "s." If the plural form ends in "s," just add an apostrophe.
Examples: This is the women's gym, but next door is the girls' gym. / These are the six mice's nests, but those are the two cats' footprints.

d A **compound noun**, a noun composed of two or more words, follows the above rules and applies them to the last word of the compound.
Example: That is my mother-in-law's house, but it is built within United States' territory.

e If two nouns own something jointly, the apostrophe is placed on the last mentioned.
Example: Maeve and Mada's book took them more than three years to write.

f If a noun comes before a gerund (verbal noun ending in -ing), use the possessive case if the gerund is the focus of what you are talking about.
Examples: We loved our brother Fred, but we never enjoyed Fred's singing. / Even though we love all music, we never liked Fred, so we even disliked Fred singing.

g Be careful not to mistake the possessive of a noun or pronoun for the noun or pronoun itself. If this occurs, it is easy to create a confusing sentence.
Example: ~~Magda's smile is her key to opening all doors.~~ WRONG: There is no word for "her" to replace because Magda is in the possessive case. CORRECT: Magda's smile is Magda's key to opening all doors.

NO PERMISSION HAS BEEN GRANTED BY N&N PUBLISHING COMPANY, INC TO REPRODUCE ANY PART OF THIS BOOK

3   **Nouns** may be singular (one) or plural (more than one). There are some helpful rules regarding how to form the plural of nouns, but considering the number of exceptions and the fact that English words come from so many other languages, the best advice is to look in the dictionary for the spelling of the plural form of any noun about which you are not certain.

a   Most nouns simply add an "s" to make the plural form.
Example: one orange / two oranges

b   Form the plural of nouns ending in "s," "sh," "ch," and "x" by adding "es" to the word.
Examples: one class / two classes; one thrush / two thrushes; one church / two churches; one fox / two foxes

c   The plural of nouns ending in "y" following a consonant (any letter other than "a," "e," "i," "o," "u") is formed by changing the "y" to an "i" and adding "es."
Example: one lady / two ladies

d   The plural of nouns ending in "y" following a **vowel**, ("a," "e," "i," "o," "u") is formed by simply adding "s" to the singular word.
Example: one monkey / two monkeys

e   The plural of nouns ending in "o" following a **consonant** is formed by adding "es," unless the word refers to music.
Examples: one tomato / two tomatoes – but – one solo / two solos

f   The plural of nouns ending in "o" following a **vowel** is formed by adding "s."
Example: one radio / two radios

g   The plural of nouns ending in "ful" is formed by adding "s" to the "ful."
Example: one handful / two handfuls

h   The plural of compound nouns is formed by making the key part of the compound plural.
Examples: mothers-in-law / attorneys-general / passersby
(Note: Passersby used to be a compound noun and keeps the "s" at the end of "passer.")

i   The plural of numbers and letters and words used as examples is formed by adding an apostrophe and an "s."
Examples: He got three "A's" on his card. / He used seven "and's" when he gave his speech. (Note: This is the **only** time that the apostrophe is used to signal the plural form.)

j   Some nouns remain the same in singular and plural form.
Examples: one deer / two deer; one sheep / two sheep

k   Some nouns retain their plural as it was formed in the language from which the word originally was taken.
Examples: alumnus (one male) / alumni (group with at least one man)
        alumna (one female) / alumnae (all women in group)
        datum (one) / data (more than one)
        analysis (one) / analysis (more than one)
        bacterium (one) / bacteria (more than one)
        crisis (one) / crises (more than one)

l   **Collective nouns** are nouns which refer to a group and are sometimes singular and sometimes plural depending on whether the group is acting as one unit or is viewed as individuals operating separately.
Examples: The team were disagreeing about which of the several players should be captain. / The team was awarded the victory.

m   Some nouns are singular but end in "s."
Examples: mathematics / measles / mumps / economics / physics

n   Some nouns are always plural.
Examples: scissors / trousers / clothes

o   Although some nouns ending in "f" or "fe" change the "f" or "fe" to "v" and add "es," others do not. These words are best learned by using a dictionary the first time you use them.
Examples: His **beliefs** about how to raise children are not impressive to me because he acts as if he were raised by **wolves**. My **belief** is that even the average **wolf** should know better than to behave the way he does. /
You can all see for **yourselves** that a cat does not have nine **lives**, but only one **life** just as I **myself** have. So you should not let your cat jump off that **cliff** or any other **cliffs**.

Now see how well you have mastered these rules about nouns.

EXERCISE 2A – NOUN USE

Directions: For each item, choose the appropriate word to complete the sentence.

Example: Mathematics (is) (are) an interesting subject.

1   (Ben and Adelle's) (Ben's and Adelle's) house is the only blue one on the block.
2   Physics (is) (are) a course that requires much concentration.
3   It was that (man dancing) (man's dancing) which started the applause.
4   He used to raise (turkeys) (turkies), but now he (trys) (tries) to raise geese.
5   Her (sister-in-law's) (sister's-in-law) recipe is the tastiest.
6   The (passerbys) (passersby) stopped to look at the strange statue.
7   As a (Sophomore) (sophomore), Taisha attended (Middletown High School) (Middletown high school).
8   I used to live in the (West) (west), but we moved to the (East) (east) last year.
9   His clothes (is) (are) all dirty from that mud.
10 Give (Mom) (mom) a hand with that laundry.
11 The Bill of Rights lists the rights which constitute my (beliefs) (believes).
12 The (children's) (childrens') reading room in the library was closed.
13 Yuna put two (handfuls) (handsful) of flour into the bowl.
14 He sells (pianoes) (pianos) for a living.
15 After two (hours') (hour's) (hours) work, he had made enough to go to the movies.
16 We read all six pages of (data) (datum) before we formed a theory.
17 The (babies) (babys) were placed in the nursery shortly after birth.
18 We study (English) (english) and (Mathematics) (mathematics).
19 The jury reached (their) (its) verdict.
20 We listened to (Aidan's singing) (Aidan singing).

PRONOUNS: SUBSTITUTE NAMERS

Pronouns provide for smooth **transitions** (passage from one idea to another). By using pronouns, you avoid unnecessary repetition of the nouns which pronouns replace. But, you must be careful to be clear, and if there is any confusion in using the pronoun rather than the noun, the noun must be used to avoid jarring the reader's focus on your writing.

However, since pronouns are highly inflected (changed in spelling to indicate a change in job, number, or gender), you have to review some basic pronoun rules.

Be sure to make your pronouns agree in **number** (singular and plural) and gender (male and female) with the **antecedent** (the word the pronoun is replacing).

In regard to whether the masculine or feminine third person pronoun should be used when speaking of both males and females, the grammatical answer is that the masculine pronoun is always correct. However, there is nothing wrong with using both (he or she) to be sensitive to all. Sensitivity to

Indefinite Pronouns	
Singular	ends in "-one," "-body," "thing" (such as "someone,..."), also "each," "either," "neither," and "another"
Plural	"both," "several," "many," "few"
Singular or Plural	"all," "any," "most," "none," "some" (These depend on the sentence to make clear whether singular or plural should be used.)

others might enhance the impact of the message you intend to send, and **sexism**, an attitude or conduct based on stereotyping sexual roles and abilities, will never end unless people consciously attempt to end it.

Now try some sentences, and see if you have mastered the right use of the indefinite pronouns.

EXERCISE 2B – PRONOUNS – PREDICATE AGREEMENT
Directions: For each item, choose the proper word.

Example: Everyone must bring (<u>his or her</u>) (their) lunch.

1   Someone has left (his or her) (their) books at home today.

2   Each member of the class must use (his or her) (their) protractor when working on the geometry problems.

3   All of the pie (has) (have) been eaten.

4   Several of the students (has) (have) given blood in order to ease the shortage.

5   Most of the performers (was) (were) professional actors.

6   Some damage from pollution (is) (are) reversible.

7   Everyone on the team should order (his or her) (their) tickets today.

8   Both (is) (are) correct.

9   Many of the rights we fought for (is) (are) endangered now.

10 Anything that (violate) (violates) our Constitution should be abolished.

☆ CAPSULE – SINGULAR OR PLURAL

Reminder: An interesting but confusing language fact is demonstrated by example 10; notice that the third person singular of an English verb in the present tense ends in "-s," while the third person plural does not (for example, "he helps," but "they help" or "he is," but "they are"). This is confusing since you are used to seeing "-s" as a sign of the plural for nouns. If you were learning English as a second language, this illogical use of language might cause you to have difficulty in using the third person singular of verbs.

"She runs."   *"They run."*
(Caution: an "s" does not always indicate plural.)

Reminder: The conjunction (word that joins) "and" creates a plural situation because joining one thing to another thing results in at least two things. However, the conjunctions "or" and "nor" may present a problem if they join one singular thing and one plural thing (eg. one man or two men). In such a situation, choose the verb form based on which noun or pronoun is closest to the simple predicate (main action or way of existing of a group of words).

For example, in the sentence, "One large man or two small men easily fit on this couch," the verb is "fit" because the plural "men" is closest to the simple predicate. However, if the sentence reads, "Two small men or one large man," the sentence is completed by saying "easily fits on this couch." In this second example, the singular "man" is closest to the simple predicate.

(Note: See page 30 for more on conjunctions.)

Before leaving this pronoun review, you should consider case (the form of the word which reflects the job of the word in the sentence).

There are three pronoun cases in English:

nominative – the case used for the subject
objective – the case that receives the action
possessive – the case that shows ownership

These cases change the spelling of the **personal pronouns** (those pronouns used to refer to people). These pronouns exist in singular and plural forms and in first person (the speaker), second person (the spoken to), and third person (the spoken about) forms.

Nominative Case		
Singular		Plural
I	1st person	we
you	2nd person	you
he she it	3rd person	they

Objective Case		
Singular		Plural
me	1st person	us
you	2nd person	you
him her it	3rd person	them

Reminder: None of the possessive pronouns use an apostrophe!

Singular	Possessive Case	
my or mine		Plural
your or yours	1st person	our or ours
his	2nd person	your or yours
her or hers its	3rd person	their or theirs

Here are some rules in regard to using pronouns.

1 Use the nominative case for the **subject** (noun or pronoun "doing" the predicate) of a **clause** (group of words which includes both a subject and a predicate).
Examples: I went. / Bill and I went.

(One trick that often works with a compound subject or **object** [receiver of the action of the predicate] is to cover one part of the compound and read the sentence. For example, "I went," instead of "Bill and I went.")

2 Use the nominative case following any part of the verb "to be."
Examples: It will be **she** who wins. / It is I. / It might have been **he.**

3 Use the possessive case before a gerund as with a noun in that position.
Example: **His** listening to her speak was a first because he is usually very rude.

4 Use the nominative case in a comparison using "than" or "as" when the pronoun is the subject of an implied statement.
Examples: He is as tall as I. ("...am tall" is implied.) / Marisa is taller than **he.** ("...is tall" is implied.)

5 Use the objective case in a comparison using "than" or "as" when the pronoun is the object.
Example: He likes her better than **me.** ("...better than he likes me" is implied.)

6 When a pronoun is renaming a noun as in a subject complement, the pronoun should be in the same case as the noun.
Example: The new patriots are **we** who speak up in defense of the Constitution.

7 Pronouns that rename nouns are in the same case as the nouns.
Example: He gave the ribbons to **us** swimmers.

8 Choose the case of the pronoun "who" based on what job is being done in the clause.
Examples: Jody is the one **who** will win. ("Who" is the subject in the clause "who will win.") / Jody is the woman **whom** I will choose. ("Whom" is the object in the clause "whom I will choose.") / **Whose** hat is that? ("Whose" shows possession, as in belonging to whom.)

9 The pronoun "which" should never be used to designate people.

10 The pronoun "that" can be used to refer to people but some form of "who" is usually preferable.

11 Avoid using any form of the pronoun "you" unless giving instructions, or writing a letter, memo, or note. This is a powerful pronoun and will often divert the reader's attention because he or she feels personally alerted.

12 Avoid the pronouns ending in "self" or "selves" if possible. They are very self-involved and will create a pompous tone unless they are essential.
Example: I saw **myself** in the mirror. (good use) / He gave some to my brother and myself. (sounds a bit pompous)

13 Use "I" if necessary when writing; however, if "I" can be omitted and the same effect achieved, then omit "I."
Example: I think that the author provided evidence. ("I think that" is unnecessary.)

14 Do not change personal pronouns within one sentence.
Examples: CORRECT: The way **you** act is often the result of **your** experience. / WRONG: The way you act is often the result of one's experience.

15 Use the objective case for objects of prepositions.
Examples: That is a matter for discussion between **me** and **her**. / She gave the book to **him**.

EXERCISE 2C – PRONOUN USE

Directions: For each item, choose the proper word and either circle it in the book or write it on a piece of paper.

Example: Did you decide (whom) (who) you like best?

1 It must have been (her) (she) on the phone this morning.

2 Ashwin is taller than (she) (her).

3 Tony gave my sister and (me) (I) (myself) two movie tickets.

4 "It is (I) (me)," she said when she answered the phone.

5 I will give this to (whoever) (whomever) asks first.

6 Ted and (me) (I) intend to go tomorrow.

7   Serena plays as well as (I) (me).

8   (We) (Us) players will win today.

9   The choices you make in life will often result in (one's) (your) success or failure.

10 Juan and (I) (me) agreed to finish the job.

11 Miranda is the girl for (which) (who) (whom) I voted.

12 Give that package to Jody and (he) (him).

13 This is between you and (I) (me).

14 President John F. Kennedy gave the medals to (we) (us) astronauts.

15 You should choose (whoever) (whomever) will work hardest.

16 We objected to (him) (his) stealing the election through trickery.

17 She is no more a thief than (I) (me).

18 The dog lost (it's) (its) collar.

19 Is that (they're) (their) (there) dog?

20 Was (him) (his) leaving a result of that fight?

CHAPTER THREE:

ADJECTIVES AND ADVERBS – THE MODIFIERS

ADJECTIVES: MODIFIERS OF NAMERS

If you were creating a language, you would need to make the words as clear as possible. **Modifiers** help to distinguish words. The **adjective** (a word which modifies a noun or pronoun) should be used to make clear the answer to one of these questions about a noun or pronoun:

Which one?
What kind?
How many?

As with verbs and nouns, adjectives should be carefully chosen for their greatest impact and precision. Excellent adjectives can be formed from verbs; these adjectives are called **participles** (a word made from a verb but used as an adjective).

Here are some rules about adjectives.

1   Most adjectives can be compared. There are three degrees of adjectives: positive ("cold"), comparative ("colder" or "more cold"), and superlative ("coldest" or "most cold").

2   No adjective may be compared by using both a suffix ("-er" or "-est") and the word "more" or "most."
Examples: Either cold**er** or **more cold** is fine as are cold**est** and **most cold**, but "more colder" and "most coldest" are always wrong.

3   Some adjectives form their comparative and superlative degree in an irregular way. To be sure about these, check your dictionary.
Examples:

Adjectives: Irregular Degrees of Comparison		
Positive	Comparative	Superlative
bad	worse	worst
far	farther	farthest
		(distance measured physically)
far	further	furthest
		(a greater extent; an advanced point)
good	better	best
ill	worse	worst
little	less	least
many	more	most
well	better	best

4   Some adjectives have no comparison: circular, dead, perfect, square, unique. (Again, check your dictionary if you are uncertain.)

5   The **comparative degree** is used to compare **two** things. If **three or more** things are being compared, the **superlative degree** is required.
Example: Jason ran farther than Hyun-Jun, but of the three people running, Yunhee ran the farthest.

6   When comparing, it is important to make clear how the thing or person relates to what is being compared.
Example: He is taller than any **other** member of the team. (We must make clear that he is also on the team.)

7   Only like things can be compared.
Example: ~~Pedro's record was better than Phil's school.~~
The example is WRONG. We cannot compare a record time and a school.
CORRECT: Because Pedro trained for many hours, his record time was better than that of Phil's school.

8   Use a comma between two consecutive adjectives if the word "and" would sound right between them.
Example: He was a sensitive, creative man.

9   Use the adjective "a" before a consonant sound and "an" before a vowel sound.
Examples: a dog / an apple / an heir

EXERCISE 3A – ADJECTIVES

Directions: For each item, choose the correct word.

Example: That dog is (<u>dead</u>) (the deadest dog).

1   Of the two men, Emmanuel is by far the (tallest) (taller).

2   Give Tom (a) (an) eighth of the estate because he is (a) (an) heir.

3   The prom was the (most perfect) (more perfect) (perfect) end to the year.

4   He was (more nearer) (nearer) my age than yours.

5   The (old Irish man) (old, Irish man) greeted us at the airport.

6   This recording of the Beatles is better (than the Monkeys.)(than that of the Monkeys.)

7   This is the (most unique) (unique) idea of the century.

8   Of all the men I know, Bill is the (most) (more) intelligent.

9   Yves studied the problem (farther) (further) than I.

10   This is the (worse) (worst) head cold I have ever had.

 CAPSULE – ADJECTIVES
Reminder: Use adjectives only when necessary to make clear which one, what kind, or how many regarding a noun or pronoun. Choose adjectives carefully. Try using participles which add to the adjective form the power of the verbs from which they come.

Now take a quick look at the other part of speech which modifies: the adverb.

ADVERBS: MODIFYING ADJECTIVES, VERBS, AND ADVERBS

The **adverb** modifies or makes clear three parts of speech, each of which is suggested by the name "adverb": **adjectives**, <u>**verbs**</u>, and other **adverbs**. The adverb answers one of these questions about adjectives, verbs, and other adverbs:

When?	To what extent?
Where?	How?

Adverbs have the same three degrees of comparison as adjectives. The comparative is formed by adding "-er" to the ending or by using the word "more."

As with an adjective, never use both "-er" and "more" together. The superlative form is made by adding "-est" to the end of the adverb or by using "most." Never use both "-est" and "most."

"No," "not," "never," "hardly," "scarcely" are all adverbs; so, although many adverbs end in "-ly," not all do. If there is any question about how an adverb is to be spelled, check your dictionary. Here are some rules to remember:

1 Avoid using a suffix in addition to "more" or "most" in comparing adverbs.

2 Use the comparative for two and the superlative for three or more things.

3 Do not use an adverb when an adjective is required. (Adjectives modify nouns and pronouns, but adverbs do not.)

4 Do not use an adjective when an adverb is required. (Adverbs modify adjectives, verbs, and other adverbs.)

5 Do not use double negatives such as "~~He hardly never steals.~~" / He never steals.

 CAPSULE – ADVERBS

Reminder: When you use "No," at the beginning of the sentence and place a comma after it, you avoid a double negative construction.

EXERCISE 3B – ADVERBS

Directions: For each item, choose the correct word.

Example: He talks (soft) (softly).
1 He did not (ever) (never) leave without saying goodbye.

2 No, he (never) (ever) told her that he loved her.

3 Ben spoke (the more eloquently) (most eloquently) of the two presenters.

4 The girl spoke (quick) (quickly).

5 Of all the five candidates, she answered (more thoughtfully) (most thoughtfully).

There remain just three parts of speech to review: prepositions, conjunctions, and interjections.

CHAPTER FOUR:
PREPOSITIONS, CONJUNCTIONS, AND INTERJECTIONS
PREPOSITIONS: JOINING NOUNS OR PRONOUNS TO THE SENTENCE

If you were to create a language, you would need connecting words. **Prepositions** join nouns or pronouns to the sentence by showing how the noun or pronoun relates to another word in the sentence.

Prepositional phrases are groups of words which start with a preposition and end with the noun or pronoun following. Prepositional phrases modify something else in the sentence and may be either adverbial or adjectival phrases. Prepositional phrases are groups of words which do not include both subjects and predicates. The following is a list of common prepositions:

about	before	concerning	off	underneath
above	behind	down	on	until
across	below	during	over	unto
after	beneath	except	past	up
against	beside	for	since	upon
along	besides	from	through	with
amid	between	in	throughout	within
among	beyond	into	to	without
around	but	like	toward	
at	by	of	under	

The subject of a sentence is never found within a prepositional phrase. Therefore, do not allow prepositional phrases to confuse you as you make the subject and simple predicate agree in number.

Example: One *of the many talented musicians* is here today. ("Of the many talented musicians" is a prepositional phrase; the subject of the sentence is "one," and the appropriate simple predicate [verb] is "is.")

Sometimes a group of words may act as a preposition ("due to," "on account of," "in spite of")

Practice choosing the verb that agrees with the subject in number, being careful not to let the prepositional phrase confuse you.

EXERCISE 4A – VERB FORM WITH PREPOSITIONS

Directions: For each item, choose the correct verb form.

Example: One of those boys (is) (are) my cousin.

1   The characters in this piece (are) (is) constantly looking for a way to change.

2   The two performers in that scene (performs) (perform) well under pressure.

3   The book with the black and white photographs (presents) (present) a good source of reference for that period.

4   The girls in the middle (have) (has) no name tags.

5   The tests from the state (insist) (insists) that the students follow this form.

CONJUNCTIONS: BINDING TOGETHER OR SETTING APART

Conjunctions are words that join or separate. The three types of conjunctions are coordinating, correlative, and subordinating. **Coordinating conjunctions** in some manner attach words, phrases, or clauses of equal value. Here are the seven coordinating conjunctions:

and	for	or	yet
but	nor	so	

Consider exactly what each does:

> "and" adds something
> "but" and "yet" present a contrast
> "nor" and "or" present options
> "for" provides the reason
> "so" provides the consequence

The **correlative conjunctions** must always be used in pairs:

either … or	neither …. nor
both … and	not only … but also
whether … or	not … so much as

(When dealing with a singular and plural united by "or" or "nor," decide on the number of the verb depending on which of the two united words is closest to the predicate.)

Examples: The one dog or the three cats <u>are</u> going to be placed in that cage. or The three cats or the one dog <u>is</u> going to be placed in that cage.

Subordinating conjunctions introduce **dependent clauses** – a group of words which includes both a subject and a predicate but cannot be a sentence by itself because of the presence of a word of dependency at or near the beginning of the clause. Here is a list of common subordinating conjunctions:

after	because	though
although	before	unless
as	if	until
as if	since	when
as long as	than	whenever

Note that many of these words sometimes appear as prepositions. Also remember that the only way you can be sure what part of speech a word is acting as is to note what job the word is doing in the sentence.

There are some adverbs which operate as conjunctions; these are called **conjunctive adverbs**. When you use these to join independent clauses, place a semicolon before them and a comma afterwards. Some common conjunctive adverbs are: *furthermore*, *however*, *moreover*, *nevertheless*, and *therefore*.

EXERCISE 4B – CONJUNCTIONS

Directions: For each item, choose the best word.

Example: The acrobats or the lion tamer (is) (are) going to perform next.

1 Not only did Boris win, (he) (but he also) set a record.

2 War is a last resort; (therefore) (therefore,) let us try to find a way to maintain peace and establish justice.

3 (Therefore,) (Therefore;) I will now admit defeat.

4 Those children or that monkey (annoy) (annoys) my father each time he visits.

5 Neither Hawthorne nor his contemporaries (excite) (excites) much discussion among shallow people today.

INTERJECTIONS – EXPRESSING EMOTION

If you create a language, you have to provide for emotion – just pure feeling. The **interjection** is a word or expression that evidences surprise or some other strong emotion. As part of a sentence, an interjection is usually set off by commas, but if it is written alone as dialogue, the interjection may be followed by an exclamation mark.

Example: I raised my hand, too quickly, to answer the question.

CHAPTER FIVE:
PROOFREADING - FINDING AND CORRECTING ERRORS

Now that you have reviewed all of these rules, try some **proofreading** (a careful reading of a text done in order to find and mark errors). No one is perfect. Proofreading is critical. This is where a parent, friend, or a member of a writer's group can be of special help. Once you have your ideas on paper, an attentive review can spot problems and your work can be polished and improved.

EXERCISE 5A – PROOFREADING ONE

Directions: Each of the following sentences has underlined items. Circle the item in which there is an error and be prepared to state exactly what the error is when the class discusses the exercise. If all of the underlined sections are correct, write "fine" at the end of the sentence.

> *Example*: Charlotte asked her (Mother) to select the better writer, Charlotte or her sister, a sophomore in college.

1   When Zeenat drove to the West to see her father, she was a senior in high school.

2   His father asked him to work for no pay; however, his father later payed his son well.

3   He sprang to his feet to see what was the matter with the geese's nests when all of a sudden their was a loud sound, and he saw that the nest had been blown apart.

4   It was too soon to tell whether his pitching arm had lost it's power, but we will all know the answer when it's time for the first game of the season.

5   He could of lied about the war, and the reporters are as responsible as he if he did because they never really investigated much or tried very hard to question him; moreover, many reporters used the opportunity to ensure their own careers.

6   All of the data that we have read seems to point to him having broken the law, but so much of the truth is not available to the public that it is hard to find sufficient evidence to confirm our beliefs.

7   Kareem plays the piano so good that all our parents have bought pianos in the hopes that we will all play beautifully too.

8   <u>Yipes</u>; I <u>broke</u> the picture <u>which</u> my mother likes <u>best</u> of the many she owns.

9   He <u>had sung</u> so <u>beautifully</u> that my mother <u>cryed</u> when she heard that he might give up his singing career and pursue another interest.

10   It was <u>me</u> <u>whom</u> you not only insulted <u>but also</u> <u>fought</u> with at every opportunity.

Check your responses. Learn the rules governing the problem areas you have.

EXERCISE 5B – PROOFREADING TWO

Directions: Each of the following sentences has underlined items. Circle the item in which there is an error and be prepared to state exactly what the error is when the class discusses the exercise. If all of the underlined sections are correct, write "fine" at the end of the sentence.

Note: Some have more or less than 4 underlined items.

Example: The <u>better</u> player of the two was Roscoe <u>who</u> had practiced <u>more</u> than Juan. FINE

1   After the patriots <u>were hung</u>, the villagers <u>cried</u> and <u>respectfully</u> placed <u>their</u> letters of sympathy on the graves.

2   Alphonso and I have <u>lent</u> our <u>copies</u> to our lab partners who were absent from <u>Chemistry</u>.

3   <u>Shakespeare's</u> sonnets, published in this old text, <u>seems</u> to speak to <u>readers</u> today <u>too</u>.

4   He is older than <u>me</u>, but <u>I have written</u> more than <u>he</u> or <u>his</u> contemporaries.

5   Of the two, Will is the <u>more</u> talkative, but Ethel is the <u>most</u> talkative person in class, and she is the one <u>which</u> I have to debate tomorrow in <u>English</u> class.

6   Either Freddie <u>or</u> his brothers <u>receives</u> fan mail daily from <u>their</u> many fans in the <u>Midwest</u>.

7   The last time <u>she</u> and <u>I</u> <u>led</u> the class in song, <u>we</u> both <u>burst</u> out laughing.

8 We objected to <u>him</u> talking while <u>she</u> and I <u>tried</u> to present <u>our</u> report to the class.

9 In <u>English</u> class <u>we</u> could <u>choose</u> any novel we wanted to read in order to <u>further</u> our language skills.

10 This tastes <u>real</u> good; <u>nevertheless</u>, it is not nutritious, and any-one <u>who</u> wants to stay in good shape will eat something else and avoid having <u>his or her</u> diet ruined.

EXERCISE 5C – PROOFREADING THREE

Directions: Each of the following sentences has underlined items. Circle the item in which there is an error and be prepared to state exactly what the error is when the class discusses the exercise. If all of the underlined sections are correct, write "fine" at the end of the sentence.

Example: Billy Collins writes poetry <u>which</u> expresses deep truth; <u>however</u>, his poems are accessible to most <u>who</u> read <u>English</u>. FINE

1 <u>Barbara Kingsolver's</u> essay about divorce is <u>her</u> thoughtful response to the questions divorce <u>raises</u> in the <u>minds</u> of many young adults.

2 Between <u>you</u> and <u>I</u>, Terence is the only one who <u>could have built</u> that shelf with so <u>few</u> tools and so little time.

3 He climbed the stairs so <u>quick</u> that Sheila and <u>I</u> almost <u>fell</u> in an effort to get out of <u>his</u> way.

4 The <u>very</u> unique idea is not <u>his</u>, but he appropriately gave credit for <u>it</u> to <u>them</u>.

5 Geraldo <u>could of</u> beaten Adrian, <u>but</u> Geraldo <u>chose</u> to work out a compromise, <u>which</u> was agreeable to both of the men.

6 Were you upset over <u>them</u> leaving so soon after the party <u>began</u>, or did you know about <u>their</u> problem with that <u>senior</u>?

7 He is the <u>most unkind</u> boy I know, and when he <u>refused</u> to lend Harry and <u>me</u> cab fare home, I knew he had lost <u>two</u> friends.

8 The soldier and <u>I</u> agreed that without a draft of everybody, it is <u>too</u> easy for people <u>to</u> send others to leave their <u>babys</u> and risk death.

9   Wanda and <u>we</u> girls went to all the <u>parties</u> that night and even invited all of the <u>passerbys</u> to join <u>us</u>.

10   Everybody should bring <u>their</u> ice cream <u>to</u> the table now, <u>and then</u> Henri and we can put the <u>two</u> toppings on each dish.

Unit Two
Writing as a Process and an Art

Chapter One: Task-Audience

How do you begin a writing response? The answer is closely connected to how you begin a speaking response: you think. Since you are dealing with written words which will be fixed in place long after the time you spent writing them, you need to be precise. Also, since you cannot use your body language, facial expression, or other words to keep explaining what you said to your audience, you need to be clear.

A **process** is a method, a way in which you proceed to attack a task. Using a process ensures that you focus on your task. Using a writing process to complete a writing task provides the probability that the writer will be as precise and clear as possible when completing the task. A process takes you from the understanding of the task through to the time when the writing is for all time permanent: published, delivered, shared, or handed in for a grade. In this text, **TASK** is an **acronym** (a word formed by using the initial letters of various other words) used to remember the steps to the writing process.

Task – the first step in the process requires an understanding of the job or assignment. The writer is responsible for this. You must understand what is required. If the task is unclear, and it is assigned by a person, you must ask that person questions: when is it due, who will read it, how long must it be, whether it requires research, etc. If the task is only written for you (as on a test), you must analyze the written task as carefully as possible, breaking it into its commands, requirements, and constraints. Underlining, highlighting, circling, or color-coding a task is often helpful if such a thing is permitted on the test.

Audience – the second step in the process requires an understanding of the spectators or listeners. Who is the intended reader? For most classroom work, the intended reader is a person who can be expected to have a full knowledge of standard English vocabulary and usage, a complete understanding of standard English grammar, and an understanding of a reasonable argument, complete with a knowledge of what constitutes worthy evidence.

Selecting – the third step in the process requires choosing the best details that you can, and based on these details beginning to decide the attitude you have about the subject. To do this, writers often brainstorm in one of a variety of ways. Writers may

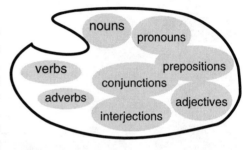

also find it helpful to assemble a **palette** (a range of colors an artist uses to create a picture) made of words rather than hues. This is the stage at which the writer may also have to do research in order to supply more details and acquire persuasive evidence.

Keeping – the fourth step in the process is holding your ideas together, getting them organized, first loosely, then according to some obvious logic. Finally, the organization provides a precise idea of form with clear transition among all of the parts. This is a step which has many segments. Writers often begin by relying on **webbing** (linking) ideas loosely along the natural divisions evident in their brainstorming. Then writers try to group some of those ideas and to add or delete others. At this point, writers often use a general outline consisting of introductory, body, and conclusion segments. Next, the rough draft is assembled by using clear transitions.

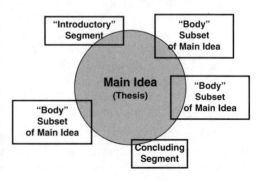

Once the rough draft is put together, writers often begin to **revise**, see the writing again, using some guidelines to craft a better piece of writing. The revision process for most classroom writing that is <u>not</u> narrative can be remembered by the acronym **AUDIENCE**.

Avoid contractions. The exception to this rule is any speech within quotation marks.

Use an introduction which includes a **motivating segment** (an attention grabber), a **bridge** (a link from the attention grabber to the thesis), and the **thesis** (a statement which expresses both your attitude and your topic).

Develop the body of the writing by explaining and validating the main points of the thesis. Here the writer must be aware of some basic logical errors to avoid, some essential aspects of valid evidence, and some criteria for worthy sources of support.

Involve the reader by offering proof as simple statements of fact, quotations and/or paraphrasing of authorities, statistics, and **anecdotes** (short narratives of one's own experience or the experience of other people).

Every paragraph must have a topic sentence.

Never jump from idea to idea. The reader is not in the mind of the writer, so the writer must supply clear **transitions** (connections from one idea to another).

Choose words which are specific, alive, and appropriate to the task, tone, and audience.

End the essay with a conclusion. If possible try to connect the conclusion to the motivating segment of the introduction.

Try to learn the TASK-AUDIENCE acronym as an easy way to remember the writing process.

CHAPTER TWO: TASK TO TEST

If the writing process is worthy of your attention, it should work with any task. So, follow a writer now in creating a piece of writing in response to a task.

Certainly every writer has a favorite relative, living or dead. To write about such a person, one must try to see through the **mind's eye** (the images stored in one's brain), and as clearly as possible imagine such a person. Through the magic of writing, one can then paint that person with words for others to see and know.

The **task** (job) is to **describe** (clearly portray) a favorite relative by using a multi-paragraph essay. The **audience** (the reader for whom the writer writes) will be the classroom teacher.

The writer now needs to start **selecting** by brainstorming some ideas about whom he will write. He sets up a piece of notebook paper putting the phrase "Favorite Person" right in the middle of the top line. Then in the left margin, he writes: "Who, What, Where, Why, When," and "How." In the right margin, he writes "See, Hear, Smell, Touch," and "Taste."

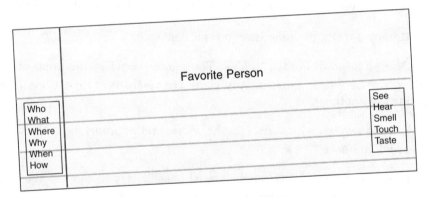

Favorite Person

Who
What
Where
Why
When
How

See
Hear
Smell
Touch
Taste

Now, in shopping list format, using only single words and phrases – no sentences if possible – the writer writes for three minutes without stopping. (Use a kitchen timer or watch.) He agrees to write whatever comes into his head with the understanding that he is the only reader of this list. If he strays off topic for four or more lines, he will refocus on the question list in the left margin or the sensory word list on the right.

Selecting well requires a wide range of choices, so he does not edit himself at this point. Later he will decide what to **keep**. For now, he just allows the ideas in his brain to fall softly on the brainstorm page. Some ideas will be gems, some ideas will be worthless, but for now, he just wants to get the ideas on the paper.

		Favorite Person		
	Uncle Ed	tough memory		
Who	too long ago	Pop		See
What	can't see Ed's face	makes me laugh still		Hear
Where				Smell
Why	can't think	played blocks		Touch
When	still can't think	read paper while I sat on his foot		Taste
How	Who?--Kevin	always looked at me when he talked to me		
	too much like me	taught me to find the words in his paper		
	dumb assignment	danced with me and did the "big finish" dip		
	I like a lot of people	thought "Pop" invented soda pop bubbles		
	little kid in me	nice voice--on key		
	bratty kid	cooked "our" noodles every day		
	loved Ma and Pop	believed in this country		
	Ma--not cool in class	Pop spoke up		
	Pop-Pop	burned the pot of macaroni-smoke alarm		
	miss him	laughing eyes with little star bursts of wrinkles on the edges		
	Pop	white, wavy, thick hair		
	"vote early and often"	joke but serious about voting		

Next, the writer begins the grouping process – deciding what to **delete** (get rid of) and what to keep. The writer can use any symbols he wants (see chart at right) but he chooses not to use numbers or letters because they imply a sequence, and he isn't sure of what he wants to keep yet.

Each person's brainstorming and use of symbols has to be unique. Remember the process is the same, but each person's product will be different. For example, this writer links the first three entries with a "+," because he feels they are closely related. But nothing else he writes seems to be in that exact group, so he creates new symbols for other groups. The first of the new symbols is a ">." He puts these next to how difficult he thinks the assignment is. Look at the sample brainstorming sheet and see how he assigns the rest of his symbols.

One Writer's Classifications	
Symbol	Meaning
+	Ideas about Uncle Ed
>	Difficulty of the assignment
~	Kevin
#	sentimental memories
*	Pop's playfulness
%	Pop's patriotism
{}	Pop's cooking
**	Pop's singing
//	Pop's physical description

Brainstorming with Grouping Symbols

Favorite Person

		# tough memory
+	Uncle Ed	# Pop makes me laugh still
+	too long ago	# played blocks
+	can't see Ed's face	* read paper while I sat on his foot
>	can't think	* always looked at me when he talked to me
>	still can't think	* taught me to find the words in his paper
~	Who?--Kevin	* danced with me and did the "big finish" dip
~	too much like me	* thought "Pop" invented soda pop bubbles
>	dumb assignment	** nice voice--on key
>	I like a lot of people	{} cooked our noodles every day
#	little kid in me	% believed in this country
#	bratty kid	* Pop spoke up
#	loved Ma and Pop	{} burned the pot of macaroni-smoke alarm
#	Ma--not cool in class	// laughing eyes with little star bursts of wrinkles on the edges
#	Pop-Pop	// white, wavy, thick hair
#	miss him	% joke but serious about voting
*	Pop	
%	"vote early and often"	

Who
What
Where
Why
When
How

See
Hear
Smell
Touch
Taste

The idea behind every brainstorming is to empty the mind of all possible ideas and then group those ideas into as many closely related groups as necessary. When you identify the elements of each different group with its own symbol, you begin to focus your ideas.

The writer was lucky with this brainstorm; he seems to have found the subject of his writing with this first attempt. Writers are not often so lucky; often writers need to brainstorm several times before finding a subject. Don't give up. Remember that the idea will come if you continue to brainstorm. Sometimes waiting for an hour or two between brainstorming exercises can yield success.

Another excellent way to unlock ideas is to talk to and listen to other writers. It is true that this approach cannot work in most testing situations, but for almost every other writing task, a writing group can help to focus your ideas. The combination of a writing group and your own brainstorming usually proves very effective. The optimum size for a writing group is four. All that is required of each member is a willingness to work to help each member do the best job he or she can on each writing piece.

For this task, the writer has created nine groups so far. However, he is not finished yet. **Keeping**, the last part of TASK, means making decisions about what to use and what not to use. Three of the groups in the brainstorm are of no value to this writer for this task. These groups are

Editing and Adding to Brainstorming

Who			Favorite Person		See
			# tough memory		Hear
~~Uncle Ed~~			# makes me laugh still		Smell
~~too long ago~~			# played blocks		Touch
~~can't see Ed's face~~			* read paper while I sat on his foot		Taste
~~can't think~~			* always looked at me when he talked to me		
~~still can't think~~			* taught me to find the words in his paper		
~~Who?--Kevin~~			* danced with me and did the "big finish" dip		
~~too much like me~~			* thought "Pop" invented soda pop bubbles		
~~dumb assignment~~			** nice voice--on key		
~~I like a lot of people~~			{} cooked our noodles every day		
# little kid in me			% believed in this country		
# bratty kid			* Pop spoke up		
# loved Ma and Pop			{} burnt the pot of macaroni-smoke alarm		
# Ma--not cool in class			// laughing eyes with little star bursts of wrinkles on the edges		
# Pop-Pop			// white, wavy, thick hair		
# miss him			% joke but serious about voting		
* Pop			# **my first baby sitter**		
% vote early and often			# **father figure when my dad left when I was three**		
# **died when I was eight**			# **lived in his house on Long Island**		

Who / What / Where / Why / When / How

the "+" group, the "~" group, and the ">" group. So the writer deletes them.

Before leaving this brainstorming, the writer goes back and consciously looks at the question and sensory words. These motivate the writer to add phrases such as "died when I was eight," "father figure when my dad left when I was three," "lived in his house on Long Island," and "my first baby sitter." These ideas the writer adds to the "#" group.

The **S**electing and **K**eeping aspects of the TASK acronym reveal that the most important job a writer does is to make choices: to choose what to put into the picture and what to leave out. As the writer decides his or her attitude about that subject, the writer must make more choices. The attitude of the author about his or her writing is called the **tone** of the writing. There are three basic tones: **positive** (I like), **negative** (I don't like), and **objective** (I have no feelings one way or the other). Within the positive and negative tones, there are a lot of slight differences which allow for many, many different tones. The writer must be very aware of exactly what attitude he has about the subject.

When you read over this author's brainstorming, you can see a definite attitude emerging. The author chose his grandfather as his subject. This grandfather was well-loved, but also you can see that the author wanted to keep a bit "cool," so humorous fondness is the tone he selected. This tone will be built by choosing just the right details and by picking just the right words. Here is where the process of writing becomes the art of writing.

CHAPTER THREE: ASSEMBLING A PALETTE

It is time for our writer to build his word palette. Visual artists use **palettes** (thin boards which are often curved with a hole for the thumb), as places to keep their assortment of colors. A rich palette provides the artist with many color choices. For the word artist (the writer), the palette is his or her vocabulary. So after completing his brainstorming and grouping of ideas, our writer compiles a rich vocabulary list working from dynamic verbs and specific nouns. The author paints with words a picture of a grandfather he knew and would like others to see. When our author thinks of his grandfather's activities, our author comes up with these actions:

Actions

1	reads	6	plays	11	baby sits
2	talks	7	votes	12	jokes
3	phones	8	teaches	13	listens
4	shows	9	walks	14	laughs
5	watches	10	asks	15	tells

Some of these actions are inside the grandfather, such as "listens" and "watches." Some actions are outside and easy for all to see, such as "talks" and "jokes." Yet, they are all actions. Notice that our author has not chosen any of the linking verbs. Instead, he chooses action verbs, which are usually more lively than verbs that link.

If the writer had had trouble finding fifteen actions, he would have checked his brainstorming list again to see the other ideas it suggested. The mind's eye approach works well if one focuses and takes time to see the pictures in one's own head.

Here are five actions the writer chose from the list of fifteen above: "reads," "plays," "baby sits," "phones," and "laughs." These are apparently chosen because the writer intends to use these actions as key strokes in painting the descriptions of the grandfather. The next step the writer takes is to acquire **synonyms** (words which have meanings very similar to each other) for each of these five words. These synonyms may allow the writer to become more focused in tone or more precise in image, or both. By the final draft, the writer may not have used all of these synonyms, but just finding those synonyms enabled the writer to make better choices.

If one has access to other writers, this would be the perfect time to work with them and ask them for at least two synonyms for any words selected for a piece of writing. While selecting synonyms, one must keep in mind what Billy Collins (Poet Laureate of the United States in 2001) has the speaker say in his poem, *Thesaurus*: "I know there is no such thing as a synonym." The speaker is correct; there are no absolutely true synonyms because each word – like each person – has a unique identity and personality. However, there are words which are like the words used, and these are the words for which the writer is searching. Choosing among these words, the writer selects exactly the tone and meaning he wants.

If, for some reason, you are working on a piece of writing and cannot or may not use a writing group, you can often use a **thesaurus** (a book in which you find lists of words which often mean nearly the same thing). Remember that the thesaurus is only a tool. Use it to select those words you know well enough to use accurately. The words which are suggested as synonyms and with which you are unfamiliar are words that you must look up in a dictionary and discuss with your writing groups and English teachers.

These identical twins look very much alike, but each is a discrete individual with ideas and a style all her own.

The first verb the writer has found synonyms for is "read." Synonyms include "contemplate, study, examine, plunge into." These are listed on the prewriting sheet at the right. The circled words are part of the palette. The author may decide to use one or more of them when painting the humorous and loving picture of his grandfather.

The entry for "plays" turns up these promising

VERBS	
read:	
contemplate	interpret
study	diagnose
examine	construe
plunge into	peruse
regard studiously	con

VERBS			
plays:	baby sit:	phone:	laugh:
entertain	minister to	dial	chuckle
frolic	shepherd	call	chortle
beguile	cherish	jingle	giggle
tickle	nurture	ring	guffaw
regale	take under one's wing		howl

words: "frolic, romp, celebrate, beguile, tickle, entertain." By the time the author finishes looking up key verbs, he places the synonyms for "baby sit" ("minister to, take under one's wing, shepherd, cherish, nurture") on the prewriting sheet along with the synonyms for "phone" ("dial, call, jingle, ring") and the synonyms for "laugh" ("chuckle, chortle, giggle, guffaw, howl"). Circled possibilities on the prewriting sheet remind the author to sharpen focus as he writes.

Nouns selected with great care should make the picture more clear, so there are also some precise nouns on the palette. The author reviews the verb group to start with because verbs are the most lively words in the language, and most verbs can easily become nouns with just a little change.

If you take the "-ing" form of a verb and use it as a noun, you create a **gerund** (word made from a verb but used as a noun). These gerunds are packed with action and also have the power to name.

Verb . . . . .Gerund
listen . . . . . . .listening
dance . . . . . .dancing
baby sit . . . . .baby sitting
phone . . . . . .phoning
read . . . . .reading

Other key namers are obvious: "grandfather," "children," "baby sitter." The author looked up these words in a thesaurus or discovered them in conversation with a writing group. The resulting synonyms are on the chart at the top of the next page. Our author has a long word palette, making his choices easier and his attitude toward his subject clearer to himself.

NOUNS			
man:	baby sitting:	grandfather:	children:
			posterity
human	watch	geezer	
person	shelter	patriarch	youth
		sexagenarian	progeny
personality	custody		
		grownup	brood
soul	shield		
	under the aegis of	adult	heirs

CHAPTER FOUR: ORGANIZING

At this point, the author begins a process of artistic decision-making which will shape his writing. The author links his remaining brainstorming groups into a webbing (or a graphic organizer).

Since this task is multi-paragraphed, the author has to make introductory and concluding paragraphs. The author chooses "Intro to Pop" as an introductory paragraph. The author makes another figure, labeling it "Conclusion," and adds to the conclusion the phrase, "died when I was eight."

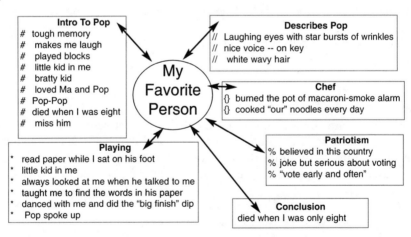

Intro To Pop
- \# tough memory
- \# makes me laugh
- \# played blocks
- \# little kid in me
- \# bratty kid
- \# loved Ma and Pop
- \# Pop-Pop
- \# died when I was eight
- \# miss him

Describes Pop
- // Laughing eyes with star bursts of wrinkles
- // nice voice -- on key
- // white wavy hair

My Favorite Person

Chef
- {} burned the pot of macaroni-smoke alarm
- {} cooked "our" noodles every day

Patriotism
- % believed in this country
- % joke but serious about voting
- % "vote early and often"

Playing
- * read paper while I sat on his foot
- * little kid in me
- * always looked at me when he talked to me
- * taught me to find the words in his paper
- * danced with me and did the "big finish" dip
- * Pop spoke up

Conclusion
died when I was only eight

At this point, the author has to write a **thesis sentence** – the control sentence for the entire essay. There are many ways to do this, but the easiest is to begin with a simple statement using the verb "to be" as a simple predicate. This statement should identify the topic of your essay and indicate the attitude or tone about the topic. Here is an example of such a statement:

"My grandfather **was** one of the most influential people in my life."

Now although the verb "to be" (used here in the form "was") is a very important verb, it is not dynamic. "To be" shows existence. The author needs a little **tension** (unsettling aspect) in the thesis, so he takes the ideas stated after the "was" and uses those ideas as the beginning of a new, dynamic thesis. To do this, the author has to change the words slightly while keeping the ideas intact.

"One of the most influential people in my life **exemplified** manhood at its best: my grandfather."

Notice that the author replaces the "to be" verb ("was") in his thesis with a livelier verb, "exemplified." Choosing this livelier verb causes the author to think about his attitude toward his grandfather as well as the content of what he wants to say in this description. "Exemplified" gives a stronger focus. After all, the author is not describing his grandfather to the police. The grandfather's height, weight, skin tone, eye color, and facial hair are not what the author is trying to emphasize. The description is about the grandfather's influence and the author's love and appreciation of the old man.

Choosing just the right verb for the thesis makes the focus sharper and the subsequent writing easier. Using a writing group to suggest words for a thesis is ideal; using a dictionary, thesaurus, or just one's own brain is a bit more challenging, but it is still possible. Just take the time to think! The more focused the thesis, the easier the writing becomes.

Try this exercise on the statement-to-thesis process just to make sure you understand how it works.

EXERCISE 3A – THESIS FORMING

Directions: Read the content and tone of the subject required by the task. Then write a simple statement using the verb "to be." Next revise that statement into a dynamic thesis. There are many correct responses to these tasks. This book merely gives suggestion of how this might be done.

Example: Content of writing and tone: a positive attitude about having driver's education offered in your high school.

– Simple Statement Using Verb "to be."
My high school should be offering driver education courses.

– Dynamic thesis:
Offering driver education courses in my high school would ensure a safe and responsible group of young drivers on our local roads.

1   Content of writing and tone: a negative tone about raising the voting age to twenty-one.
    – Simple Statement Using Verb "to be."

_____

_____

    – Dynamic Thesis:

_____

_____

2   Content of writing and tone: a positive attitude about keeping work places free of smoke.
    – Simple Statement Using Verb "to be."

_____

_____

    – Dynamic Thesis:

_____

_____

Now that the author has a thesis, he can begin to outline his writing in a more formal manner. He will place the thesis at the beginning of his outline just to remind himself of his focus.

THESIS: One of the most influential people in my life exemplified manhood at its best – my grandfather.

    I.   Introduction segment
        A.   Motivator
        B.   Bridge
        C.   Thesis

> ☆ : The author took these topics from his webbing.

    II.   Body
        A.   Interaction
        B.   Chef
        C.   Physical description
        D.   Patriotism

    III.   Conclusion

Notice that there are three elements in the introduction segment: a motivator (attention-grabbing part of the introduction), a bridge (connection between the motivator and the thesis), and the thesis (control statement of the entire essay).

A good motivator should be more general than the thesis but some-how connected to it. For instance, this thesis is about a grandfather's positive influence on a little boy, so the author might find a motivator about influences in general or grandfathers in general or little boys in general. Here are three possible motivators.

Example: One never sees the wind, but its influence on the direction of things is always present in nature. (influences in general)

OR

Example: Grandfathers' influences have been the subject of literature from Heidi's grandfather in the Alps to Charlie's Grandpa Joe of Roald Dahl's chocolate factory fame. (grandfathers in general)

OR

Example: The negative image of little boys as being composed of "twigs, and snails, and puppy dogs tails" in the anonymous nursery rhyme may capture some of the challenging aspects of caring for little boys. (little boys in general)

The motivator about the wind seems most appealing to this writer. Next, the author has to be sure that the motivator has the proper tone (positive, but humorous) and that it can be connected with the thesis (grandfather's influence is like the wind). The author's choices appear in his **rough draft** (first full writing attempt at responding to the task).

WRITING THE ROUGH DRAFT
Here is a rough draft by this writer:

One never sees the wind, but its influence on the direction of things is always seen in nature. When I was three, I was dumped by a fierce wind and then guided by a gentle one. When I was three, my father's problems got the better of him, and he abandoned my mother and me. So my mother and I went to Long Island to live with her father in his two- story white house with its circular red brick front stoop and its long, sloping gravel driveway. Pop was a widower, and when he took us in, he had been retired for five years. I loved my mother and father, and I was angry about the move, so although I was his progeny, Pop was heir to the temper tantrums of a little brat. Officially, he was my baby sitter; unofficially, he was my guiding light. One of the most influential people in my life exemplified manhood at its best – my grandfather.

(Following the outline, the next step is writing the body of the essay. As you write, keep an eye on your palette. Notice that two words were taken from the palette for the introductory paragraph – "progeny" and "heir.")

Nurturing was what Pop did best although he had been a mailman by profession. It makes me laugh still to think of Pop's lesson in driveway safety. Every morning before I would be able to play on the driveway, Pop would set up my stuffed bear and rabbit in my wagon and give them a strong push with his foot. They would clatter over the gravel until they bounced out on the stones near the bottom of the slope.

These crash test dummies were my reminder to be slow and safe in my wagon. They were far more effective than a lecture. Though a tall man, he would sit on the floor and play blocks with me, always looking at me when I talked, always <u>chuckling</u> at my stories about pirates and dinosaurs. When he read his paper, he would either let me play horse and sit on his foot as he bounced his leg or put me in his lap and let me pick out the words "and" and "the." Sometimes we <u>entertained</u> my mom when she looked particularly sad. We would dance across the linoleum while he sang with his lovely, low voice and end with a "big finish" at which point I would fly on to her lap. He taught me to put the feelings of others ahead of my own and keep an eye out for my mom. By the time we were finished with our dance or burping contests (Pop told me he had invented soda pop bubbles), my mom was smiling again and we were once more a family that could cope with whatever happened.

Pop's exploits as a chef were his most famous. He could not cook — no matter how hard he tried. His best dish was chicken soup from a can; he would always tell my laughing mom how hard he had to work cooking the noodles for that soup. The only time he tried to make dinner from scratch, he set off the fire alarm.

Pop's face is still in my mind: mostly I see his smile; which starts with his laughing green eyes. At the edges of these eyes, there were star bursts of wrinkles that got deeper and deeper as he smiled. His white, wavy hair added to his "Santa" charm. Often as I tried to fight sleep, he would rock me on his shoulder and I would pat that silken hair. He was my personal <u>shelter</u>; his image was one of warmth and security.

Even as young as I was, I was aware of Pop's love for this country. He had a joke on election day, a time when he and I went to the polls to vote. "Vote early and often," he would say with a <u>chortle</u>. When I was old enough to ask why he only voted once, he took the opportunity to explain that each <u>adult</u> got only one vote and had an obligation to use it in every election. He believed in the *United States Constitution* and in the country which it fashioned.

(In the concluding paragraph, notice how the author tries to connect to the introductory paragraph. A two sentence conclusion is fine. The conclusion should remind the reader of the topic and the tone, and then end with a powerful statement.)

So, my maternal grandfather will always be one of my favorite people. I consider myself blessed to have been related to such a wind of positive change.

REVISING

Now the writer must proofread the writing with an eye to **revising** (seeing the work again with all of the possibilities that changing the text might offer).

To change the text for the better, the writer probably bears in mind some rules which British author George Orwell suggested:

- Never use a figure of speech which you are used to seeing in print.
- Never use jargon or foreign words when an English word will do.
- Never use a long word when a shorter word will do as well.
- If you can cut out a word, cut it out.
- Never use the passive voice when the active will do.
- Break any of these rules rather than say something very awkward.

In the introductory paragraph, the author could have the sentence, "One never sees the wind, but its influence on the direction of things is always seen in nature" to "One never sees the wind, but in nature its influence on the direction of things is always seen." (This change tightens the sentence.) Also, the author might change the second use of "wind" to "gentle breeze."

The author also revised the sentence, "When I was three, my father's problems got the better of him, and he abandoned my mother and me." A tighter form would be "My father's problems overwhelmed him."

The author must have noticed the overused metaphor, "*guiding light*," in the sentence, "He was my baby sitter, officially, but unofficially he was my *guiding light*." He revised it to read, "He was my baby sitter, officially, but unofficially he was my inspiration."

In sentence two of paragraph two, the author moved the word "still" to "still makes me laugh." He also made three shorter paragraphs from this long one because the focus switched. Notice how this improves the flow.

Nurturing was what Pop did best although by profession he had been a mailman. It still makes me laugh to think of Pop's lesson in driveway safety. Every morning before I would be able to play on the driveway, Pop would set up my stuffed bear and rabbit in my wagon and give them a strong push with his foot. They would clatter over the gravel until they bounced out on the stones near the bottom of the slope. These crash test dummies were my reminder to be slow and safe in my wagon. They were far more effective than a lecture.

Though a tall man, Pop would sit on the floor and play blocks with me, always looking at me when I talked, always <u>chuckling</u> at my stories about pirates and dinosaurs. When he read his paper, he would either let me play horse and sit on his foot as he bounced his leg or put me in his lap and let me pick out the words "and" and "the."

Sometimes Pop and I <u>entertained</u> my mom when she looked particularly sad. We would dance across the linoleum while he sang with his lovely, low voice and end with a "big finish" at which point I would fly on to her lap. He taught me to put the feelings of others ahead of my own and keep an eye out for my mom. By the time we were finished with our dance or burping contests (Pop told me he had invented soda pop bubbles), my mom was smiling again, and we were once more a family that could cope with whatever happened.

So here is the author's second (final) draft composed after he revised his rough draft:

FINAL DRAFT

One never sees the wind, but in nature its influence on the direction of things is always seen. When I was three, I was dumped by a fierce wind and then guided by a gentle breeze. When I was three, my father's problems overwhelmed him, and he abandoned my mother and me. So my mother and I went to Long Island to live with her father in his two story white house with the circular red brick front stoop and the long, sloping gravel driveway. Pop-Pop was a widower, and when he took us in, he had been retired for five years. I loved my mother and father, and I was angry about the move, so although I was his <u>progeny</u>, Pop was <u>heir</u> to the temper tantrums of a little brat. He was my baby sitter, officially, but unofficially he was my inspiration. One of the most influential people in my life exemplified manhood at its best – my grandfather.

Nurturing was what Pop did best although by profession he had been a mailman. It still makes me laugh to think of Pop's lesson in driveway safety. Every morning before I would be able to play on the driveway, Pop would set up my stuffed bear and rabbit in my wagon and give them a strong push with his foot. They would clatter over the gravel until they bounced out on the stones near the bottom of the slope. These crash test dummies were my reminder to be slow and safe in my wagon. They were far more effective than a lecture.

Though a tall man, Pop would sit on the floor and play blocks with me, always looking at me when I talked, always chuckling at my stories about pirates and dinosaurs. When he read his paper, he would either let me play horse and sit on his foot as he bounced his leg or put me in his lap and let me pick out the words "and" and "the."

Sometimes Pop and I entertained my mom when she looked particularly sad. We would dance across the linoleum while he sang with his lovely, low voice and end with a "big finish" at which point I would fly onto her lap. He taught me to put the feelings of others ahead of my own and keep an eye out for my mom. By the time we were finished with our dance or burping contests (Pop told me

he had invented soda pop bubbles), my mom was smiling again, and we were once more a family that could cope with whatever happened.

Pop's exploits as a chef were his most famous. He could not cook no matter how hard he tried. His best dish was chicken soup from a can; he would always tell my laughing mom how hard he had to work cooking the noodles for that soup. The only time he tried to make dinner from scratch, he set off the fire alarm.

Pop's face is still in my mind. Mostly I see his smile which starts with his laughing green eyes. At the edges of these eyes, there were star burst of wrinkles that got deeper and deeper as he smiled. His white, wavy hair added to his "Santa" charm. Often as I tried to fight sleep, he would rock me on his shoulder and I would pat that silken hair. He was my personal shelter; his image was one of warmth and security.

Even as young as I was, I was aware of Pop's love for this country. He had a joke on election day, a time when he and I went to the polls to vote. "Vote early and often," he would say with a chortle. When I was old enough to ask why he only voted once, he took the opportunity to explain that each adult got only one vote and had an obligation to use it in every election. He believed in the United States Constitution and in the country which it fashioned.

So, my maternal grandfather will always be one of my favorite people. I consider myself blessed to have been related to such a wind of positive change.

This is the author's final draft which he handed in for a grade. What grade would you have given him and what advice would you have given him? You might discuss the answers to these questions with your writing group.

UNIT THREE
PARAPHRASING OTHERS' WRITING

CHAPTER ONE:
TREATING OTHERS' IDEAS RESPONSIBLY

Writing is a very powerful means of communicating. Through writing, you have the opportunity to influence many more people than you may actually ever personally meet in your lifetime. So, when you use the words or ideas of others in your writing, you have some serious social obligations. You must honestly and accurately reproduce the words or ideas of others, even if you disagree with what they have written or said. You must never use the words of another without giving credit to that speaker or author. Also, you must be sure to put those exact words in quotation marks. In addition, you must never use the original ideas of others without giving credit to the speaker or author and making sure that those ideas are faithful to the speaker's or writer's actual language and intent.

Presenting the ideas of another when not using the exact words of that person is called **paraphrasing**. Paraphrasing is extracting the idea of another person from his or her words and putting that idea into your own words. It is a key technique for successful communication, both oral and written. To ensure clarity when you speak to another person about a critical issue, it is a good idea to repeat in your words the idea you think that other person has just expressed to you.

For instance, if you are discussing a subject about which you disagree, paraphrasing can help you understand just how much you actually disagree. Or it can provide a common ground for you to proceed in resolving your disagreement.

Paraphrasing is essential in all writing which responds to the words of another. As a writer, you owe others

Red Sox and Yankee fans might benefit from paraphrasing properly.

the courtesy of accurately conveying their ideas and crediting them for these ideas. The ability to convey the ideas of others is paraphrasing, and as with writing in general, there is a process to help ensure your focus and success.

In writing a research paper, paraphrasing is key. You need to extract the ideas of others, **cite** (give credit to the author) those ideas, and then put those ideas on your paper in your own words. Such a use of the ideas of others ensures that your paper will be rich in evidence while maintaining your voice.

Paraphrasing skills are basic also in taking notes from oral presentations. In this situation, there is usually not time for transcribing the exact words of others, so paraphrasing allows you to get the ideas down in your own words.

The first step in paraphrasing is use of a dictionary for all difficult words. On a test, usually this is not possible, but in every other circumstance, it is not acceptable to ignore words about which you are not sure. Stop and look up the words before you present them.

Here is an excerpt from President George Washington's *Farewell Address* to his Cabinet delivered on 17 September 1796:

"Promote, then, as an object of primary importance, institutions for the general diffusion of knowledge. In proportion as the structure of a government gives force to public opinion, it is essential that public opinion should be enlightened."

To unlock a piece of reading, always find the simple predicate first and then its subject. The first simple predicate is "promote" and the subject is "you." (Although this subject is not written out, it is understood since this first part is a command or request.) Next, ask what it is that "you" should "promote." The answer is "institutions for the general diffusion of knowledge." You know what these are: schools of all kinds. So the first sentence is telling the Cabinet to encourage schools.

The second sentence is more difficult because there are three **clauses** (a clause is a group of words with both a subject and a simple predicate) in it. This sentence tells why the cabinet should encourage schools. The simple predicate of the first clause of the second sentence is "gives" and the subject is "structure." The kind of "structure" is "government," and what it "gives" is "force."

The simple predicate of the second clause of the second sentence is "is" and the subject is "it." Here, you need to know what the antecedent of "it" is. "It" stands for the something "essential" or necessary.

The simple predicate of the third clause of the second sentence is "should be" and the subject is "public opinion." The answer to what "should be" is "enlightened public opinion."

Try to put these ideas together now. Government "structure" (or form) "gives" (or bestows) "force" (or power) to "public opinion," so there is a need to see that the "opinion" is "enlightened" or informed. After finding the subjects and simple predicates, you must look at the qualifiers such as "in proportion." This was a hard piece, but unlocking the idea was worth the trouble. Here is how one might paraphrase these two sentences:

"Encourage schools because it is important to make sure that public opinion is informed to the degree that the public makes governmental decisions."

Now try this excerpt from Newton Minow's "Television and the Public Interest" speech delivered to the Thirty-ninth Annual Convention of the National Association of Broadcasters on 9 May 1961. (Newton Minow was Chairman of the Federal Communications Commission.)

"We all know that people would prefer to be entertained than stimulated or informed. But your obligations are not satisfied if you look only to popularity as a test of what to broadcast. You are not only in show business; you are free to communicate ideas as well as relaxation. You must provide a wider range of choices, more diversity, more alternatives. It is not enough to cater to the nation's whims; you must also serve the nation's needs."

The first sentence has two clauses. The first clause uses the simple predicate "know" and the subject "we." The second clause uses the simple predicate "would prefer" and the subject "people."

Looking at the key qualifying words in that sentence, the idea becomes clear that everyone understands that human beings would pick amusement over controversy or enlightenment.

The second sentence has two clauses. The simple predicate of the first clause is "are" and the subject is "obligations." The second clause uses the simple predicate "look" and the subject "you."

By scanning the important qualifying words, you can conclude that the second sentence basically says that the duty of the listeners (the broadcasters to whom this speech was delivered) is to look beyond mere ratings as a way to decide what to broadcast.

The third sentence has two clauses. The simple predicate of the first is "are" and the subject is "you." The simple predicate of the second clause is "are" and the subject is "you." Qualifiers modify this sentence radically since one of them is "not." The essential idea is that broadcasters are not merely showmen but are also responsible for transmitting ideas.

The fourth sentence has only one clause. The simple predicate is "must provide" and the subject is "you." After scanning the qualifiers, the meaning emerges that Minow demands that the broadcasters offer a diverse menu of shows.

The fifth sentence has two clauses. The simple predicate of the first is "is," and the subject is "it." The antecedent of "it" is that thing that would be enough to do. The simple predicate of the second clause is "must serve" and the subject is "you." After examining qualifiers in these clauses, this sentence appears to tell broadcasters that they must not just offer what people enjoy and are amused by, but members of the broadcast industry must also provide programming for the necessary enlightenment of the population.

Here is a third quotation to paraphrase. The passage is an excerpt from a speech by Hubert H. Humphrey, Jr. to the Democratic National Convention in 1948. The speech is entitled "In Support of Civil Rights."

"We cannot use a double standard of measuring our own and other people's policies. Our demands for democratic practices in other lands will be no more effective than the guarantees of those practiced in our own country."

The first sentence has only one clause; the simple predicate of which is "can(not) use" and the subject is "we." That which "we cannot use" is one set of regulations which is applied differently to measure either our own policy or that of other people. The second sentence uses "will be" as the simple predicate and "demands" as the subject. The important qualifiers convey the meaning that those practices which we insist on as appropriate in other societies will only occur in other societies to the degree to which they are adhered in our society.

So, the key to the paraphrase is to find the simple predicate, the subject, and all important qualifiers. Here is a quotation from a letter written by Thomas Jefferson in which it is clear that besides the simple predicate, the subject, and the qualifiers, it is imperative to be aware of figurative language – language which says more than, or other than, what the words mean.

"We are not to expect to be translated from despotism to liberty in a featherbed."

This quotation is one sentence using "are" as the simple predicate and "we" as the subject. "Translated" must mean something different from changing one language to another in order to understand it. "Translated" also means to change in form, so this makes sense. However, to make sense of the entire sentence, "featherbed" has to be seen as a **metaphor** (something which is identified with another thing essentially different because of some similarity between the two). A "featherbed" is a luxury, a thing of comfort. So Jefferson is telling his reader that one cannot change one's situation from living under a dictator to living a free life by being comfortable.

Always examine that which you are paraphrasing for figurative language.

****

Now you will proceed to prepare for the final examination in English. The next part of the book brings you to writing for certification. You need to do well on this examination in English in order to validate your competency in English. This type of writing is task driven, but you can take control of it by deciding to do your best and by putting all that you know about writing as process and writing as art to work for you. Think of this next part of the text as preparation for yet another evaluation. It is rather like passing the driving test. In the driver's seat, you can put all of the power of writing to work for you. Good luck.

Unit Four
Writing for Certification

After having practiced the TASK–AUDIENCE process and the writer-artist's vocabulary palette, you will next apply your new skills to three sample English comprehensive tests. At this point your focus will be much the same as when you are preparing for the tests to get a driver's license: you will need to know how the test is set up, what skills are required, and how the exam is evaluated. Prepare to take the driver's seat on your way to English language certification.

YOU ARE IN THE DRIVER'S SEAT

If you were to take a driver's license test and you had never seen a car or a street or a traffic light, the chances of your passing that test would be very minimal. In a similar way, if you need to prepare for an English comprehensive test, most of which will evaluate your ability to respond appropriately in multi-paragraph essays, and you know little or nothing about the writing process, mechanics, or sentence structure, there is very little likelihood that you will do your best on such a test. To do well on any test, you need to know the basics of the subject on which you will be tested. You need to practice using those basics over and over again, and you need to be prepared to respond to questions that you have never seen before.

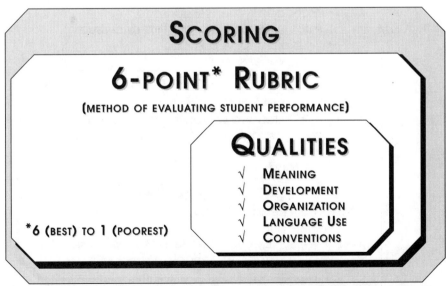

SCORING

6-POINT* RUBRIC

(METHOD OF EVALUATING STUDENT PERFORMANCE)

QUALITIES

√ MEANING
√ DEVELOPMENT
√ ORGANIZATION
√ LANGUAGE USE
√ CONVENTIONS

*6 (BEST) TO 1 (POOREST)

ENGLISH LEARNING STANDARDS

(OVERALL INSTRUCTIONAL OBJECTIVES)

READ, WRITE, SPEAK, & LISTEN FOR ...*INFORMATION AND UNDERSTANDING*
...*LITERARY RESPONSE AND EXPRESSION*
...*CRITICAL ANALYSIS AND EVALUATION*
...*SOCIAL INTERACTION*

As you slip into the driver's seat, you will become familiar with the structure of the language, the rules which govern the way language is used, and the general types of questions that the examiners will most likely use to test your language ability. If you learn the basics, sufficiently

COMPREHENSIVE ENGLISH TEST

SESSION ONE PART A

Standard: Listening and writing for information and understanding

TASK:
• Extended written response to a speech
• 6-8 Multiple-choice on key ideas

SESSION ONE PART B

Standard: Reading and writing for information and understanding

TASK:
• Extended written response to informational materials (text and visual)
• Multiple-choice on basic comprehension

SESSION TWO PART A

Standard: Reading and writing for literary response

TASK:
• Extended written response to two linked passages of different genres
• Multiple-choice on key ideas, details, and vocabulary

SESSION TWO PART B

Standard: Reading and writing for critical analysis and evaluation

TASK:
• Extended written response to literature read for school

practice the skills, and prepare for the possible questions, you will have a better chance of receiving the equivalent of a state driver's license for English, a passing grade on the Comprehensive Test in English.

THE FOUR ENGLISH STANDARDS

As you work your way through the English test question types, you will refer to the writing process and to the English Learning Standards, and you will become aware of how each test question type focuses on certain of these Standards.

These Standards are as follows:

1a Be able to read and write for **information and understanding**.
1b Be able to speak and listen for **information and understanding**.

2a Be able to read and write for **literary response and expression**.
2b Be able to speak and listen for **literary response and expression**.

3a Be able to read and write for **critical analysis and evaluation**.
3b Be able to speak and listen for **critical analysis and evaluation**.

4a Be able to read and write for **social interaction**.
4b Be able to speak and listen for **social interaction**.

These are the four focal points on the English Comprehensive Test. The Learning Standards impress on you that the English language does many jobs in our lives. In a way, these Standards could be seen as the essential questions that any language user should ask before starting out; these are the language equivalents of the driver's checklist before starting the engine. In language use, this would mean asking yourself if your focus in a certain use of language will be on information and understanding, or on literary response and expression, or on critical analysis and evaluation, or on social interaction.

So, writers, fasten your seat belts, adjust the rearview mirrors, start the engines, take a good look, and ease onto the information highway using the skills you are about to review.

☆ An important part of this section of the book, your "writer's / driver's guide" to success on the English Comprehensive Test, is the **Glossary/Index** found on the last pages. Although most of the key terms are explained somewhere within this guide, a quick reference is always available in the glossary pages. After all, if you had to change a tire on an unfamiliar car and did not know where the jack and tire iron were located, you could check the owner's manual that most drivers keep in their glove compartments. In other words, don't neglect one of the most useful parts of this guide, the Glossary/Index.

INTRODUCTION TO THE STANDARDS AND RUBRICS

You have just seen the Learning Standards. Understand that each of the four parts of the English Comprehensive Test will focus on one of the first three Standards. The Fourth Standard, social interaction, receives less emphasis on this English Comprehensive  Test than do the other three Standards, but it may appropriately be perceived as the desired outcome of the  other three. Review the four Standards and get used to seeing the icons which represent them. When you see the icon for a Standard, know that this Standard is a focal point of the task on which you are working.

The English Comprehensive Test will assist you in answering the questions by providing you with guidelines and a scoring rubric to follow when responding to the questions in each of the four parts. There is a *Guideline* section of each of the four parts of the test. Learn to follow these *Guidelines*; use them to proofread and edit. They are similar to road maps and will keep you from getting lost. The *Guidelines* (related to the rubric qualities) for each of the tasks will remind you that you will be judged on your  ability to

- **show a clear understanding** of the task, including making some reference to the text and/or visual part of the question itself,

- **develop your response** specifically and convincingly,

- **organize your writing** coherently using proper introduction, body, and conclusion elements which have smooth transition,

- **use vocabulary appropriately**, and

- **apply the rules of Standard English** writing.

☆ The five qualities of the rubrics can be remembered by the initials: **MDOLC** (*pronounced "em-dolk"*).

A helpful **mnemonic** (a memory device) for **MDOLC** is:

Mature Drivers Obey Legal Constraints

Mature (Meaning)	=	**M**
Drivers (Development)	=	**D**
Observe (Organization)	=	**O**
Legal (Language Use)	=	**L**
Constraints (Conventions)	=	**C**

Below is a sample of the **MDOLC** rubric scoring sheet for Session One, Part A of the English Comprehensive Test. You will use a similar rubric scoring sheet for every task in this text. View it as a survival sheet for the language user who wishes to excel. Drive yourself to a good score by making these qualities part of everything you write.

Remember: ***Mature Drivers Obey Legal Constraints.***

PART A SCORING RUBRIC - Listening and writing for information and understanding (see Appendix for complete Scoring Rubric – check evaluation box for each quality scored)	
Quality	Commentary The response:
Meaning: the extent to which the response exhibits sound understanding, interpretation, and analysis of the task and text(s)	
Development: the extent to which ideas are elaborated using specific and relevant evidence from the text(s)	
Organization: the extent to which the response exhibits direction, shape, and coherence	
Language Use: the extent to which the response reveals an awareness of audience and purpose through effective use of words, sentence structure, and sentence variety	
Conventions: the extent to which the response exhibits conventional spelling, punctuation, paragraphing, capitalization, grammar, and usage	

Note on Grading – using the Scoring Rubric's 6-point system:

For simplicity, in this book the Sample Responses and their Scoring Rubrics have been simplified to show general "average" ratings by rating all 5 qualities with a uniform score (e.g., "6," "3," or "1").

In "real" grading, a teacher could rate each of the five qualities differently (Meaning = "6" but Development = "2," Organization = "4," Language = "3," and Conventions = "5"). The actual final score would be an average of the individual quality scores (6 + 2 + 4 + 3 + 5 = 20 divided by 5 (qualities) = final average score of 4).

CHAPTER ONE: MEANING

QUALITY ONE ON THE TEST SCORING RUBRICS

The first quality, **Meaning**, is the quality of the rubric which indicates that you will be graded in part on your ability to understand what you read in the text and visuals. Reading is one of the things which you can do outside class to enhance your language ability. In addition to school assigned readings, you should try to read other works of interest for at least fifteen minutes a day. If you do this and also do your assigned reading, you will probably notice an improvement in your reading level.

Sometimes even good readers have problems with understanding what the writer means, because some readers have difficulty understanding the author's tone. **Tone** is the author's attitude toward what he or she is saying. There are as many tones in writing as there are attitudes in speaking (e.g., angry, satiric, humorous, authoritative, business-like, sympathetic). You can unlock the tone if you realize how important it is and learn how it is constructed. When you become an expert on tone, you can enhance your own writing as well as your reading.

☆ CAPSULE – TONE

Tone is comprised of some combination of use of **figurative language** (language used to mean more than or other than what the dictionary meanings actually expressed); use of **rhetorical** and **literary devices** (those techniques such as repetition, rhyme, arrangement of words in a sentence, explanations, and interruptions used in order to convince a reader); **diction** (word choice); **selection of detail**; and **sentence structure**. We can remember this combination by the initials *FRDSS* (pronounced "*ferds*").

Figurative language	=	*F*
Rhetorical and literary devices	=	*R*
Diction	=	*D*
Selection of detail	=	*S*
Sentence structure	=	*S*

Tone = FRDSS

FIGURATIVE LANGUAGE

When you use language to mean exactly what the words indicate in the dictionary, you are using the language **literally**. When you use language to mean more than or other than what the dictionary meaning of the words indicate, you are using language **figuratively**.

The following are some common figures of speech you need to know:

- **Metaphor = an identification of two essentially different things which the maker of the metaphor identifies based on some similarity which he or she perceives.** This identification is usually constructed using some part of "to be" (e.g., is, am, was, were, will be, has, or had been) when nouns are linked; however, if one verb is identified with another verb, just switch the verb and do not use part of "to be."
  Examples: Ben is a brick. / Ben pulverizes the punching bag.

  The metaphor is the biggest lie one can tell (if only taken literally) because it is obvious that the two things identified are really not the same. But the intention of the maker of the metaphor is not to deceive but rather to emphasize some less than obvious similarity that the maker of the metaphor sees between the two things.

  Examples: If I wish to show that Oprah and a rose share the quality of beauty, I can use a metaphor:
  Oprah is a rose.
  He watched, consuming her with his eyes.
  ("watched" is replaced by "consuming.")

  Note: Never write a metaphor which you have often heard or seen. Such a metaphor is tired out and will not increase the power of your writing.

- **Simile = a similarity between two essentially different things expressed using the words "like" or "as."** Similes are not as powerful as metaphors, but similes make the similarity obvious.

  Examples: Oprah is as beautiful as a rose. / When Ian pitches, his curve ball sinks like an anchor.

  Note: Never write a simile which you have often heard or seen. Such a simile is tired out and will not increase the power of your writing.

- **Personification = giving the qualities of a person to a non-person.**
  Examples: The cat laughed.
  The car died on the road and had to be towed.

- **Hyperbole = extreme exaggeration.**
  Examples: I told you this meaning a billion times.
  Everybody in the world is doing this dance.

RHETORICAL AND LITERARY DEVICES

- **Repetition = stating something more than once in order to intentionally stress the words or the idea**.

  Examples: I came, I saw, and I conquered.
  Crowded halls, crowded cafeterias, and crowded classes greeted them on the first day of school.

- **Rhyme = the repetition of similar or exact sounds**.

- **Onomatopoeia = words or phrases, the meaning of which imitates the sounds associated with the objects or actions to which they refer**.

  Examples: The slap of his hand echoed.
  The loud buzz of the saw disturbed the peace.
  A murmur moved across the room as the beautiful bride slowly moved down the isle

- **Alliteration = the repetition of initial consonant sounds of successive words.**

  Examples: "Fred," said his mother, "phones frequently."
  Circus clowns are serious about their work.

- **Arrangement = position of words in a sentence.**

  Examples: Him, I know. (Here the stress is on the object "him.")
  That, I expected. (Stress is on "That.")

- **Explanation = all definitions and explications are intended to operate as devices to convince.**

  Examples: The teacher, a person trained in that skill, illustrated how to do it correctly by demonstration.
  Music, lilting and peaceful, calmed the crowd.

- **Interruption = a break in the sentence**

  Examples: "If I get my hands on you, I'll..."
  "I... I love you," he stammered.

DICTION

- **Diction = word choice.**

  Examples: Dad, may I borrow the car?
  Give me the car, old man!

SELECTION OF DETAIL

- **Selection of detail = what facts you choose to include**

  Examples: Dinner was tasteless.
  Dinner was lukewarm water and white store-bought bread.

SENTENCE STRUCTURE

- **Sentence structure = selection of a variety of the four kinds of structure: simple, compound, complex, compound-complex.**

  Examples: I know. (simple)
  Do you think that I would ask you if I didn't know? (complex)
  You are conceited, and I do not want to talk to you. (compound)
  If you ever want to talk to me again, you need to apologize, and you must promise never to be obnoxious again. (compound-complex)

✍️ EXERCISE ON TONE ASSESSMENT

Try this exercise to see how well you understand tone.

Directions: ·For each of these tone exercises, try to select the tone which is present. Give an example (from the selection) that describes *each* of the **FRDSS** elements listed after the selection. Be sure to discuss your selection with your writing group.

Reminder: Tone is constructed by some combination of **FRDSS**. When choosing the type of tone, it may be necessary to use all of **FRDSS** or some part of it.

Figurative language = **F**
Rhetorical and literary devices = **R**
Diction = **D**
Selection of detail = **S**
Sentence structure = **S**

Tone selection one:

He was unable to stop his own tremors. He looked like a whipped puppy that had been cast alone on a deserted road. His eyes were swollen from crying, and anyone could see the regret which shrouded his whole form. That regret would be his constant companion for the rest of his sad life.

1a Which elements (parts) of **FRDSS** were used?

F = simile: _____

metaphor: _____

personification: _____

R = repetition: _____

D = diction: _____

S = selection of detail: _____

S = sentence structure: _____

_____

_____

1b The tone for selection one is _____.

Tone selection two:

The foolish man was at last unmasked for all to see. What a sight they did see! He sat in the board room among those he had formerly terrorized. His gumdrop shape shook with every sob, which reverberated several times through all the ripples and dimples of flesh. His blotched face was that of a naughty cherub, caught with his plump little fingers in the cookie jar.

2a Which elements (parts) of **FRDSS** were used?

F = metaphor: _____

R = repetition: _____

onomatopoeia: _____

D = diction: _____

S = selection of detail: _____

S = sentence structure: _____

_____

_____

2b The tone for selection two is _____.

Tone selection three:

I looked into his beady, cramped eyes and tried to speak. After taking several deep breaths, I had enough control to shout. "You, you are such an absolute moron. Do you have any idea how much I despise you? If I were not such a decent person, I would, I would...." He sat there quaking on a register of ten on the Richter scale. He was a mound of quivering chicken fat. I walked away, but not before I turned and spat on the floor in front of that blob.

3a   Which elements (parts) of **FRDSS** were used?

F   =_____

_____

R   =_____

_____

D   =_____

_____

S   =_____

_____

S   =_____

_____

_____

3b   The tone for selection three is _____.

Now, shift into second gear to the next *Guideline* of the rubrics: the quality of **Development**.

CHAPTER TWO: DEVELOPMENT

QUALITY TWO ON THE TEST SCORING RUBRICS

This part of the grading rubric calls your attention to the necessity to be precise in your response to the task. Precise means exact. Precision requires specific reference to facts. The facts of the task are present in the task itself, so you need to make relevant reference to the text and/or visuals of the task. Such reference requires that you give credit to the text and/or visuals. You can give this credit right within the sentences you write by **paraphrasing** the text and/or visuals and then making clear that you obtained the information from the text and/or visuals. You can also make reference to the text and/or visuals by using the exact words from either or both. If you use the exact words of another, either spoken or written, you must use quotation marks. Also, you must give credit to the author by either citing the name of the author and/or the title of the text or visual within the sentence or at the end of the sentence by parenthetically noting the page and the author and/or title.

QUOTATION MARKS

You need to review **quotation marks** just a bit here. Here are the essential rules:

1   Use commas around the tag, the "who said" part, begin the quotation with quotation marks, and end with quotation marks if the quotation is a complete sentence or does not smoothly fit into the larger sentence.

    Example: Franklin D. Roosevelt said, "I hate war."

2   Even if the quotation is short and fits smoothly into the larger sentence, it still needs quotation marks but does not have to be set off by a comma or commas.

    Example: "It is a question of feeding the poor" was the slogan of the campaign.

3   If the quotation is of lines of poetry, use a " / " to show that one line has ended and the next, begun.

    Example: Hamlet said to his best friend Horatio, "Since my dear soul was mistress of her choice / And could of men distinguish her election" (III. ii. 57-58).

4   If the quotation runs more than four lines of text, then set the entire quotation off in a block form (ten spaces indentation is suggested). (In this case, do *not* use quotation marks or back slashes.)

Example: Hamlet said in Act III, scene ii, lines 57-69:

> Since my dear soul was mistress of her choice,
> And could of men distinguish her election,
> Sh' hath sealed thee for herself, for thou hast been
> As one in suff'ring all that suffers nothing,
> A man that Fortune's buffets and rewards
> Hast ta'en with equal thanks; and blest are those
> Whose blood and judgment are so well co-mingled,
> That they are not a pipe for Fortune's finger
> To sound what stop she please: give me that man
> That is not passion's slave, and I will wear him
> In my heart's core, ay in my heart of heart,
> As I do thee.

When you need to quote from the text, never just throw the quotation on the page without explanation. Always be sure to introduce who said the quotation, what credentials the speaker had, and under what pertinent conditions the words were said. After you have used the quotation, be sure that you use your words to explain how that quotation was important to your response.

☆ *Remember*: Quotations are not just dialogue. Any words you take exactly as another said or wrote them are then quotations in your paper.

Now you need to review parenthetical documentation.

PARENTHETICAL DOCUMENTATION

This process refers to using parentheses to enclose the author, title of the work, and/or page numbers of some paraphrased idea or quotation you have used. Here are the basic forms:

1   If the author and work are made clear in the text, just put the page number in a parentheses at the end of the sentence.

Example: Ms. St. Onge in her essay "The History of Punctuation" states that grammar "has a purpose" (2).

Note: Notice that the period of the sentence goes after the parenthesis.

2   If there is more than one article by the same author referred to in the paper you are writing, include the title of the article.

Example: Then again, when Sheila St. Onge looks at Roman writing, she says, "The Romans did not wish the average person to be able to read this" ("Keeping Writing for the Privileged" 3).

3   If you are quoting from more than one author, and you did not make clear in your text which author you are referring to, do so in your parentheses.

Example: (St. Onge 3)

☆ *Note:* The basic concept here is common sense and clarity. If you have only one author quoted in a piece of writing, after the initial citation, you only need to cite page numbers in the parentheses. If an author has more than one piece referred to, then use the title of the piece in the parentheses unless your text makes clear which piece is being cited. If you are referring to more than one author, then make clear in the text or in the parentheses to which author you are referring.

In Session One, Part B of the Comprehensive Test in English, the Development quality requires you to make specific reference to the text and/or visuals of the task. Make sure when you refer to the text and/or visuals that you give credit to the author and/or title of the task and/or visual. That is why quotation marks and parenthetical documentation are important. Give reference and give credit for that reference.

Now that you have reviewed the first two qualities of the scoring rubric, Meaning and Development, get moving to the next quality, Organization. Clutch twice, and slide into third gear.

CHAPTER THREE: ORGANIZATION

QUALITY THREE ON THE TEST SCORING RUBRICS

Here is where your knowledge of the writing process will be of great value. In order to evidence organization to your reader, you must have it. The organizational procedures that you have learned included: pre-writing; use of introductory, body, and conclusion elements; and proofreading and revising. These procedures will give you the best possibility of organizing your work.

Here again are the steps of the writing process. Review them and use them whenever you write. These steps help you to understand and follow the process. It is important to recognize that the writing process is part of the Learning Standards.

The Writing Process

I   Know your task.
II   Have a clear sense of audience.
III   Be aware of what you already know about the task and what more you need to know.
IV   Group your ideas.
V   Delete those ideas that don't seem related or valuable.
VI   Organize your groups and include an introduction and conclusion.
VII   Write a first draft.
VIII   Proofread and edit your draft.
IX   Revise.
X   Write your final draft.

These are the basic rules of the writing road. You must know them in order to be in the driver's seat as a successful writer.

All of the tasks of the English Comprehensive Test require **multi-paragraph responses**. Therefore you must have at least three paragraphs for each response: introduction, body, and conclusion. The best introductory paragraphs will follow this form: motivator concept begins the introduction; one or more bridge sentences bring the reader from the motivator to the thesis; and the thesis is the last sentence of the introduction. Try to find a motivator concept which can be picked up again in the conclusion paragraph so that you have a power-packed finish.

Two essential keys to successful writing are (1) understanding your **audience** and (2) organizing your *task* so that it will be clearly understood.

Task
Audience

Remember that you have learned that the TASK–AUDIENCE formula is an innovation designed to enhance proofreading by using an acronym. Experience has shown us that the open-ended writing process, the "parts" of which are inextricably connected, is more accessible to many students if some type of step–by–step process is used to explain it. TASK–AUDIENCE is simply an extension of this approach.

Test yourself. Do you remember that each of the "lettered parts" of the TASK–AUDIENCE acronym should be self-explanatory (see Unit Two, pages 35-37). The TASK–AUDIENCE proofreading formula focuses your attention on the two most basic concepts in any piece of writing:

- **understanding the task**

- **awareness of the audience**

The TASK–AUDIENCE formula specifies the major points that any author should consider when proofreading her or his work on the Comprehensive Test in English. In addition, this method will succeed in making students attentive to the primary concerns in editing any piece of writing.

In high performance cars, fourth gear is intended for cruising. The fourth quality of the test scoring rubric is Language Use. The student who writes with the rules of Language Use in mind expresses himself/herself well and cruises much more easily through the tasks. Having worked through the qualities of Meaning, Development, and Organization, you are ready for sentence construction, Chapter 4.

Chapter Four: Language use

Quality Four on the Test Scoring Rubrics

This chapter focuses on sentence structure and the appropriate level of vocabulary for the audience. Begin by reviewing how a sentence is constructed.

How a Sentence is Built

In English there are four main structures from which to choose when building a sentence. Just as a good driver knows the basics about how the gearshift functions to smooth the transition between speeds, a good language user knows how the sentence is structured to make the writing smooth. Understanding these structures will help you to avoid writing run-ons and fragments. Also, if you understand how a sentence is built, you can learn when and where to place commas. All of this should really improve your performance on the exam.

First, you need to remember that for *any* sentence of *any* type there must be *at least one* independent clause. So you need to review phrases and clauses, both dependent and independent.

A **phrase** is a group of words that does not include both a subject and a predicate. A **simple predicate** is the main action of a group of words or a way of existing. A **complete predicate** is the part of the clause that states something about the subject. If you are a bit shaky about finding a predicate, try these four rules.

Rules for Finding the Simple Predicate

1 Look for a part of the verb "to be" or an action word. Parts of the verb "to be" include am, is, are, was, were, will be, has, or have been.

   Examples: He <u>was</u> here. (part of the verb "to be")
   I often <u>rushed</u> through dinner in order to go out later. (action word)

2 Make sure that there is no "to" in front of the suspected simple predicate.

   Example: On the way to his house to see him, I <u>fell</u> down. (Because there is a "to" in front of "his" and "see," I know that the simple predicate here is "fell" and not "his" or "see.")

3   In your mind, try putting one of the following pronouns in front of the suspected simple predicate; if it sounds right with just one of these pronouns, go on to the next step.

Pronouns to try: I, you, he, she, it, they

Example: The last day of school seems so near now.
                ("It seems" sounded right to you, and so you go to step 4.)

4   Make sure that somebody or something in the sentence is performing the action of the predicate.

Example: The last day of school seems so near now.
                ("It seems" sounded correct and there is something in that group of words that "seems." <u>Day</u> <u>seems</u>. Good, you have found your predicate.)

Here is another approach to finding the simple predicate that often helps students. Put a time word such as "tomorrow" or "yesterday" in front of the sentence. The word(s) that changes so that the sentence takes on a new meaning is the predicate.

Example: He represented his client in court.
                <u>Tomorrow</u> he will represent his client in court.
                ("Represented" had to change, so that must be the simple predicate, and it is.)

Now that you know how to find the simple predicate, finding the subject of a group of words is easy because a subject is the "do-er" of the predicate.

Example: <u>Menemsha</u> creates beautiful patterns of knots.
                (Following the rules for finding the simple predicate and the suggestion to put a time word in front of the sentence, you have discovered that "creates" is the simple predicate. The proper noun "Menemsha" is the do-er of "creates," so "Menemsha" is your <u>subject</u>.)

Knowing the definition of a simple subject and a simple and complete predicate allows you to differentiate between a phrase and a clause. You know that a phrase is a group of words which does not include both a subject and a predicate.

A clause is a group of words that includes both a subject and a predicate. So far this is not too difficult. If you were to write a phrase all by itself, you would create a **fragment**, *not* a sentence. However, there is more to creating a sentence than just writing a mere clause. There are two types of clauses.

The first type of clause can be a sentence all by itself because it is independent and can stand on its own. This type of clause is called an **independent clause**. An independent clause requires a subject and a predicate and the stating of a complete thought.

Example: He is.
(In this sentence the simple predicate is a part of the verb "to be," and the subject is "He." Although you do not know any more about "he" than that this being is male and that he "is," there is a kind of completion to this knowledge. You know he exists in some way. Therefore, this is an <u>independent clause</u> and as such can exist all by itself as a sentence.)

However, if you were to take a word of **dependency** (also referred to as a subordinating conjunction) and add it to the beginning of the clause, the result would be a **dependent clause**. Dependent clauses cannot stand on their own since they are incomplete thoughts.

COMMONLY USED WORDS OF DEPENDENCY

if	who	unless
since	whom	where
that	which	whenever
because	although	when
while	as if	until
after	than	as long as

Here are some examples of dependent clauses created from the independent clause "He is."

<u>if</u> he is	<u>who</u> he is	<u>than</u> he is
<u>since</u> he is	<u>whom</u> he is	<u>unless</u> he is
<u>because</u> he is	<u>which</u> he is	<u>where</u> he is
<u>while</u> he is	<u>although</u> he is	<u>whenever</u> he is
<u>after</u> he is	<u>as if</u> he is	<u>as long as</u> he is

Not one of these groups of words which begin with a word of dependency is a sentence because not one of these groups includes an independent clause. Every sentence must have *at least one* independent clause in order to be a sentence.

This information will become much clearer as you practice building sentences using independent and dependent clauses. Only the clauses in a sentence are important to the structural type. Phrases are interesting, but they do not affect sentence type. You can add or drop phrases as you choose without changing sentence type.

Now try your skill with an exercise.

Directions: Place the letters **IND** on the line next to an independent clause and **DEP** on the line next to a dependent clause. Then write the letter **S** for sentence next to all of those **IND** answers that you have because each independent clause by itself is a sentence.

✍ CLAUSE ASSESSMENT

1 In the early light, I could see the outline of the tree. ___

2 Because it was such a large and majestic oak. ___

3 My friend Flick and I used to play under it on hot days. ___

4 When we were young and had few responsibilities. ___

5 Which was a very long time ago. ___

6 Every summer's day we played there until dark. ___

7 I really miss those days. ___

8 Now everybody and everything is different. ___

9 Then it was a lot easier. ___

10 Soon, though, I will be out of the house and on my own. ___

11 After I graduated from high school and moved to the city. ___

12 Then things will change a bit. ___

13 If I get a good education. ___

14 I'll be able to really change my life. ___

15 I'm tough and determined. ___

16 I can stick with school and get ready to make some real money. ___

17 I'm in the driver's seat. ___

18 Whenever I get overwhelmed. ___

19 I try to remember that. ___

20 It usually works for me. ___

Although there are many makes and models of cars, sentences are classified in four structure types.

SENTENCE TYPE #1

The Simple Sentence

There is *only one* independent clause in a **simple sentence**. Remember that it is not possible to judge sentence type based on length alone.

Examples: Here are two simple sentences.
1   She is.
("She is." – the one independent clause)

2   In the early part of the day at the top of the hill by the barn, the rooster crowed.
("the rooster crowed." – the one independent clause)

SENTENCE TYPE #2

The Compound Sentence

There are *at least two* independent clauses in a **compound sentence**; the last *two* of these clauses are joined by a coordinating conjunction preceded by a comma. The coordinating conjunctions include *and, but, or, nor, for, yet,* and *so*.

Examples: Here are two compound sentences.
1   She is, <u>and</u> I am too.
("She is," and "I am too." – the two independent clauses)

2   In the early part of the day at the top of the hill by the barn, the rooster crowed, <u>and</u> the noise awakened Adelle, our new granddaughter.
("the rooster crowed," and "the noise awakened Adelle." – the two independent clauses)

SENTENCE TYPE #3

The Complex Sentence

A **complex sentence** includes *only one* independent clause and *at least one* dependent clause.

Examples: Here are two complex sentences.
1   Since she is, I am too.
("Since she is," – the dependent clause; "I am too." – the independent clause)

2   I woke up because the rooster crowed in the early part of the day at the top of the hill by the barn.

("I woke up" – the independent clause; "because the rooster crowed ...," – the dependent clause)

SENTENCE TYPE #4

The Compound-Complex Sentence

A **compound-complex sentence** includes *at least one* dependent clause and *at least two* independent clauses, the last *two* of which are joined by a coordinating conjunction preceded by a comma.

Examples: Here are two compound-complex sentences.

1   Since she is, I am too, but neither of us is happy about the situation.

("Since she is" – the dependent clause; "I am too," – the 1st independent clause; "neither ..." – the 2nd independent clause)

2   Adelle awoke because the rooster crowed in the early part of the day at the top of the hill by the barn, and she was not able to sleep through any type of noise.

("Adelle awoke" – the 1st independent clause; "because the rooster ... by the barn," – the dependent clause; "she was not able to sleep ..." – the 2nd independent clause)

✍ FOUR SENTENCE TYPES ASSESSMENT

This activity pinpoints mechanics as you have reviewed them here. It also emphasizes Standard #1 in its focus on reading, writing, and listening for information and understanding, as well as Standard #4 in its focus on social interaction and the need to read, write, and listen to others.

Directions: The class should divide into writing groups. Four per writing group would be best. The following list of details should be dictated, and each group should write four separate paragraphs. Each paragraph will use all of these details and have a good topic sentence, but each will be written in *only one* sentence type. One paragraph will be only simple sentences, one only compound, one only complex, and one only compound-complex. Each student in the group could take the responsibility of writing one of the paragraphs, but remember that each group will be successful only if all four paragraphs contain perfectly composed sentences; therefore, each group should help each member to write perfectly.

The list to be dictated is as follows:

- some multiple-choice questions
- Comprehensive Test in English
- pressure
- about seventy-five per cent of the exam is essay response
- qualities to be assessed
- ability to understand the task and the readings and visuals on the exam
- ability to develop logical, accurate, and specific answers
- ability to use word choice and sentence structure well
- ability to organize ideas well
- ability to use conventions of spelling, punctuation, paragraphing, usage, and grammar
- practice is the answer
- it can be done
- start now

Now, write your four paragraphs.

FOUR PARAGRAPH SUMMARY

Constructing these four paragraphs should have given you a feel for the power of the individual sentence type. The simple sentence has a staccato effect – a powerful, single punch. The compound sentence gives a balanced approach to ideas. The complex sentence provides for further explanation as soon as an idea is introduced. The compound-complex sentence provides for a balanced explanation.

One difference between a race car and your family car is the fuel used in each. The high performance racer requires high octane; whereas most cars used on public highways can run well on much lower octane fuels. Just as the proper fuel is critical to smooth performance, the appropriate use of vocabulary is essential in effective writing. Keep your audience in mind as you write in Standard English. With this in mind, review the vocabulary that you will use in the four parts of the English test (vocabulary found on the next pages).

Understanding the proper use of the Key Terms on the following pages may greatly improve your writing.

KEY TERMS

Just as you cannot start the car easily without the key, so also you cannot respond to the four English Comprehensive Test tasks unless you know some key terms. If you want to excel quickly, look through this list and make a 3x5 flash card for every word the meaning of which you don't immediately know. Review these cards often.

GROUP ONE: PHRASES HAVING TO DO WITH WRITING WORDS

1 **genre** = (n.) kind or type as in novel, short story, poem, fiction, nonfiction

2 **literary** = (adj.) having to do with books

3 **technique** = (n.) method

4 **convention** = (n.) practice (how something is done) of Standard English as used in grammar, usage, or spelling

5 **tone** = (n.) author's attitude toward his or her work

6 **level of language** = (n.) degree of difficulty and/or appropriate formality of diction and sentence structure

7 **quotation marks** = (n.) punctuation signs which indicate that the exact words of a speaker are being used

8 **rhetorical question** = (n.) question asked for dramatic reasons and not intended to evoke a response

9 **rhetorical devices** = (n.) effective language tools used to persuade

10 **figurative language** = (n.) language which says more than or other than what the meaning of the words alone indicates

11 **literal language** = (n.) language which says exactly what the words mean

12 **metaphor** = (n.) identification between two essentially different things

13 **simile** = (n.) comparison using "like" or "as" made between two essentially different things

14 **personification** = (n.) giving the qualities of a person to a nonperson

15 **hyperbole** = (n.) obvious exaggeration

16 **irony** = (n.) difference between what is and what is expected or between what is and what seems to be

17 **onomatopoeia** = (n.) figure of speech in which the sound of the words imitates the meaning of the words

18 **allusion** = (n.) reference to something outside the realm of the writing piece such as myths, the Bible, or history

19 **diction** = (n.) word choice and use in writing and speaking

20 **point of view** = (n.) angle from which the story is told as in first person, second person, third person, or omniscient

21 **omniscient** = (adj.) all-knowing, like a god

22 **apostrophe** = (n.) figure of speech in which a non-person, absent person, or deceased person is addressed

23 **denotation** = (n.) dictionary meaning of a word

24 **connotation** = (n.) general idea or meaning associated with a word in addition to its literal sense

✍ EXERCISE WITH "WRITING WORDS" ASSESSMENT

Here is an exercise using these words. Refer to the list above for meanings if you need help.

Directions: Place the appropriate word from the list above in the proper blank.

1 "She is a rose" is an overused example of a figure of speech called a _____.

2 "She is like a rose" and "she is as lovely as a rose" are two examples of a figure of speech called a _____.

3 "The cat laughed" and "the door attacked me" are two examples of the figure of speech called _____.

4 When I look in the dictionary, I find the _____ of a word.

5 When I use a word such as " naughty," I know that I cannot use it to describe a drug dealer even though the dictionary tells me that it means " improper" because the _____ of the word tells me that the community would never use "naughty" to refer to conduct as repulsive as dealing in drugs.

6 "I have told you this a billion times" is a figure of speech called _____.

7 Poems and short stories are two different kinds of _____.

8 One frequently used kind of tone is _____ which indicates an attitude that makes clear the difference between what is and what is expected or between what is and what seems to be.

9 Choice of words is called _____.

10 Spelling and grammar are examples of _____ in English.

GROUP TWO: WORDS DESCRIBING PEOPLE, PLACES, THINGS, OR IDEAS

(Note: All of these words are adjectives.)

1 **salient** = (adj.) outstanding, dominant

2 **relative** = (adj.) having a connection with another

3 **fluent** = (adj.) flowing effortlessly, polished

4 **accurate** = (adj.) without error

5 **specific** = (adj.) precise, exact

6 **logical** = (adj.) evidencing reason

7 **coherent** = (adj.) marked by orderly and logical unity

8 **relevant** = (adj.) on the topic

9 **consistent** = (adj.) uniform, in agreement

10 **dominant** = (adj.) outstanding

11 **valid** = (adj.) convincing

✍ EXERCISE WITH "DESCRIBING WORDS" ASSESSMENT

Here is an exercise for these words. Refer to the list above for assistance.

Directions: Place the appropriate word in the appropriate blank.

1   He doesn't ever change in his kindness to others, and this
_____ courtesy is most appreciated by others.

2   The _____ characteristic of a unicorn is its single horn in the middle of its head.

3   That discussion about his nephew's soccer skills had no place in our debate about air pollution because the nephew's story was not

_____.

4   If you merely generalize in your writing, your prose will lack the convincing effect of _____ references.

5   My Spanish teacher speaks Spanish well and quickly because she is
_____ in the language.

GROUP THREE: WORDS NAMING CONCEPTS

(Note: All of these words are nouns.)

1 **distinction** = (n.) differentiating characteristic

2 **perspective** = (n.) point of view

3 **criteria** = (n.) basis for judgment

4 **repetition** = (n.) act of doing or saying again

5 **factor** = (n.) element

6 **bullet** = (n.) as used in printing, the circle placed before a word to emphasize it

7 **tendency** = (n.) inclination

8 **task** = (n.) job

9 **purpose** = (n.) reason for doing

10 **situation** = (n.) set of circumstances

11 **overview** = (n.) the big picture of a situation

12 **element** = (n.) part

13 **interpretation** = (n.) way of perceiving

14 **visual** = (n.) capable of being seen

✎ EXERCISE WITH "CONCEPT WORDS" ASSESSMENT

Here is an exercise for these words. Refer to the list above for assistance.

Directions: Place the appropriate word in the appropriate blank.

1   It is her _____ to be the valedictorian of the class.

2   Your goal is your _____.

3   The job is the _____.

4   We agreed because his _____ was the same as mine.

5   Color has a _____ appeal.

GROUP FOUR: ACTION OR COMMAND WORDS

(Note: These are all verbs.)

1 **interpret** = (v.) to explain the meaning of

2 **analyze** = (v.) to take something apart in order to understand

3 **explicate** = (v.) to fully explain

4 **evidence** = (v.) to provide facts

5 **specify** = (v.) to give detail

6 **propose** = (v.) to suggest

7 **discuss** = (v.) to present and explain fully

8 **develop** = (v.) to present fully

9 **assume** = (v.) to suppose without proof

10 **criticize** = (v.) to offer personal reaction to the quality of

11 **signify** = (v.) to indicate

12 **illustrate** = (v.) to picture

13 **mention** = (v.) to state without explaining

14 **state** = (v.) to merely mention

15 **delineate** = (v.) to clearly picture

✍ EXERCISE WITH "ACTION WORDS" ASSESSMENT

Here is an exercise for these words. Refer to the list above for assistance.

Directions: Place the appropriate word in the appropriate blank.

1   When you _____ another's writing, always be aware that feelings are involved.

2   If he does _____ something, that doesn't mean you have to accept it.

3   You may _____ that to be true if you like, but you have no proof.

4   Take this idea apart and _____ it before you accept it.

5   Proof is required to _____ something.

GROUP FIVE: PHRASES NAMING VARIOUS WRITING FORMS

(Note: These are all nouns.)

1 **text** = (n.) writing

2 **feature article** = (n.) special piece of writing in a newspaper or magazine

3 **thesis / support paper** = (n.) research paper presenting a point of view and documented proof to support that point of view

4 **essay** = (n.) a personal viewpoint

5 **chart** = (n.) a sheet presenting information as a map or graph

6 **graph** = (n.) visual device used to present some numerical concept

7 **anecdote** = (n.) short, personal narrative used as a type of proof

8 **critical lens** = (n.) English Comprehensive Test quotation used as a basis for analysis and interpretation on Session Two, Part B of the exam

9 **dictation** = (n.) material read aloud for analysis or transcription

✎ EXERCISE WITH "WRITING FORMS" ASSESSMENT

Here is an exercise for these words. Refer to the list above.

Directions: Place the appropriate word in the appropriate blank.

1 This newspaper carried a _____ about that movie star's early career.

2 When the teacher read the _____, the entire class was silent.

3 An _____ can be very dramatic proof, as it usually represents a limited number of cases.

4 Session Two, Part B of the English Comprehensive Test uses the _____.

5 I absolutely must provide documented proof for a _____.

Can you imagine the chaos on our highways if there were no signs or pavement markings to help motorists follow the "rules of the road?" In much the same way, there is a need for a few rules of Standard English, "rules of the language road." This chapter reviewed the structure of sentences; now examine the various ways that that structure can be arranged in the next chapter on English Conventions.

CHAPTER FIVE: CONVENTIONS

QUALITY FIVE ON THE TEST SCORING RUBRICS

A **convention**, as the term is used with language, means a rule or method accepted by general consent.

You may know these rules of the language road as punctuation, mechanics, usage, spelling, or just the general term "**grammar**." Using these rules properly is the sign of an educated user who chooses to steer the language as carefully as possible. This user engages in the flow of communication most clearly with as many people as possible without accidentally injuring someone or excluding someone from the conversation.

PUNCTUATION

As Sheila St. Onge observed in her analysis of the reason for punctuation, "... the system of punctuation has developed into an essential tool for precisely expressing individual thought" (*Keeping Writing for the Privileged* 3). Precision on the road helps you avoid accidents. When driving, you have road signs that tell you exactly what you must do in certain circumstances. So also with language, you have writing signs called **punctuation marks**.

Examples: Let's forget Bill and still be friends.
Let's forget, Bill, and still be friends.

These two sentences mean very different things, and only the proper placing of commas makes clear exactly what is meant. So review some very basic comma rules starting with the rule that makes such a difference in the example sentences.

CONVENTION: KEY COMMA (,) RULES

1 Use a comma to set off the name of the audience to which the sentence is directed.

Example: Let's forget, Bill, and still be friends.
(Here we are speaking to Bill, not about him as in the sentence: Let's forget *Bill* and still be friends. The use of the commas before and after the word, "*Bill*," allows the reader to know that Bill is the audience to whom the sentence is directed.)

2 Use a comma after every element in a series (three or more items) except for the last.

Example: We invited Jacinder, Lindsay, Madeline, and Tom.

3 Use a comma after two adjectives that would "sound correct" with an "and" between them.

Example: The tall American man spoke Spanish fluently.
                    (Here "tall" and "American" would not sound correct with an "and" between them, so you should not use a comma.)

However, in this following sentence, a comma would be required:

Example: The tall, educated man spoke Spanish fluently.
                    (Here "tall" and "educated" would "sound correct," so instead of using the "and" which would be an extra word, you are expected to use the comma.)

4 Use a comma after an introductory prepositional or participle phrase. A **preposition** is one of those fairly short words which ties a **noun** or a **pronoun** to the rest of the sentence in what is called a **prepositional phrase** (*example*: <u>in</u> the morning). A **participle** is a verb ending in -<u>ing</u> or -<u>ed</u> (*examples*: <u>excited</u> by the cheering or <u>exciting</u> the crowd).

Examples: In the morning, I was awakened by the rooster. (introductory prepositional phrase)

                <u>Excited</u> by the rooster's crowing, the old man removed his shoes and danced. (introductory participle phrase)

                <u>Exciting</u> the crowd, the rooster seemed to imitate popular rock stars. (introductory participle phrase)

5 Use a comma to separate the tag of a quotation from the rest of the sentence. The tag is the "he said" part.

Examples: "I am," <u>he said</u>, "the best baseball player in the city."

                <u>He said</u>, "I am the best baseball player in the city."

                "I am the best baseball player in the city," <u>he said</u>.

6 Use a comma before the coordinating conjunction used to join two clauses in a compound or compound-complex sentence.

Examples: Elias swims, <u>and</u> Marisa does too.
(Here you have two independent clauses joined by ", and" in a compound sentence.)
Elias swims, <u>and</u> Marisa does too when she has the time.
(Here you have two independent clauses joined by ", and" in a compound-complex sentence.)

7 Use a comma following an introductory dependent clause.

Example: Because T.J. likes to fish, Sundeep bought a rod for T.J. as a birthday present.
("Because T.J. likes to fish" is an introductory dependent clause.)

8 Use a comma after short introductory expressions such as "yes," "no," and "well."

Example: <u>Yes</u>, it is very necessary to know punctuation rules.

9 Never use a comma to separate two parts of a two-part subject, two-part predicate, or two-part complement.

Examples: Eduardo and Kareem excelled in school.
(Eduardo and Kareem are both parts of the two-part subject.)
Eduardo listened to music and wrote many tunes of his own.
(Eduardo both listened and wrote as two parts of the two-part predicate.)
Kareem composed lyrics and songs.
(Kareem composed two things: lyrics and songs, a two-part complement.)

10 Avoid comma-splice run-ons by using a comma to join sentences only if that comma precedes a coordinating conjunction.

Example: Writing with appropriate punctuation is not too hard, but practice is required.

11 Use a comma to set off interruptions in the sentence. These interrupters might be words, phrases, or entire dependent clauses.

Examples: Mr. Kim, principal, attended the meeting of the PTA last night.
Janelle, the captain of the squad, led the cheer.
My sister, who is younger than I, lives next to Mr. Smith.

✍️ COMMA RULES ASSESSMENT

Here is a chance to practice your comma rules.

Directions: In each of the following sentences, choose **A, B, C,** or **D** as a place which should have a comma. Write your letter choice on the first line provided. On the second line, write the number of the comma rule which you followed when you decided to place the comma in that particular spot.

Example: No_A I did_B not know that_C you_D and Alli had dated.
(position) **A**   *(rule)* **8**

1   Jarnelle, Mindy_A and Claudia_B were all happy to hear that he had won the lottery_C and had been written up in the paper_D for all to see.
*(position)*_____ *(rule)*_____

2   Georgio_A the president of our club, often plays both football_B and baseball with the little children_C on our block_D and in our neighborhood.
*(position)*_____ *(rule)*_____

3   Alahandro_A and I_B cannot understand_C but Shawnee says that she knows the answer_D and the reason behind it.
*(position)*_____ *(rule)*_____

4   "I do not know anything about your lost bracelet_A"_B said Marlin, "but I will try to help you to find it_C and determine who_D did take it from your room."
*(position)*_____ *(rule)*_____

5   Trying very hard to appear studious_A Naveen opened his book_B and took out his pen_C and pencil, and everyone else in the room_D smiled.
*(position)*_____ *(rule)*_____

Convention: Key Semicolon (;) Rules

1   Use a semicolon as you would a period between two closely connected independent clauses. When you use the **semicolon**, you should not capitalize the word which follows it.

   Example: I have lost this match; perhaps I did not practice enough.

2   Use a semicolon before a **conjunctive adverb** (also, besides, for example, however, nevertheless, in addition, instead, meanwhile, then, and therefore) that joins two independent clauses. Be sure to put a comma immediately after such an adverb.

   Example: The work is hard; however, the pay is good.

3   Use a semicolon to separate groups of words that contain other necessary commas.

   Example: They went with Mama, the oldest sibling; Uncle Petrov, the baby of the family; and Aunt Helga, the middle child.

✍ Semicolon Assessment

   Directions: Now apply what you have learned with the semicolon by indicating where one should be placed (**A**, **B**, **C**, or **D**) and citing which of the three rules you are following in placing that semicolon.

1   He wanted to leave$_A$ and to return home$_B$ however, he was afraid to$_C$ ask permission of the captain$_D$ who had never shown much sympathy for those who had family problems.
   (position)_____ (rule)_____

2   At the food market$_A$ I purchased flour for a cake for Uncle Bob, who is having a birthday$_B$ litter for my cat which never goes outside$_C$ and$_D$ a sugar free cola for myself because I've been so good on my diet.
   (positions)_____ (rule)_____

CONVENTION: KEY COLON (:) RULES

1   Use a colon after the salutation of a business letter.

Example: Dear Mr. Scott:

2   Use a colon before a word, phrase, or clause that explains the
    independent clause.

Example: This was his most important test: he had to pass this
                 or lose the love of his child.

3   Use a colon to introduce a formal quotation.

Example: Franklin Delano Roosevelt said: "I hate war."

4   Never use a colon immediately following a verb.

Example: He gave me these: candy and cookies.

Wrong: ~~To me he gave: candy and cookies.~~

✍ COLON ASSESSMENT

Directions: Now apply what you have learned about the colon by
                 indicating where a colon should be placed (*A*, *B*, *C*, or
                 D) and which of the four rules you are following by
                 placing that colon at that place in the sentence.

1   He wanted$_A$ to remember the words of Lincoln$_B$ "Fourscore$_C$ and
    seven years ago our fathers brought forth upon this continent a new
    nation conceived in liberty and dedicated to the proposition that all
    men are created equal.$_D$ "
    (position)____ (rule)____

2   Dear Susan$_A$
    Dear Dr. Zeus$_B$ "
    Dear Aunt Fanny$_C$
    Dear Mom$_D$ "
    (position)____ (rule)____

✍ SENTENCE PUNCTUATION ASSESSMENT

Now try your hand at punctuating these sentences.

1   Since Tyler arrived early he needs to ask you to move your car so that he can leave and pick up his brother. *[needs one comma]*

2   I want to ask her to the concert but I don't have the money right now because I haven't been paid yet. *[needs one comma]*

3   Yes Jung Shoo can play football well but he also is an excellent student. *[needs two commas]*

4   After putting the dog inside Moe forgot to close the gate and the dog ran right after him. *[needs two commas]*

5   Josh and Koreen agreed with me and voted for my candidate but Ali chose to vote for his friend. *[needs one comma]*

✍ PARAGRAPH PUNCTUATION ASSESSMENT

Directions: Place eight commas, two colons, and one semicolon where they should be in this writing piece.

The Comprehensive Test in English will focus on four questions one on listening and writing for information and understanding one for reading and writing for information and understanding one for reading and writing for literary response and one for reading and writing for critical analysis and evaluation. This might seem very difficult at first but the reality is that the tasks are not too difficult if one is well prepared. The scoring rubric used for each of these tasks will concentrate on five points meaning development organization language use and conventions. Students who review the writing process will be preparing well for this English Test students should set aside time to study and practice in order to really do well on this test.

With this assessment on paragraph punctuation, you have reached the last page of your "English Driver's Manual." What you need to do next is practice. Assuming that you had completed a driving course and finished reading your state's Department of Motor Vehicles Driver's Manual, you would not take your road test without first practicing what you had learned. You need "road time." Although this book has reviewed with you the qualities of the Learning Standards on which you will be evaluated on the exam, the review has been brief. You need practice to achieve a realistic skill level.

If you were to take a survey of students' results on the English Comprehensive Test, you would most likely discover that most of the students' scores were directly related to the amount of effort that they had put into practicing their writing skills – the more the study, the better the score.

Go back through this book again. Do all of the exercises for a second time. Was it easier and quicker the second time around? How many items did you have to look up for a second time? You know if your skills are up to the challenge. Treat the rest of your test preparation as if you were an Indy 500 driver and your life depended on the proper execution of what you had learned.

Practice Tests A, B, & C will give you vital experience for the actual English Comprehensive Test. However, if you take the easy road instead of joining Robert Frost on "The Road Less Traveled," don't expect a grade higher than the effort you make. It is easy to complete these three practice tests because there are many helpful hints and sample answers along with the questions. Before you accept the sample responses, do the work yourself. Use the answers to check your work.

"Now, Ladies and Gentlemen, start your engines!"

UNIT FIVE
PRACTICE TESTS A, B, AND C
WITH STEP-BY-STEP GUIDANCE

PRACTICE EXAM A

REVIEW OF SKILLS NEEDED FOR SUCCESS ON SESSION I, PART A

The focus of the Session I, part A question is on your ability to listen, take notes, and then write a response for a specific audience. This question begins with an oral reading (selection) by the proctor, most probably a speech, and you are encouraged to take notes on what you hear at any time during the readings. You are not permitted to see the material which is read to you. The reading is presented to you only twice.

REMEMBER THAT NOTE TAKING IS CRITICAL TO THIS TASK.

Note taking is really one aspect of the writing process; the difference is that the piece is already written, and it is your job to be a kind of detective and to find the skeletal structure and essential ideas which the original author used as he or she was putting the piece together.

A good driver recognizes the railroad crossing sign as a place to use all senses. The driver only proceeds across the tracks after listening and looking carefully. Session One, Part A questions require listening to a passage twice and carefully noting the critical information before proceeding to respond.

At a stop sign, the driver must look down all the intersecting roads for approaching traffic before proceeding through the intersection. Session One, Part B questions require analyzing two or more documents before expressing a written response to a situation.

Since note taking is so closely allied to the writing process, you can use any of the several ways to take notes that you might use when you are trying to organize your own pieces of writing.

In the writing process, after you have a clear idea of the task and the audience, you then attempt to become aware of what you already know through a process of brainstorming. This brainstorming results in a listing of ideas. You then group these ideas, deleting those which are inappropriate.

At this point, you need to organize the remaining groups. Use a webbing or outlining process or both. You know that listening to a written work will be easier if you think along the lines that the author of the work thought when he or she wrote. So you must attempt to make a web that the author might have used.

You can do this because you know that all the English Comprehensive Test dictations must have a *beginning*, a *middle*, and an *end*. Get your outline set up and ready before the speaker starts to read the dictation.

Construct this sample *Webbing Form* on your paper:

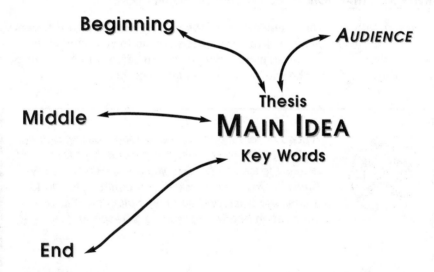

Even before you hear the dictation, you will get some help from the **"Overview"** which is printed on your copy of the exam and which you may read as the proctor reads it with you. The instructions will tell you the main idea of the speech. Write it in your web right away so that you do not lose focus as you listen.

Then carefully read the **Situation** part of the instructions. It will tell you why you are listening to this speech, what information you need to get from it, what you will have to write, and who your specialized audience will be. Write the audience above your web because you want to keep in focus exactly whom you need to address.

As you hear the dictation for the first time, listen for those things that you, as a good writer, will do. Under the part called "**beginning**," you will write the motivator (a hook idea) that the author of the speech used to grab your attention.

Then you must listen for a clear statement of the point of the speech. This is what you as a writer refer to as the thesis statement. Next to "**Thesis**" in your web, you will write the few key words that help you focus on the thesis.

Note: **Do not try to write every word you hear. You must listen and write just a few key ideas.**

When you hear the speaker begin to get very detailed about one part of the thesis, you will move to the "**Middle**" section of your webbing. Put a capital letter "**A**" and write only a word or two to remind yourself about this first big point. You may write a "**1**" or "**2**" under the "**A**" words if you hear some very clear detail that you think your audience might need to know. Remember that if you miss anything on the first reading, you need not worry since the piece is read twice to you.

Write as many capital letters as you need as you hear different ideas presented to develop the thesis. Some of these capital letters will have no numbers under them, and some will have a few numbers under them. That is to be expected.

If you hear a closing transition phrase such as "In conclusion," or "Therefore we can see," you will skip to your "**End**" section. Here, as writers, you know that you will hear the thesis idea repeated in different words. So, listen to make sure that you have the thesis idea correct.

As you know, writers try to end their works with a memorable finish. This finish idea might be one that would be impressive for you to use in your piece of writing about this speech. So put down a couple of key ideas about that finish.

Then you will listen to the dictation a second time. This time as you listen, you will focus on your outline and see whether you are correct or need to add a few details. Then you are ready to write.

PRACTICE ENGLISH TEST A

SAMPLE EXAM A: SESSION ONE, PART A – SAMPLE QUESTION

Try to take notes on this Session One, Part A sample question using the webbing form just described.

Overview: For this part of the exam, you will listen to a speech about the qualities of folk heroes, answer some multiple-choice questions, and write a response based on the *Situation* described below. You will hear the speech twice. You may take notes anytime you wish during the readings.

Situation: As an officer of the high school outreach counselors to the local middle school, your responsibility is to raise the consciousness of the middle school student about role models. Your faculty supervisor has asked you to attend a lecture by William Edwards, a noted lawyer and teacher of English, about the folk hero and then use the information you gain to write about traditional heroic qualities. You will publish this writing piece in the *Outreach Newsletter* which will be sent to each of the high school student counselors in your club. Be sure to use relevant information from this speech to write your essay.

Your Task: Write an essay to your fellow student outreach counselors to help them to be aware of traditional heroic qualities so that they might discuss some of these with the middle-schoolers whom they counsel about role models.

Guidelines:
- Tell your audience what they need to know to help them understand the qualities of the folk hero

- Use accurate, specific, and relevant information from the lecture to support your discussion

- Use a tone and level of language appropriate for an essay addressed to your peers and appearing in the school newsletter

- Organize your ideas in a logical and coherent manner

- Be sure to indicate any words taken directly from the speech by using quotation marks and by referring to the speaker

- Follow the conventions of written Standard English

Directions: The following is the text to be read aloud. Try to have a classmate or instructor read this to you without allowing you to see it first. Ask him or her to read it slowly, clearly, and carefully two times aloud.

Passage

So having had a chance at our first session to discuss why students have so few heroes in our modern culture and at our second session to investigate some of the folk heroes as they appeared in literature from various parts of the world at different times, let us now see what might be done to improve the heroic outlook in this country. If we can begin to see what the traditional human community considered important in its heroes, we might begin to look for those qualities in people we elect to office and in people we admire as celebrities. We have agreed that the essential qualities of a folk hero are six. Today I'd like to discuss three of these.

The first quality of a folk hero is that the hero must embody the values of his or her culture. In each of the stories we discussed, the hero needed to be a good community member who put the needs of that community above his or her own personal needs. As we saw, for instance, in the English epic, Beowulf risks his life personally and all alone combats a monster who terrorizes a community. That is an essential requirement of a traditional hero: self-sacrifice.

Do you think we see much of that today? Are our celebrities and public officials risking much for their colleagues, teams, peers, neighborhoods, and/or country? Of course some are, but are most of the people whom we see on TV or read about in the paper willing to sacrifice self? If not, why do we as a nation pay so much attention to these people? Is it because the only value that the community or country has is money or extensive recognition? We need to really think about this one.

What are the values which our celebrities and public officials embody? Do they value classical strength, the willingness to undergo pain without complaining? Are there many in the headlines who demonstrate this?

What about the need for intelligence as a societal value? We saw it time and again as we examined various, diverse myths. Are our public officials intelligent? Are our celebrities intelligent? We need to spend some time talking about that in our small group meetings today.

The second quality of a folk hero is the hero's willingness to leave the familiar in order to quest for something of value. The quest need not be for the Holy Grail of the Arthurian legend. The familiar that is left behind by the hero need not be one's country. The hero merely needs to be open to the unknown, willing to risk all to attain a worthy goal.

Are our celebrities and politicians willing to try new paths, risk fortune and fame, and/or follow undiscovered trails in order to achieve a worthy goal? We'll discuss that today in small groups also.

The third quality under discussion today is the folk hero's willingness to seek help from others, either spiritual or physical mentors. Odysseus gratefully took counsel from Athena. Once again, do we find our celebrities and public officials seeking help from those whose wisdom and insight are acknowledged as sound? This will be our last topic of group discussion.

My words today have raised far more questions than I've attempted to answer.

However, in discussion with each other we may begin to arrive at a solution to our current lack of heroes among our youth. In looking at these three essential qualities of folk heroes, we may begin to see how our culture might improve the images children view in the media. Our cartoons, our movie ads, our sports pages, our legal battles, and our political debates are the stuff of our daily epic in this twenty-first century America. So we must create our epic carefully, keeping in mind what qualities we want our children to emulate.

****

Instructions by Test Proctor:
"You may take a few minutes to look over the *Situation* and your notes. (Pause) Now I will read the passage aloud a second time." (Read the passage a second time.) After the second reading say: "Now answer the multiple-choice questions and continue with the task. You may now begin."

Here are sample notes on this speech:

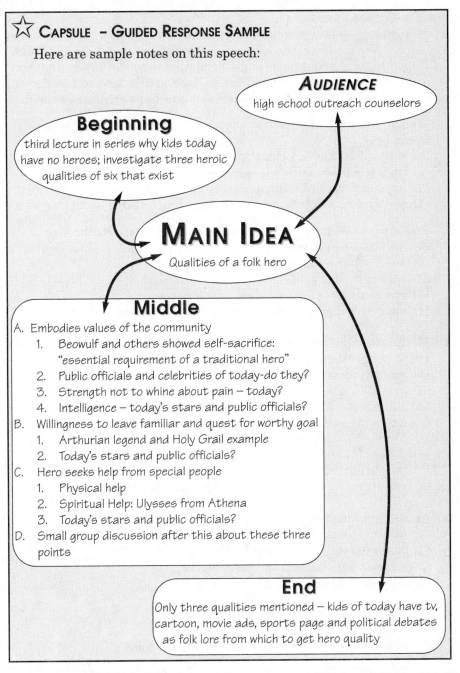

AUDIENCE
high school outreach counselors

Beginning
third lecture in series why kids today have no heroes; investigate three heroic qualities of six that exist

MAIN IDEA
Qualities of a folk hero

Middle
A. Embodies values of the community
   1. Beowulf and others showed self-sacrifice: "essential requirement of a traditional hero"
   2. Public officials and celebrities of today-do they?
   3. Strength not to whine about pain – today?
   4. Intelligence – today's stars and public officials?
B. Willingness to leave familiar and quest for worthy goal
   1. Arthurian legend and Holy Grail example
   2. Today's stars and public officials?
C. Hero seeks help from special people
   1. Physical help
   2. Spiritual Help: Ulysses from Athena
   3. Today's stars and public officials?
D. Small group discussion after this about these three points

End
Only three qualities mentioned – kids of today have tv, cartoon, movie ads, sports page and political debates as folk lore from which to get hero quality

After you finish your notes and before you write, you will read and respond to the short answer multiple choice questions about this speech. The questions themselves might well give you some more information about the speech or help you to check that you have received the correct impression from the text.

Multiple-Choice Questions

Directions: Use your notes to answer the following questions about the lecture. The questions may help you think about ideas and information from the lecture that you might want to use in your article for the newsletter. You may return to these questions anytime you wish.

1   Who do you think the speaker's *intended* audience for this speech would be?
(1) people who know nothing about heroes
(2) high school students who are counseling younger students
(3) anyone who liked folk music
(4) people who had listened to two preceding lectures about this topic

2   According to William Edwards, what was the source for the six qualities of a folk hero?
(1) one myth from ancient times
(2) only epic poetry
(3) group discussion about various folk heroes
(4) popular TV, ads, cartoons, and political speeches

3   Mr. Edwards' reference to Beowulf, Arthurian quests, and Odysseus might be an attempt to
(1) confuse those new to the lecture series
(2) give allusions as specific evidence
(3) name some of the discussion group members
(4) cite some authors

4   Mr. Edwards extensively uses
(1) double entendre   (3) sarcasm
(2) repetition   (4) allusions to cinema

5   According to the text, intelligence
(1) was often mentioned in diverse myths
(2) is unimportant if one is good-looking
(3) was not important in the early myths
(4) was only important in European myths

6   The Holy Grail was part of the legend of
(1) Beowulf   (3) Greece
(2) Athens   (4) Arthurian tales

7   Mr. Edwards states that he knows that
(1) he is very knowledgeable
(2) he knows very little
(3) his lecture is boring
(4) he raised more questions than he answered

8   The tone of this speech is
   (1) humorous   (3) questioning
   (2) pompous   (4) ridiculing

☆ CAPSULE – APPLYING THE PROCESS

As you work on your response writing and create your newsletter article, you must remember the writing process and apply it. You know *Your Task* and your audience. Your brainstorming consists of the notes you took on the speech. Now pull out the major ideas that you listed in the Middle section of your notes. Use these ideas as an outline for the body of your own newsletter essay.

Before doing anything else, look at *Your Task* directions. You were told to "Write an essay to your fellow student outreach counselors to help them become aware of traditional heroic qualities so that they might discuss some of these with the middle schoolers whom they counsel about role models."

In the introductory segment of your outline, you will have to be sure that you make your thesis clear to your audience. You should also try to start with a motivator of some kind. For this outlining of your own writing, you will use a more formal outline because you are not as rushed as you were when you took notes on the dictation.

Now you are ready to make your outline.

I.   Introductory segment:
   A. Motivator: How can we help middle school students find good role models?
   B. Thesis: Investigating some of the qualities of traditional folk heroes might help present day students think about the qualities of their role models.

II. Body paragraphs:
   A. Three qualities of traditional folk heroes
   B. Are these qualities in present day celebrities?
   C. Do things need to change?

III. Conclusion:
   A. Use other words to restate the thesis idea
   B. Use a reference or quotation from the original speech

Now you are ready to follow your outline and write.

Once your rough draft is complete, proofread, edit, and revise it. But, before you do so, you must check *Your Task* and *Guidelines* and see that you have fulfilled all of the requirements.

☆ CAPSULE CONTINUES ON NEXT PAGE

Have you fulfilled the following requirements?

- You told your audience what they need to help them understand the qualities of a folk hero.
- You used accurate, specific, and relevant evidence from the lecture.
- You used a tone and level of language appropriate for your peers who will read this in a school newsletter.
- You organized your ideas in a logical and coherent manner and double checked to make sure that the conventions of written Standard English were followed.
- You identified the words from the speech used by the author.
- You followed the conventions of written Standard English.

Once you have finished proofreading, editing, and revising, you will write your final draft.

After you have completed your essay, read these three sample responses which were evaluated as a #6 (the highest score), a #3 (a mid-range score), and a #1 (a poor score).

****

Here is a sample response which has been rated as a #6 (the highest rating).

Session One, Part A – Sample One Response

How can we help middle school students to find good role models? One way might well be to consider some of the qualities of a traditional folk hero. At a lecture last week, I heard Mr. William Edwards, teacher and lawyer, discuss contemporary society and traditional heroes. Mr. Edwards believes that by investigating some basic qualities of folk heroes, we may help both adults and young people think about how our media presents those celebrities whom we want our youth to emulate.

According to Mr. Edwards, there are at least three essential qualities of most traditional folk heroes. The first quality of a traditional folk hero is that of one who embodies the values of his/her community. Some of these traditional values were willingness to sacrifice for the community, an "essential quality of a traditional hero," the ability to endure pain and not complain, and the ability to exercise intelligence. A second quality of a folk hero is the willingness to leave the familiar and quest for something worthy, much as was done in the Arthurian tales. The last quality of a hero is the willingness to seek help from someone in order to gain either spiritual or physical power. For instance, Odysseus was willing to accept help from the goddess Athena, but that is merely one example, for these qualities were demonstrated through many tales from many cultures.

Are these qualities of the traditional folk hero present in contemporary America? Does the media feature public officials and celebrities who are noted for their willingness to sacrifice for the community? Do present day local, county, state, or world leaders speak about the need to give to others, let alone demonstrate a willingness to give of themselves? Is intelligence prized or does the media contribute to ridiculing those who have outstanding intellectual ability? Do our celebrities make headlines because of their willingness to endure hardship without complaining? Do our public officials and celebrities gain media attention by seeking spiritual guidance? These are things to consider because it is through the media attention that young people today form ideas of what is valued by the culture.

If we need to change our representation of what is of value in America, we can start by having our middle school friends ask questions such as I've just asked. Rather than tell our middle school students what should be of value to them in a hero, we need to start by telling our young friends whom we counsel exactly what some traditional heroic values were. Then we need to ask what they think of these customary values. And finally, we can raise the consciousness of these growing minds to the level that they will begin to question what they see and hear about the celebrities in the news. This is an important first step to bring back worthy role models to our American youth. The epics of today are written by the media on a daily basis, but the media ultimately will respond to public pressure. We must help our middle school friends to ask the right questions.

Look at the comments about this #6 as they appeared on the six point rubric chart, **MDOLC** in action.

SESSION ONE, PART A SCORING RUBRIC - Listening and writing for information and understanding (See Appendix for complete Scoring Rubric)	
Quality	**6 - Response at this level:**
Meaning: the extent to which the response exhibits sound understanding, interpretation, and analysis of the task and text(s)	- in-depth analysis of the text. Makes insightful connections between information in the speech and the assigned writing task
Development: uses specific allusions to the text and at least one quotation from it appropriately set off by quotation marks and a reference to the speaker	- specific allusions to the text and at least one quotation from it which is appropriately set off by quotation marks and a reference to the speaker
Organization: there is a fine motivator and thesis in the introduction as well as well developed body paragraphs which have clear transition. Further, there is a good, tight conclusion with a powerful closing statement.	- has a fine motivator and thesis in the introduction as well as developed body paragraphs which have clear transition - good, tight conclusion with a powerful closing statement
Language Use: the language is precise and sophisticated. There is a definite sense of student voice talking to peers.The sentence length is appropriately varied as are the types.	- language is precise and sophisticated - definite sense of student voice talking to peers - sentence length is appropriately varied as are the types
Conventions: there are virtually no errors in this sophisticated use of language.	- virtually no errors in this sophisticated use of language

Now Here is another essay response to this same question. However, this response was rated as a #3 (a paper in need of work).

Session One, Part A – Sample Two Response

Folk heroes are important. Youth today need to admire good people. Folk heroines were such people of the past. Maybe if we study these folk heroes and they're qualitys we can help students to have role models.

Edwards said that there are three qualities of a folk hero in the hole world. One quality is being a good community person. Is this true today? What about our judges, stars, and politicians? Secondly a folk hero must be willing to search for something. Are our stars willing to do this and risk their popularity? Thirdly the folk hero must be willing to seek help from others as Odysseus did from Athena. Do our celebrities do this today?

We need to help kids ask these questions so that they can decide what qualities there role models should have.

Look at the comments about this #3 rating as they appeared on the rubric. (Drive through this evaluation with confidence in your **MDOLC**.)

SESSION ONE, PART A SCORING RUBRIC -
Listening and writing for information and understanding
(See Appendix for complete Scoring Rubric)

Quality	3 - Response at this level:
Meaning: the extent to which the response exhibits sound understanding, interpretation, and analysis of the task and text(s)	– basic understanding of the text and makes some implicit connections between that information and the ideas in the assigned task
Development: uses specific allusions to the text and at least one quotation from it appropriately set off by quotation marks and a reference to the speaker	– develops some ideas more clearly than others, but uses relevant specifics from the dictation
Organization: there is a fine motivator and thesis in the introduction as well as well developed body paragraphs which have clear transition. Further, there is a good, tight conclusion with a powerful closing statement.	– ideas presented are logical, but the introduction is not strong – body lacks internal consistency – paragraphing and better transition is needed
Language Use: the language is precise and sophisticated. There is a definite sense of student voice talking to peers. The sentence length is appropriately varied as are the types.	– appropriate language with some awareness of the audience – occasionally varies sentence structure or length
Conventions: there are virtually no errors in this sophisticated use of language.	– some errors, but they do not greatly hinder comprehension

Here is the third and final essay response to this same Part I task. However, this response was rated #1 (very poor).

Session One, Part A – Sample Three Response

Heros are good I ust to have a hero when I was young but do kids today, No it is the fault of the stars and big shots you should tell others to be polit and not be pushy or jst conceted. Odyssues was a big shot but he helpt Athens. Tell kids not to not do drugs just sey know.

Look at the ratings for this response as they appeared on the rubric.

<table>
<tr><td colspan="2">SESSION ONE, PART A SCORING RUBRIC -
Listening and writing for information and understanding
(See Appendix for complete Scoring Rubric)</td></tr>
<tr><td>Quality</td><td>1 - Response at this level:</td></tr>
<tr><td>Meaning: the extent to which the response exhibits sound understanding, interpretation, and analysis of the task and text(s)</td><td>– no evidence that the writer understands either the text or the assigned piece of writing</td></tr>
<tr><td>Development: uses specific allusions to the text and at least one quotation from it appropriately set off by quotation marks and a reference to the speaker</td><td>– only one attempt at a paragraph and it lacks any relevant reference to the text</td></tr>
<tr><td>Organization: there is a fine motivator and thesis in the introduction as well as well developed body paragraphs which have clear transition. Further, there is a good, tight conclusion with a powerful closing statement.</td><td>– no focus and little organization</td></tr>
<tr><td>Language Use: the language is precise and sophisticated. There is a definite sense of student voice talking to peers. The sentence length is appropriately varied as are the types.</td><td>– level of language is minimal</td></tr>
<tr><td>Conventions: there are virtually no errors in this sophisticated use of language.</td><td>– minimal use of conventions and the result is great confusion regarding meaning</td></tr>
</table>

☆ **CAPSULE – QUESTION FOCUS**

The focus of this question is on your ability to read and write for information and understanding. You have to read both a text and examine some visuals in order to acquire sufficient information and understanding in order to write a response as required by the task. As with the first English test task, you will be evaluated by how well you reflect the qualities of the rubric, your **MDOLC**. IT IS EXTREMELY IMPORTANT THAT YOU INTEGRATE INFORMATION FOUND IN BOTH THE TEXT AND THE VISUALS INTO YOUR RESPONSE.

Directions: Read the text and study the graphs on the following pages, answer the multiple-choice questions, and write a response based on the *Situation* described below. You may use margins to take notes as you read. You may use scrap paper to plan your response.

Situation: The drama club in your school is planning its fall production. Your class has been promised some of the proceeds of this production to defray some of your class expenses such as the dance, the trip, and the day at the amusement park. The drama club is inviting members of your class to suggest the play to be performed. You decide to write a letter suggesting two appropriate play.

Your Task: Write the body of the letter to the president of the drama club. Using relevant information from the text and graphs, discuss the factors that you feel should be considered in the choice of a play for your school. Suggest two plays which you believe meet the criteria of the *Guidelines* suggested by the text and the graphs.

Guidelines:
- Tell your audience what they need to know about factors that should be considered when choosing a high school play
- Discuss how the two plays you have chosen for presentation are worthy choices because of how they reflect the important factors to be considered in choosing plays

- Use specific, accurate, and relevant information from the text and the graphs to develop your discussion
- Use a tone and level of language appropriate for a letter to the president of the drama club
- Organize your ideas in a logical and coherent manner
- Be sure to indicate any words taken directly from the article by using quotation marks and by referring to the author
- Follow the conventions of written Standard English

"Theater Still Thrives" by Vic Shun

1   Cars fill the lots; children, teens, parents, and senior citizens hasten to take their seats before curtain. The house is filled to capacity as the pit orchestra finishes the last fine tuning and the lights dim. Is this the Great White Way, the hub of culture,
5   the defining point of every professional actor's career? No, this is opening night at any one of the fifteen or so high schools in the area. The theater still thrives, the thespians are our children, and we, as the audience, play our part as one of the three factors that a district drama club must consider before select-
10   ing a play to produce.

      Most of the money which districts spend on the drama clubs is generated from the ticket sales of the last play. Therefore, the district-appointed advisors must give some thought to producing at least one fairly well-attended play
15   each school year. Part of the audience for the play will, of course, be the student body itself; part will be the faculty, administration, and staff; and part will be the parents and relatives of the actors and crews who are involved in the play.

      However, to fill a house, it is requisite that the drama club
20   attract other members of the community and, if possible, surrounding communities. Therefore, the drama group must consider which plays are most reliable as money makers. Musicals top this list, and traditional musicals seem to be those most preferred. For instance, although staging Gilbert and Sullivan pro-
25   ductions can be pricey (and the plays are somewhat dated), the general audiences have seemed to come out for them in recent years; so, we can expect to keep seeing them for a while.

      The cost of production is a second important factor which
30   helps to determine what play the high school drama club will

choose. The club must consider the payment of royalties to the various services which hold the rights to the plays and music. Then there is the outlay of money for sets and costumes. Even with parents willing to construct the sets and help make most of the costumes, this is an expensive element of play production. Then the element of lights and special effects can add another impressive sum to the burgeoning cost. Add to this cost the additional cost of make-up for an average group of ten, props, program, advertising costs, and promotions to encourage a full house and you have the reason why even high school theater tickets have become more expensive lately.

The more students involved in a production, the more most drama supervisors are pleased. As Ms. Su Nakitom, director of District 111's production of The Pirates of Penzance, said, "We were willing to pay for this expensive production because as a Gilbert and Sullivan piece we know we have a potentially large audience, and more importantly, we know that we can put many more students on stage and in the various crews with this play than we could have with the other play under consideration. We exist to give as many students as we can the possibility of becoming a part of a high school play. All students have a right to be involved. We see the issue as another case where somehow the state must guarantee entitlement to extra-curricular activities, sports as well as drama." So the number of students who could be involved is key to many district drama clubs. The choice of play genre (musical, comedy, or tragedy) then is also determined by what kind of talent the club has the most of in any given year. If there are few singing voices, but great comedic actors, the choice may be to stage a comedy. For Ms. Nakitom with her many gifted singers this year, the choice was a musical.

So what's it to be this year in your district? Will it be a musical, a comedy, or a tragedy? Well, you know the three important factors: audience interest, cost, and the numbers of students who can be involved. Whatever it is, go out and support your school and your kids, and have a good time.

Graph 1-a

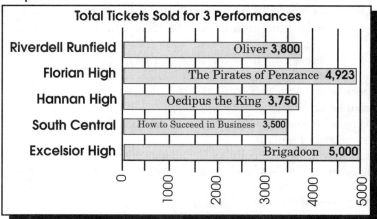

Total Tickets Sold for 3 Performances

School	Production	Tickets
Riverdell Runfield	Oliver	3,800
Florian High	The Pirates of Penzance	4,923
Hannan High	Oedipus the King	3,750
South Central	How to Succeed in Business	3,500
Excelsior High	Brigadoon	5,000

Graph 1-b

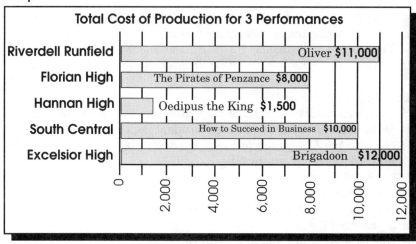

Total Cost of Production for 3 Performances

Riverdell Runfield	Oliver	$11,000
Florian High	The Pirates of Penzance	$8,000
Hannan High	Oedipus the King	$1,500
South Central	How to Succeed in Business	$10,000
Excelsior High	Brigadoon	$12,000

Graph 1-c

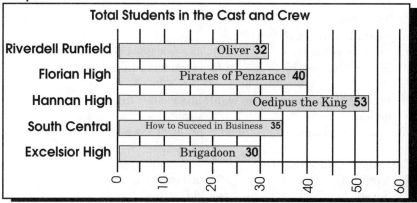

Total Students in the Cast and Crew

School	Production	Students
Riverdell Runfield	Oliver	32
Florian High	Pirates of Penzance	40
Hannan High	Oedipus the King	53
South Central	How to Succeed in Business	35
Excelsior High	Brigadoon	30

Multiple-Choice Questions

Directions: Answer the following questions. The questions may help you think about the ideas and information you might want to use in your letter. You may return to these questions anytime you wish.

9 The purpose of the article is to
  (1) criticize local theater groups
  (2) describe what audiences prefer and what considerations districts face in choosing a play
  (3) explain how a high school play is put together
  (4) argue for more professional theater groups to locate in the area

10 In line 19, the word "requisite" means
  (1) greatest   (3) necessary
  (2) limited   (4) least

11 According to graph 1-b, what was the most expensive play that a high school in the area produced last year?
  (1) *The Pirates of Penzance*   (3) *How to Succeed in Business*
  (2) *Oedipus the King*   (4) *Brigadoon*

12 According to graph 1-c,
  (1) these schools like to feature plays that use only a few students
  (2) *Oedipus the King* used the most students of this grouping
  (3) *Oedipus the King* was the least expensive play
  (4) no students tried out for *Oliver*

13 Ms. Su Nakitom is
  (1) the star of *The Pirates of Penzance*
  (2) a principal
  (3) the director of production at District 111
  (4) unhappy about the expense of theater

14 The text implies that a district which chooses a comic performance rather than a musical
  (1) has few students   (3) has few good singers that year
  (2) is choosing poorly   (4) is ignoring his advice

15 Ultimately Mr. Shun says he wants his reader to
  (1) become actors   (3) support school theater
  (2) read his column   (4) produce fewer musicals

16 The tone of this article is
  (1) annoyed   (3) informative
  (2) harsh   (4) ridiculing

⭐ CAPSULE – THE OUTLINE

So now you can respond after reading the article carefully, reviewing the information in the multiple-choice questions, and reading the material presented in the graphs. Use the **MDOLC** approach which is emphasized also in your *Guidelines* section of the question as a key to your response outline. You know you have to use the form for the body of a letter. First you will outline your multi-paragraph response. Each Roman numeral will be a paragraph.

I. Recommend two plays: one tragedy, one musical (*Oedipus the King*, *The Pirates of Penzance*)

   A. Remind receiver why the letter is being sent

   B. Simply state the selection suggestions

II. Explain first recommendation (*Oedipus the King*) with specific reference to article and visuals:

   A. Criteria of audience interest (REFER TO GRAPH 1-a): in the curriculum, Sophocles revival year at Greek center

   B. Criteria of cost (REFER TO GRAPH 1-b): no royalties, no sets, modern day costuming

   C. Criteria of student participation (REFER TO GRAPH 1-c): chorus could be open – no cuts from stage actors!

III. Explain second recommendation (*The Pirates of Penzance*) with specific reference to article and visuals:

   A. Criteria of audience interest (REFER TO GRAPH 1-a): big success last year at Florian High in neighboring district

   B. Criteria of cost (REFER TO GRAPH 1-b): low royalties

   C. Criteria of student participation (REFER TO GRAPH 1-c): very large cast, we have required fine voices

IV. Closing paragraph

Now you are ready to write your rough draft letter body. Although a business letter such as this has a sender's address, date, receiver's address (which is the same as what will be on the envelope), salutation, body, and closing, this task requires *only* the body, the part between the salutation and the closing. Write your final draft.

Compare your work with these three evaluated responses, a #6, a #3, and a #1 respectively.

Session One, Part B – Sample One Response

You and the club were kind enough to offer some part of the proceeds from this fall's production to be added to our class treasury. You also asked for suggestions as to what play might be the best to produce this fall. I've just finished reading in our local paper Vic Shun's article and the accompanying graphs about productions by high schools in our area last year, and I think that I can offer two good choices to you. Mr. Shun said that in choosing a high school play it is a good idea to use three criteria: audience interest, cost of production, and number of students involved. Using his criteria and studying the productions of five high schools last year in terms of these criteria, I've selected two plays. I know that clubs like to have choices when making decisions; however, the final choice is up to you. For the fall production, I'm suggesting the tragedy <u>Oedipus the King</u> or the musical <u>The Pirates of Penzance</u>.

<u>Oedipus the King</u>, an ancient Greek tragedy, meets the three important criteria set out by Mr. Shun. First, since this play is required reading for eleventh graders in our district, many students might want to come to watch what they have read. This fact and the fact that we know that there was a Sophocles revival at the Greek center last year that drew large crowds should lead us to expect ticket sales at least as large as Hannan High saw last year. Sophocles was the author of this tragedy, so we could expect many of those same people who went to the Greek center to come here also. Further, this play is great in regards to finances. There are no royalties to pay, no sets to build, and no costumes to rent if you use modern clothes. In the case of Hannan High, its drama club decided to rent costumes but still held the cost of the entire play to only $1,500. As regards the third criteria of student involvement, you could have on stage any actor who tried out because there is no limit to the number of people you could put into the chorus. Hannan High used 53 students in its production last year. So on all three criteria points, <u>Oedipus the King</u> seems to be a winner.

<u>The Pirates of Penzance</u> is a musical which also fulfills Mr. Shun's criteria. Last year, at Florian High, this play was a real crowd pleaser. The royalties for score and script are comparatively low when compared to such musicals as <u>Brigadoon</u>, <u>How to Succeed in Business</u>, and <u>Oliver</u>. The cast is large, so lots of students could be involved, and this year, as you know, we have the fine voices required for such a production. I'm sure Mr. Shun would concur that <u>The Pirates of Penzance</u> is a good choice.

Thanks for offering the class some of your profits, and thanks for asking for our suggestions. No matter what you choose, I hope your production is a success.

Look at the comments about this #6 as they appeared on the six point rubric chart, **MDOLC** in action.

SESSION ONE, PART B SCORING RUBRIC - Reading & writing for information & understanding (see Appendix for complete Scoring Rubric - check evaluation box for each quality scored)	
Quality	**6 – Response at this level:**
Meaning: the extent to which the response exhibits sound understanding, interpretation, and analysis of the task and document(s)	– *fine analysis of the text and the graphs –makes insightful use of information from the graphs and the text and uses these with understanding in the response*
Development: the extent to which ideas are elaborated using specific and relevant evidence from the document(s)	– *refers to the author by name and to the graphs included with the article by Shun*
Organization: the extent to which the response exhibits direction, shape, and coherence	– *clear transition (reference to Shun's criteria) and appropriate* – *introduction has clear thesis concept in response to the task* – *good sustained focus on the assigned task of discussing elements of choice and suggesting plays*
Language Use: the extent to which the response reveals an awareness of audience and purpose through effective use of words, sentence structure, and sentence variety	– *skillful reference to the graph and text which shows clear awareness of purpose and audiece. Diction shows peer audience respect*
Conventions: the extent to which the response exhibits conventional spelling, punctuation, paragraphing, capitalization, grammar, and usage	– *fine use of Standard written English in a thorough discussion*

Now here is another essay response to this same question. However, this response was rated as a #3.

Session One, Part B – Sample Two Response

Thanks for asking for our help in choosing a play. I read a great article in the paper and it suggested some ways to choose a play. Based on that I suggest these two plays to be considered for the fall production.

Oedipus the King and The Pirates of Penzance. These are good money makers and have lots of kids in them and don't cost too much to put on.

Oedipus the King I read in junior year. I really liked the plot. I never could imagine what it would be like to wake up one day and find out that you had married your mother, yuck! The article said that a good play should sell a lot of tickets, and I think this would because lots of kids know the story. Also this is a good play to put on because not only will a lot of people want to see it, but it costs them very little to put on, and lots of kids can be involved.

The Pirates of Penzance is a musical that lots of people will come to see because they know it is an old story. Not only will a lot of people come to see it, but a lot of kids can be in it, and it doesn't cost too much to produce. It follows the three guidelines of the newspaper article.

So these are my suggestions for the play so you can tell them. Both will be fairly inexpensive to produce, will attrat a good audience, and will use lots of kids. Good luck in your final decision.

Look at the comments for this #3 as they appeared on the six point rubric chart, **MDOLC** in action.

SESSION ONE, PART B SCORING RUBRIC - Reading & writing for information & understanding (see Appendix for complete Scoring Rubric - check evaluation box for each quality scored)	
Quality	**3 – Response at this level:**
Meaning: the extent to which the response exhibits sound understanding, interpretation, and analysis of the task and document(s)	- *conveys a basic understanding of the text by identifying the three criteria and then responding by making a suggestion of two plays* - *response fails, however, to include any reference to the graphs or to specifics from the graphs*
Development: the extent to which ideas are elaborated using specific and relevant evidence from the document(s)	- *develops ideas briefly but does not use criteria from text*
Organization: the extent to which the response exhibits direction, shape, and coherence	- *keeps focus in general but tends to digress as with reference to author's personal reading of the play*
Language Use: the extent to which the response reveals an awareness of audience and purpose through effective use of words, sentence structure, and sentence variety	- *use of "they" and "you" seem to indicate confusion over intended audience. Use of "kids" non-standard*
Conventions: the extent to which the response exhibits conventional spelling, punctuation, paragraphing, capitalization, grammar, and usage	- *some sentence structure problems*

Now here is the last essay response to this same question. However, this response was rated as a #1.

Session One, Part B – Sample Three Response

Okay, so here is a good idea. Let everybody who wants to be in a play be there so knowbody fels leftout or stoopid. Its like sports when i trye out in 7 grade and didnt mak the teem so i figer why bother and be stoopid? so how come they dont have teems for everybody or plays that everybody can be in. I think they should make a rule that the paly you put on is one any-body can get a part in. How about LesMs?

Look at the ratings for this response as they appeared on the rubric chart (**MDOLC**).

SESSION ONE, PART B SCORING RUBRIC -
Reading & writing for information & understanding
(see Appendix for complete Scoring Rubric - check evaluation box for each quality scored)

Quality	1 – Response at this level:
Meaning: the extent to which the response exhibits sound understanding, interpretation, and analysis of the task and document(s)	– conveys no understanding of the text, graphs, or task
Development: the extent to which ideas are elaborated using specific and relevant evidence from the document(s)	– reference to a play suggestion but no indication that there are any criteria involved in the choice
Organization: the extent to which the response exhibits direction, shape, and coherence	– no introductory segment or conclusion – the one paragraph lacks coherence
Language Use: the extent to which the response reveals an awareness of audience and purpose through effective use of words, sentence structure, and sentence variety	– no awareness of the specific audience
Conventions: the extent to which the response exhibits conventional spelling, punctuation, paragraphing, capitalization, grammar, and usage	– sentence, usage, spelling, and capitalization problems

The third of the English Comprehensive Test tasks is evaluating your ability to read and write for literary response.

☆ CAPSULE – THE KEY CONCEPT OF GENRE

One of the key concepts here is genre, the form in which the literature exists such as poetry, play, short story, letter, journal, feature article, or novel. You are asked to read two examples of literature, each from a different genre, and then you are asked to write a response in which you make reference to the two pieces in regard to their similarities or differences in treating closely related issues. You need to read with pencil in hand, underlining key ideas as you see them, and then you need to apply the writing process to your response, being sure to do pre-writing in a web and then a formal outline. Your response will be multi-paragraphed.

Directions: Read the poem "Adjective Wives" and the essay "Can't a Guy Ever Get a Break," and then answer the multiple-choice questions. Next, write the essay described in *Your Task*. You may use the margins to take notes as you read and scrap paper to plan your response.

Your Task: After you have read the passages and answered the multiple-choice questions, write a unified essay about the attitude toward women as revealed in the poem and the essay that you read. In your essay, use ideas from both passages to show how, though each selection presents an opposing attitude about women and their relationships, each uses a similar tone and effective literary techniques to emphasize that particular point of view.

Guidelines: (*MDOLC*)
* **Meaning**: Discuss the conflicting attitudes towards women and their relationships that are revealed in each selection
* **Develop**: Show how the use of specific literary elements (e.g. setting, characterization, structure), and techniques (e.g. figurative language, irony, symbolism) helps to convey the attitudes expressed in each selection
* **Organize** your ideas in a unified and coherent manner
* **Use Language** that communicates ideas effectively
* Follow the **Conventions** of written Standard English

Use a guided response to this sample Session Two, Part A question.

Texts: "Adjective Wives" by Siobhan McCabe
"Can't A Guy Ever Get a Break?" an essay by E. Ponymous

Passage I: "Adjective Wives" by Siobhan McCabe

1   Beware, young lady, of the fairy tale prince with his
        smiles and charm.
    He bows and he kisses and he looks so polite
    And he leaves every ball with a girl on each arm.
    He uses one name in each of his lives;
5   He's known as "the Prince" by his adjective wives.
    Snow White, Sleeping Beauty, and all of the rest,
    They don't see a problem; they think he's the best.
    Blindly, they love this idea of a man
    Who comes home, pets, and loves them whenever he can.
10   He's saved them from death, and from work, and from
        thought!
    He allows them to speak, whenever they ought.
    Permitted to hope, the wives wish, with laughter,
    And silently dream of happily ever after.

    Beware, young lady, the fairy tale prince with his smiles and
        charm.
15   He's all that you wanted: he's a fairy tale hero.
    Ask his adjective wives –
    He's got one on each arm.

Passage II: "Can't a Guy Ever Get A Break?" by E. Ponymous

1   I'm all for equal rights for women, no question. I mean you'd have to be a Neanderthal not to believe that every person has the right to speak his or her thoughts, live his or her life.

    However, I'm getting weary of men always being the
5   heavies in relationships, as if women were always perfect and men were all jerks waiting for a chance to control, or hinder, or be insensitive. There's plenty of proof as to the traditional controlling, hindering, and insensitive nature of women. Why, just look at the nursery rhymes and the fairy tales.

10   The Old Woman who lived in that shoe was a real child abuser and control freak. She forced her brood to live in a shoe, and then she whipped them all soundly and put them to bed. It's right there for anybody who learned that version to see.

    What about Beauty, you ask? Well, let's talk about Beauty
15   of "Beauty and the Beast." Why was it that Beauty's father encountered the Beast in the first place? Beauty's father

encountered the Beast because Beauty's father was stealing from the Beast, and what was the old man stealing?

20   The father was stealing the one thing that Beauty had requested as a present: a rose. So, the whole mess was caused by Beauty's insensitive request. Where else was the father to find a rose outside its normal growing season than in the garden of a bewitched being?

25   There are others we could consider. There was The Little Girl Who Had the Little Curl Right in the Middle of Her Forehead, that perverse child; Red Riding Hood, the disobedient little scamp; and Mistress Mary Quite Contrary, the name says it all. But, the point is clear. Women have been just as controlling, hindering, and insensitive as men. It's time we face the truth.

Multiple-Choice Questions

Directions: Answer the following questions. The questions may help you think about the ideas you might want to use in your essay. You may return to these questions any-time you wish.

(Questions 1-4 refer to Passage I – the poem)

1   The tone of the poem is enhanced by the use of reference to children's literature, a device known as
     (1) metaphor   (3) simile
     (2) allusion   (4) onomatopoeia

2   The tone present in the phrase "this idea of a man" in line 8 of "Adjective Wives" is one of
     (1) respect   (3) ridicule
     (2) joy   (4) gravity

3   In line 10 of the poem, the tone of irony is further enhanced by the idea of
     (1) saving someone
     (2) risking oneself for another
     (3) saving someone from thought
     (4) the mention of death

4   Lines 3 and 17 of the poem use the rhetorical/literary device known as (the)
     (1) rhetorical question   (3) inversion
     (2) repetition   (4) simile

(Questions 5-7 refer to Passage II – the essay)

5   In "Can't a Guy...," Ponymous alludes to his culture's
    (1) love of mankind   (3) achievement
    (2) stereotypes   (4) changes

6   The word "heavies" in line 4 of the essay is an example of
    (1) a simile   (3) non-standard word
    (2) a metaphor   (4) transition

7   With what retorical device does line 14 begin?
    (1) metaphor   (3) rhetorical question
    (2) hyperbole   (4) simile

8   One literary technique used by both Siobhan McCabe and
    E. Ponymous is
    (1) extended metaphor
    (2) allusion to fictional evidence
    (3) organizing in a cause/effect manner
    (4) introducing their works with quotations

 CAPSULE – OUTLINING

After you have finished these questions, review *Your Task*, and the *Guidelines* and write your response to Session Two, Part A. You may use scrap paper to plan your response.

Here is a sample of an outline for a response to this task.

I.   Introduction:
    A.   Motivator: mention how two genres can discuss same topic
    B.   Thesis: state how this poem and essay reveal conflicting attitudes about women and their relationships, but how each work uses a similar tone and effective literary techniques to make its point.

II.   Body:
    A.   Poem
       1.   Attitude toward women and their relationship: ironic (the women seem happy but still dream of happiness)
          a.   Dream prince saved them from death and thought
          b.   Dream prince has several of them but there is only one of him
       2.   Literary devices and techniques
          a.   Allusions to fairy tales as evidence
          b.   Use of rhyme
          c.   Use of image
          d.   Speaker addresses young women in mock caution about meeting princes at balls

☆ CAPSULE CONTINUES ON NEXT PAGE

B. Essay:
    1. Attitude toward women and their relationship: ironic (men seem to be the "heavies," but really women have always been as bad in relationships)
        a. Women of fairy tales were controlling, hindering, and insensitive
        b. Victims were children, fathers, and others
    2. Literary devices and techniques
        a. Allusion to fairy tales as evidence of thesis
        b. Use of rhetorical question
        c. Casual diction (heavies)

III. Conclusion:
    A. Use other words to restate the thesis
    B. End with ironic similarity as conveyed through allusions and diction in both pieces

After you have completed your essay, compare it to the following samples. This text evaluated the first as a #6 using the **MDOLC** rubric guide.

Session Two, Part A – Sample One Response

Writers write about the same issues but sometimes do so using different forms: poems, essays, journal entries, memories, newspaper columns, etc. In "Adjective Wives" by Siobhan McCabe and "Can't a Guy Ever Get a Break" by E. Ponymous, the authors write about the same issue, women and their relationships, and take very different points of view on that issue while using a similar tone and effective literary devices to emphasize their points of view.

"Adjective Wives" by Ms. McCabe presents women as the victims of bad relationships caused by the vulnerable women allowing themselves to be carried away by their "idea of a man": the same prince who saves them all from death and thought. These women then become his adjective wives who are permitted only to dream of better times and some future, obscure "happily ever after."

All then is ironic, not what it appears to be. Through rhyming couplets and images such as "bows" and "kisses," McCabe has allowed us memorably to see the suave prince bedazzle the unsuspecting women. However, because it is unlikely that most young women these days will be in danger of being swept away by fairy tale princes at balls, the author emphasizes the satiric nature of her tone. Further, her use of diction in lines 10-12 in which the Prince is seemingly praised, upon careful analysis, is ridiculing the Prince for his saving "[the wives] from thought," allowing them "to speak," and permitting them "to hope." So Ms. McCabe uses diction and allusion to children's fiction in order to present a satiric point: women must be careful not to allow themselves to lose their identities by being swept away by the empty, superficial charm of some men.

"Can't a Guy Ever Get a Break," an essay by E. Ponymous, ironically presents a point of view which differs greatly from that of McCabe's poem. Ponymous pleads for the public to see women as being just as damaging to relationships as men, who have borne all the weight of blame.

Ponymous uses as proof the same type of fairy tale allusions as does the poem. He points to the Old Woman of "The Old Woman Who Lived in a Shoe" as being abusive and controlling and Beauty of "Beauty and the Beast" as causing havoc by being insensitive in her request to her father. Ponymous uses proof from fiction to make a valid point: all people are essentially alike. Using fictional children's stories as proof allows the author to make his satiric tone clear. Further his use of diction, such as "heavies" creates a casual, humorous voice which allows the reader to see the author's point as being valid but not preachy.

Perhaps the greatest irony of these two pieces which have very different attitudes about the relationships of women is that each uses two literary devices in common: allusion to children's literature and precise diction.

So McCabe and Ponymous take different stands on the role of women in their relationships, but both share a similar satiric tone. Further, both use some convincing literary devices to make their points.

Now read the evaluation on the **MDOLC** rubric chart for this #6.

SESSION TWO, PART A SCORING RUBRIC - Reading & writing for Literary Response (see Appendix for complete Scoring Rubric - check evaluation box for each quality scored)	
Quality	**6 – Response at this level:**
Meaning: the extent to which the response exhibits sound understanding, interpretation, and analysis of the task and text(s)	- conveys clear understanding of both texts with their differing views yet similar tone - focus on task is clear in analysis of how each is same and different
Development: the extent to which ideas are elaborated using specific and relevant evidence from the text(s)	- makes use of quotations from poem and essay - good clear thesis which is well discussed in multi-paragraph body - conclusion clear and to the point
Organization: the extent to which the response exhibits direction, shape, and coherence	- good transition between proof and analysis
Language Use: the extent to which the response reveals an awareness of audience and purpose through effective use of words, sentence structure, and sentence variety	- appropriate to a literary analysis-omniscient voice
Conventions: the extent to which the response exhibits conventional spelling, punctuation, paragraphing, capitalization, grammar, and usage	- thorough discussion affords opportunity to use grammar, syntax, paragraphing, spelling, and capitalization well

Now here is another essay response to this same question. However, this response was rated as a #3.

Session Two, Part A – Sample Two Response

These are two good discussions of women and relationships. Ms. McCabe's poem places the blame on charming men, and Mr. Ponymous places the blame on women as well as men. Both use the tone of satire. Both use diction well.

"Adjective Wives" talks about a Prince who has several wives he picked up at balls. He never lets them do more than dream about happy endings. They are too thoughtless to realize they've been had. McCabe uses good diction to make her point about "the Prince." What a jerk!

"Can't a Guy Get an Even Break" is an essay about women in relationships and how the women are just as bad as the men. The Old Woman in the Shoe and Beauty and the Beast for instance. The author thinks that these stories prove his point. He uses comical language from old gangster movies.

These two authors had different points of view but were both making fun of some old ideas. They used good word choice too.

Look at the comments for this #3 as they appeared on the six-point *MDOLC* rubric chart.

SESSION TWO, PART III SCORING RUBRIC - Reading & writing for Literary Response	
(see Appendix for complete Scoring Rubric – check evaluation box for each quality scored)	
Quality	**3 – Response at this level:**
Meaning: the extent to which the response exhibits sound understanding, interpretation, and analysis of the task and text(s)	– recognizes the similarity of tone but not of allusion
Development: the extent to which ideas are elaborated using specific and relevant evidence from the text(s)	– observes the texts but doesn't use quotations
Organization: the extent to which the response exhibits direction, shape, and coherence	– good paragraphing but needs smoother transitions
Language Use: the extent to which the response reveals an awareness of audience and purpose through effective use of words, sentence structure, and sentence variety	– suitable for audience
Conventions: the extent to which the response exhibits conventional spelling, punctuation, paragraphing, capitalization, grammar, and usage	– fragment problem

Now here is another essay response to this same question. However, this response was rated as a #1.

Session Two, Part A – Sample Three Response

I want to show you how these two are the same. They both talk about women. One makes fun of fair tails and princes and the other makes fun of rimes and beasts. Both wer okay but I liked the poem best it was funnier with the stupid wives droling over this guy who treted them like dirt.

Look at the ratings for this response on the **MDOLC** rubric chart.

SESSION TWO, PART A SCORING RUBRIC - Reading & writing for Literary Response	
(see Appendix for complete Scoring Rubric – check evaluation box for each quality scored)	
Quality	**1 – Response at this level:**
Meaning: the extent to which the response exhibits sound understanding, interpretation, and analysis of the task and text(s)	– *doesn't seem to understand the texts or the task*
Development: the extent to which ideas are elaborated using specific and relevant evidence from the text(s)	– *there are no specifics which could document a thesis*
Organization: the extent to which the response exhibits direction, shape, and coherence	– *one rambling attempt at a paragraph proves confusing*
Language Use: the extent to which the response reveals an awareness of audience and purpose through effective use of words, sentence structure, and sentence variety	– *some words totally unclear*
Conventions: the extent to which the response exhibits conventional spelling, punctuation, paragraphing, capitalization, grammar, and usage	– *spelling and diction problems prohibit clear understanding as do lack of paragraphing and run-ons*

☆ CAPSULE – PREPARING FOR THE QUESTION

PROCEDURE FOR CATALOGING LITERATURE

This Session Two, Part B asks you to rely on your reading of worthy literature. That which you have read in class in high school is probably your best bet for handling this question. In preparing for the test, review all of the literature that you can remember and make a simple study guide for each work so that you can review the night before the test. Your writing group can share these study guides as you study for the test together.

Sample Study Guide for novels and short stories:

I.	Title:
II.	Author:
III.	Genre:
IV.	Setting:
	A. Time:
	B. Place:
V.	Point of view of narration:
VI.	Main characters and brief description:
	A.
	B.
VII.	Minor characters and brief description:
	A.
	B.
VIII.	Major conflict(s):
IX.	Climax:
X.	Denouement (resolution):
XI.	Ending:
XII.	Theme:
XIII.	Tone:
XIV.	Major symbols if any:

Once you have reviewed the literature, carefully read the *Critical Lens* (a statement about literature). First analyze it. Then, agree or disagree with it by fully discussing evidence from the literary works that you think are good examples of what the statement was saying.

READING & WRITING

Your Task: Write a critical essay in which you discuss *two* works of literature you have read from the particular perspective of the statement that is provided for you in the *Critical Lens*. In your essay, provide a valid interpretation of the statement, agree or disagree with the statement as you have interpreted it, and support your opinion using specific references to appropriate literary elements from the two works. You may use scrap paper to plan your responses.

Critical Lens: One statement about literature is attributed to John Hersey: "The final test of a work of art is not whether it has beauty but whether it has power."

Guidelines:

- Provide a valid interpretation of the *Critical Lens* that clearly establishes the criteria for analysis
- Indicate whether you agree or disagree with Hersey's statement as you have interpreted it
- Choose *two* works you have read that you believe best support your opinion
- Use the criteria suggested by the *Critical Lens* to analyze the works you have chosen
- For each work, do not summarize the plot but use specific references to appropriate literary elements (for example, theme, characterization, structure, language, point of view) to develop your analysis
- Organize your ideas in a unified and coherent manner
- Specify the titles and authors of the literature you choose
- Follow the conventions of written Standard English

☆ **CAPSULE – WRITING THE ANSWER**

Once again these task *Guidelines* provide you with a review of **MDOLC**. Now begin your writing.

First paraphrase the quotation; put Hersey's meaning into your words. This will allow you to interpret what he is saying. Hersey speaks of a "final" test of a work of art. "Final" means ultimate or most important. Literature is one type of a work of art. So when Hersey speaks of beauty and power here, he speaks of beauty and power as two ways to evaluate literature. Beauty is something attractive in itself, a sunrise, a flower, a handsome face. Power is something that is capable of causing a reaction in someone or something else.

☆ CAPSULE CONTINUES ON NEXT PAGE

Hersey says that the test of good literature is not its ability to be attractive but rather its ability to cause a reaction. Hersey is saying that literature can make the reader react, even though that which the reader is reacting to may be ugly, or sad, or hateful.

Now that you have analyzed what Hersey is saying, you must agree or disagree with his statement and then use *two* works of literature which you have read as evidence of your opinion about Hersey's comment.

Consider Hersey's statement based on the literature you have read and reviewed before this exam. You know that you were more impressed by literature which was based on sad or ugly things than on the literature which was simply a lovely story. Think of two works which stand out in your mind as being powerful although the subject that was written about was not necessarily attractive.

For example, what follows is based on John Steinbeck's novel *Of Mice and Men* and the poem "Dulce et Decorum Est" by Wilfred Owen.

Now you are ready to outline using the *Guidelines* as your key.

I.   Introduction:
     A. Paraphrase and explain Hersey's quotation
     B. State my agreement and two selected works I offer as evidence

II. Discuss Steinbeck's novel:
     A. Painful subject: murder of a friend to keep him from being taken
         prisoner for murder
     B. Memorable
         1. Characterization
         2. Plot
         3. Setting
         4. Theme
     C. My reaction

III. Discuss Owen's poem:
     A. Ugly subject: gas attack during World War I
     B. Memorable
         1. Setting
         2. Tone
         3. Images
         4. Allusion
     C. My reaction

IV. Conclusion:

After you have completed your final draft, compare it to the following three sample responses.

Session Two, Part B - Sample One Response

John Hersey believed that the ultimate test of literature is not the appeal of the subject matter of the piece, but rather the ability of a piece to make the audience react. He said, "The final test of a work of art is not whether it has beauty, but whether it has power." Considering that John Steinbeck's novel Of Mice and Men and Wilfred Owen's poem, "Dulce et Decorum Est" both deal with unattractive subjects yet cause powerful reactions, it is clear that Hersey's statement is correct.

Of Mice and Men deals with the friendship of two hard-working migrant farmers. They are not particularly attractive people; they have low paying jobs, are always on the move, and one of them, Lennie, has some developmental disabilities. The power of the story comes from the spirit that Steinbeck shows in his characters. Lennie is completely loyal to his friend George, as is George to Lennie. They share a dream which no one can take from them. This powerful characterization makes these men real, and because they become real they cause the reader to react to them with true concern for their welfare. The Salinas Valley becomes real in all its uncertainty for these characters who work for their daily bread and save for their dream ranch. Curley, the son of the owner, is a totally unattractive antagonist whose crude attitude toward his own wife causes the reader to be repelled. The reader is shocked when Lennie accidentally kills Curley's wife and George decides to shoot Lennie to save Lennie from the indignities of being caged in prison. Such incidents of plot have no beauty but have the power to stay in the memory of any attentive reader.

Wilfred Owen deals in his poem "Dulce et Decorum Est" with a gas attack on the battle field in World War I. The imagery of the setting allows the reader to hear the choking and see the men grabbing for their gas masks. Neither picture is pretty, but both become etched in the mind of the careful reader. In the poem, Owen says that if the reader could hear the blood gurgling from the seared lungs, the reader would no longer picture dying in war as "sweet" [dulcet]. Well, the reader does "see" that ugly picture because Owen writes well enough using imagery and onomatopoeia to delineate the horror for the reader. This is one of the ugliest scenes in poetry, but it is one of the most memorable. The power of this poem supercedes the lack of beauty in the subject. Owen did create a true work of art in this powerful piece of writing.

Hersey was correct. These two pieces hold the reader even after he or she has finished reading them, and yet neither has a beautiful subject to present. The true test of literature is in its ability to have the audience react.

Here is the **MDOLC** rubric chart for this #6 response.

SESSION TWO, PART B SCORING RUBRIC - Reading & writing for Critical Analysis (see Appendix for complete Scoring Rubric - check evaluation box for each quality scored)	
Quality	**6 – Response at this level:**
Meaning: the extent to which the response exhibits sound understanding, interpretation, and analysis of the task and text(s)	– *provides clear interpretation of the critical lens that is true to the original statement* – *using this interpretation, the author then agrees and focuses on the analysis of the two texts in light of the lens.*
Development: the extent to which ideas are elaborated using specific and relevant evidence from the text(s)	– *discussed application of Hersey's quotation to the two works using specific examples*
Organization: the extent to which the response exhibits direction, shape, and coherence	– *good introduction with clear thesis* – *body supports the thesis and shows focus and clear transition* – *conclusion returns to thesis and emphasizes it*
Language Use: the extent to which the response reveals an awareness of audience and purpose through effective use of words, sentence structure, and sentence variety	– *fine use of omniscient voice in presenting personal experience of the two texts*
Conventions: the extent to which the response exhibits conventional spelling, punctuation, paragraphing, capitalization, grammar, and usage	– *demonstrates control with virtually no errors*

READING
& WRITING

YIELD

FOR CRITICAL ANALYSIS

Now here is a sample response to this same task. However, this response was rated as a #3.

Session Two, Part B – Sample Two Response

I strongly agree with this quotation from Mr. Hersey. I have interpreted this statement to mean that all really good literture must be powerful more than it must be beautiful I think this is true. Beauty is only skin deep boy do I know that. But how a thing controls you is really important.

Of _Mice_ _and_ _Men_ was about two guys, one who was retarted,Lenny. They had a hard life working on other people's farms. They had some ugly times like when the villain Curley was disrespectful to Lenny. But I remember the story because it was about how sometimes friendship asks you to do some ugly stuff. Like, George had to decide to kill Lenny so Lenny didn't go to jail and suffer for accidentally killing Curley's wife. A powerful, good book.

We read _"Dulce et Decorum Est"_ in social studies last year. It was about the trench warfare in World War I and how soldiers died of posion gas. The poem talked about how ugly the guys deaths were from the gas. But that poem changed my thinking about war. That was not a pretty poem, but it was powerful.

Hersey was right on targut here. Really good books are not always pretty but are alwasys powerful.

Here is the **MDOLC** rubric chart for this sample #3.

SESSION TWO, PART B SCORING RUBRIC - Reading & writing for Critical Analysis	
(see Appendix for complete Scoring Rubric - check evaluation box for each quality scored)	
Quality	**3 – Response at this level:**
Meaning: the extent to which the response exhibits sound understanding, interpretation, and analysis of the task and text(s)	- does seem to understand the lens and apply it to two works - focus drifts a bit
Development: the extent to which ideas are elaborated using specific and relevant evidence from the text(s)	- uses references to the works - neglects citing authors
Organization: the extent to which the response exhibits direction, shape, and coherence	- good division into introduction, body, and conclusion - transition a bit weak - confuses point of view
Language Use: the extent to which the response reveals an awareness of audience and purpose through effective use of words, sentence structure, and sentence variety	- fragment and run-on problem
Conventions: the extent to which the response exhibits conventional spelling, punctuation, paragraphing, capitalization, grammar, and usage	- spelling is confusing as are punctuation problems

Now here is a sample #1 response to this task.

Session Two, Part B – Sample Three Response

John nos his stuf. Sum girls are prety but they are mean so what good is that? You have to have power. Art is very like this. In art class they do sum powerful stuf. I lik power. Beauty is ok but sometimes its not.

Here is the **MDOLC** rubric chart for this sample.

SESSION TWO, PART B SCORING RUBRIC - Reading & writing for Critical Analysis	
(see Appendix for complete Scoring Rubric – check evaluation box for each quality scored)	
Quality	**1 – Response at this level:**
Meaning: the extent to which the response exhibits sound understanding, interpretation, and analysis of the task and text(s)	*– confused and incomplete, with no analysis of the point of the quotation in regard to literature*
Development: the extent to which ideas are elaborated using specific and relevant evidence from the text(s)	*– gives no reference to literature*
Organization: the extent to which the response exhibits direction, shape, and coherence	*– one, rambling attempt at a paragraph*
Language Use: the extent to which the response reveals an awareness of audience and purpose through effective use of words, sentence structure, and sentence variety	*– incoherent in spots*
Conventions: the extent to which the response exhibits conventional spelling, punctuation, paragraphing, capitalization, grammar, and usage	*– very needy*

End of Practice English Comprehensive Test A

Practice English Comprehensive Test B follows. Now that you have completed one practice exam, you should be able to apply what you have learned on the Practice English Test A. You will do more of the work yourself on this second practice exam. For example, the Session One and Session Two, Parts A and B Scoring Rubrics have not been filled out for you. You will evaluate each of the sample responses based on the Rubric Qualities (**MDOLC**).

PRACTICE ENGLISH TEST B

PRACTICE TEST B: SESSION ONE, PART A – SAMPLE QUESTION

☆ CAPSULE – REMEMBER *MDOLC*

Now try another Practice Test – Session One, Part A question.
Remember that you are being asked to do the following:

M Listen for **meaning**, take notes on the meaning, and write a
response which clearly evidences that you understand and can
communicate the meaning of what you have heard

D **Develop** with specific and relevant evidence the specifics of
what you have heard and then write a well developed, precise
response

O **Organize** your notes based on the organization of the listening
passage and then organize your writing well so that your reader
may clearly follow your presentation

L Use your **language** to show an awareness of your audience by
using good diction and effective and varied sentence structure

C Follow the **conventions** of Standard English
in regard to spelling, punctuation,
paragraphing, capitalization, grammar, and
usage

Try to take notes on this Practice English Test –
Session One, Part A question using the webbing form
described on page 100-101.

Overview: For this part of the exam, you will listen to a speech
delivered at a local Board of Education hearing,
answer some multiple-choice questions, and write a
response based on the *Situation* described below. You
will hear the speech twice. You may take notes anytime you wish during the readings.

Situation: As a part of your community service requirement for
graduation, you have been asked to write an essay
about the value of teaching Shakespeare's *Hamlet* to
seniors in high school English classes in your district.
In preparation for writing your essay, you will listen
to a speech made by a parent who has considered this
issue carefully. Use relevant information from the
speech to write your essay.

Your Task: Write an essay for your Social Studies 12 class on the
topic of the value of teaching *Hamlet* to seniors in
English classes in your district.

Guidelines:

In your article be sure to do the following:

- Tell your audience what they need to know to help them to understand the issue and how this one, informed parent feels about it
- Use specific, accurate, and relevant information from the speech to support your discussion
- Use a tone and level of language appropriate for an essay for your Social Studies 12 class
- Organize you ideas in a logical and coherent manner
- Be sure to indicate any words taken directly from the speech by using quotation marks and referring to the speaker
- Follow the conventions of written Standard English

Directions: The following is the text to be read aloud. Try to have a classmate or instructor read this to you without allowing you to see it first. Ask him or her to read it slowly, clearly, and carefully two times aloud.

Passage

I have sat patiently and waited for this opportunity to speak here today because I am happy to sit anywhere at the end of my long day. I work in the local grocery mart as a cashier. I have worked there since my oldest, who is now a senior, was three. When I started, I was a clerk, and I am a cashier now. I have no real complaints about my job, and as a single parent now I am thankful for the security it offers us, but I could have done more with my life if I had had an opportunity to increase my skills.

Where I work, knowing or not knowing *Hamlet* would never be a question anyone would spend much time discussing. But I have heard many intelligent and well educated people discuss this question, and since my son is a senior and my other two will be seniors some day, and my tax money helps to support this district, I listened carefully to all of the arguments presented.

I read in the paper that some kids say Shakespeare has nothing to teach in this new computer age. I hear others say that the time would be better spent on learning a keyboard.

I hear some say that we need more literature about real American students, kids like my three boys.

I hear that there are some who say that some of the language in that play is very rude. There are, I guess, some insulting lines that Hamlet says to his mother.

I hear from neighbors whose children have substance abuse problems that kids would be better off with more counseling and fewer plays from long ago.

But, most importantly before I came here tonight, I heard from my son the senior. He is not the best student, but he wants to learn so he won't have to be in the same low paying job for the next twenty years. So he does care, and he is usually fair.

I heard from my son that there is a lot of very hard vocabulary in that play. He told me that his teacher made up vocabulary lists and exercises from the play before they read it. He said that he learned a lot of new words. He sometimes even says some of the lines from the play to me. I don't know what all the words mean, but he does.

I heard from my son that the main character, Hamlet, is a very confused young man who sometimes is tempted to want to end his life because his family problems are so bad. My son knows something about such things. My son could see when Hamlet was being selfish and self-pitying and when Hamlet really deserved pity. My son could see that some of Hamlet's decisions were bad. And when my son saw these bad decisions, my son could see the bad results without ever getting hurt himself. That is a good thing for my son: to see poor choices made and not have to really deal with the results. He could learn from this what anger and vengeance do to people. He could learn what happens when a person loses hope.

We aren't from England. My parents didn't even speak English, but somehow my son is learning something from somebody who lived hundreds of years ago on a tiny island which he has never visited. I think that is good. Maybe that is what being a human is all about. Maybe that is what makes this play so good. This play is not about an old Englishman or an old Dane. This play is about human nature as it is found in men and women then and now.

I want my son to learn the English vocabulary. I want him to learn to talk about anger without just yelling obscene words. I want him to see that all families are not perfect, but that this is no reason to give up hope. I want my son to see that people are people.

I was happy to sit and wait for my turn to speak because I heard a great deal that made me think. What I think is that we should teach Shakespeare's *Hamlet* and teach it so well that all students will see what my son saw and then some. *Hamlet* sounds so good that my son said that if I wait until he has some time, he will teach it to me.

Directions from the proctor: "You may take a few minutes to look over the *Situation* and your notes." (Pause) "Now I will read the passage aloud a second time." Read the passage a second time. After the second reading say, "Now answer the multiple-choice questions and continue with the task. You may begin now."

☆ CAPSULE – AFTER THE SECOND READING

After the second reading, jot down notes in the format of speech beginning, speech middle, and speech end. Then you will know what to list as the main idea of the speech. Repetition of ideas and extensive use of specifics will allow you to see those ideas as being of major importance.

AUDIENCE
School Board and meeting audience

Beginning
glad to sit anywhere after long day as cashier

MAIN IDEA
question of whether <u>Hamlet</u> should be taught in senior English classes in this district

Middle

- heard kids – negative, Shakespeare has nothing to teach the new computer age-better to spend same time on learning the keyboard
- heard kids – negative, need more literature for and about today's American youth
- heard others – negative: play has some rude language
- heard neighbors – whose son has substance abuse problem: better to have more counseling and fewer plays "from long ago"
- heard son – "most importantly" from own son – positive: hard vocabulary but he is learning it. Hamlet is confused and "tempted to want to end his life because his family problems are so bad."
- her son knows something about such things, her son can see bad decisions but not get hurt
- her family not from England, her "parents didn't even speak English" but her son can learn that the play is about "human nature" as it is found in men and women then and now"

End

She wants her son to learn English vocabulary. She wants her son to learn to talk about anger without obscenities. She wants her son to see no family is perfect but not a reason to give up hope. She wants her son to learn <u>Hamlet</u>, and if he has time, teach it to her.

After you finish your notes and before you write, you will read and respond to the short answer multiple-choice questions about this speech because the questions themselves might well give you some more information about the speech or help you to check that you have received the correct impression from the text.

Multiple-Choice Questions

Directions: Use your notes to answer the following questions about the speech. The questions may help you to think about ideas and information from the speech that you might want to use in your essay. You may return to these questions anytime you wish.

1   The speaker was obviously
  (1) a woman with a sense of concern for her children
  (2) annoyed at having to wait so long to speak
  (3) disrespectful to those whose views she did not share
  (4) uninterested in the views of those who were not adults

2   The speaker uses which technique to keep the audience focused on the speech?
  (1) threats   (3) repetition of phrases
  (2) allusions to historical events   (4) rhetorical questions

3   The tone of this speech is
  (1) sad   (3) ridiculing
  (2) thoughtful   (4) objective

4   According to the speaker, the most convincing argument came from
  (1) a teacher
  (2) a Board member
  (3) the neighbor whose son has a substance abuse problem
  (4) a senior student who had studied *Hamlet*

5   The speaker implies that she
  (1) has had a difficult life   (3) is a single parent
  (2) has three children   (4) works for a living

6   The speaker comes from parents who
  (1) beat her
  (2) did not speak English
  (3) sent her to college
  (4) never got interested in her education

7   The speaker likes the idea that through *Hamlet* her son can
  (1) learn about Denmark
  (2) see poor decisions made and not suffer personally from their consequences
  (3) learn to act
  (4) appreciate college level material

8   The speaker hopes that her son will
  (1) get a job in her store
  (2) clean his room
  (3) teach her all of this new vocabulary
  (4) teach her about *Hamlet*

☆ CAPSULE – THESIS FORMATION

Your Response: After you have finished answering these questions, review the *Situation*, *Your Task*, and the *Guidelines*. Underline the commands and major constraints of the task.

Your Task: Write an essay for Social Studies on the topic of the value of teaching *Hamlet* to seniors in English classes in your district.

Now refer to the notes you took on the speech. Decide upon your point of view. Make an assertion and then a thesis on the task.

Simple Assertion using Verb "To Be"
There is a value to teaching *Hamlet* to seniors in English classes in this district.

Dynamic Verb Thesis Made from Assertion:
The value of teaching Shakespeare's play *Hamlet* resounded in the words of a supportive parent at the District Board of Education meeting last Tuesday evening.

Now pull out the major ideas that you listed in the Middle section of your notes. Use these ideas as notes from the body of your essay. Group and delete your notes. When this is done to your satisfaction, make an outline. In your outline include the introductory and conclusive elements of your letter. Try to begin your introduction segment with a good attention grabber, a motivator.

Here is an outline of the essay that you might write:

I.   Introductory segment:
   A. Motivator: Shakespeare would have been very pleased with the voice of a citizen whose ancestors not only were not English but also didn't even speak the English language.
   B. Thesis: The value of teaching Shakespeare's play <u>Hamlet</u> resounded in the words of a supportive parent at the District Board of Education meeting last Tuesday evening.
II. Body paragraphs:
   A. Expression is improved
   B. Understanding of the flawed nature of families and the need to make good choices
   C. People are people now and then

III. Conclusion:
   A. Restate in other words the thesis idea
   B. Use a quotation from the speech for a powerful ending

Three responses to this task follow. Since ultimately the task will be graded on a score of #1 (poorest) to #6 (best), try to evaluate these three responses yourself much as the graders will. You must use your **MDOLC** rubrics guide as the criteria here.

MEANING
DEVELOPMENT
ORGANIZATION
LANGUAGE USE
CONVENTIONS

Here is the first response. Evaluate it as a #6 (very good), a #3 (writing in need of work), or a #1 (very poor).

Session One, Part A - Sample One Response

It is an excellent idea to teach Hamlet by Shakespeare to seniors in high school English classes. The play is well written and seniors are old enough to understand that kind of stuff, also some members of the community are really in favor of the play and so it should be taught.

Seniors are old enough to understand Shakespeare. It is difficult but it is worth it. Things that are worth doing are worth doing well I know because it took me a year to get my driver's license.

Seniors as the oldest high school students should be given a chance to do more than learn the keyboard and get counseling. They should be given a chance to read important stuff and Shakespeare is that important.

Some adult members of the community also think that seniors are old enough to read Hamlet. It is good even if it is difficult and the language is tough seniors need to know these words and ideas. Seniors need to know that families all have problems like this. One parent even said that her son should be able to read it and even he should teach it to her.

So, Shakespeare's Hamlet should be taught to seniors in high school. They are old enough to learn good stuff even if it is hard.

Now rate this response using the **MDOLC** chart on the next page.

Remember: From the dictation, you have made your outline and essay response. Compare the quality of the sample essay and your own. When evaluating both the sample given here and the response you wrote, consider the following questions: Does the sample response clearly and specifically give good evidence from the speech to support the value of teaching *Hamlet* to seniors in English classes? Is there an introduction, a middle which has specific proof, and an end? Is there good transition? Are there sentence structure errors? Do these errors sometimes make the writing confusing?

I would rate this first example as _____.
I will list my reasons under the parts of **MDOLC**.

SESSION ONE, PART A SCORING RUBRIC - Listening and writing for information and understanding (see Appendix for complete Scoring Rubric – check evaluation box for each quality scored)	
Quality	**Commentary** The response:
Meaning: the extent to which the response exhibits sound understanding, interpretation, and analysis of the task and text(s)	
Development: the extent to which ideas are elaborated using specific and relevant evidence from the text(s)	
Organization: the extent to which the response exhibits direction, shape, and coherence	
Language Use: the extent to which the response reveals an awareness of audience and purpose through effective use of words, sentence structure, and sentence variety	
Conventions: the extent to which the response exhibits conventional spelling, punctuation, paragraphing, capitalization, grammar, and usage	

Now share your chart with your writing group.

Now here is the second response to be rated.

Session One, Part A – Sample Two Response

This was a good spech about how a mother loves her son. Today many parents do not give there kids enough credit I know my mother doesn't and that bothers me a. lot. My mother is alweys buggin me, and she hardly never lets me read magazines that I want becuz she says that I'm waisting time. I think seniors should be able to do whatever they want, even reading junk. I hope you agreee.

Using your **MDOLC** chart, rate this second response.

Remember: From the dictation, you have made your outline and essay response. Compare the quality of the sample essay and your own. When evaluating both the sample given here and the response you wrote, consider the following questions. Does the sample response clearly and specifically give good evidence from the speech to support the value of teaching *Hamlet* to seniors in English classes? Is there an introduction, a middle which has specific proof, and an end? Is there good transition? Are there sentence structure errors? Do these errors sometimes make the writing confusing?

I would rate this second example as _____.

I will list my reasons under the parts of **MDOLC**.

SESSION ONE, PART A SCORING RUBRIC - Listening and writing for information and understanding (see Appendix for complete Scoring Rubric – check evaluation box for each quality scored)	
Quality	Commentary The response:
Meaning: the extent to which the response exhibits sound understanding, interpretation, and analysis of the task and text(s)	
Development: the extent to which ideas are elaborated using specific and relevant evidence from the text(s)	
Organization: the extent to which the response exhibits direction, shape, and coherence	
Language Use: the extent to which the response reveals an awareness of audience and purpose through effective use of words, sentence structure, and sentence variety	
Conventions: the extent to which the response exhibits conventional spelling, punctuation, paragraphing, capitalization, grammar, and usage	

Now share your chart with your writing group.

Now here is the third response to be rated.

Session One, Part A – Sample Three Response

Shakespeare would have been very pleased with the voice of a citizen whose ancestors not only were not English but also didn't even speak the English language. The value of teaching <u>Hamlet</u> resounded in the words of a supportive parent who spoke at school last night.

A hard- working single parent and taxpayer spoke eloquently defending the value of teaching <u>Hamlet</u>. Her first point was that in teaching the play, students like her own senior son have a wonderful opportunity to enhance their vocabularies. This lady told how her son's teacher had constructed lists of words from the play and used these lists to increase the vocabulary level of the students. Further this mother of three spoke of how she is pleased that her son may now have the ability to express even anger without merely using obscenities.

The speaker then made some very valid points about the level of understanding that a student, such as her son, could receive from the play. She mentioned that <u>Hamlet</u> is the story of a young man who nearly lost the will to live because of his dysfunctional family. She then stated that her son had had some experience with family problems and that it was very important that he saw that no family is perfect, but that lack of perfection is also no reason to lose hope. This is counseling on a dramatic level. Such a vivid story certainly would make an impression on some students who have similar family problems. This parent then said that her son needed to see the results of poor choices without having to pay the cost of the poor choices. These powerful examples helped me to see the social implications of the teaching of this tragedy.

The ability of the play to help people to connect with others who come from different backgrounds was next made very clear by this speaker. She said that her parents had not spoken English and she was not English but that the play was able to say something to her son about life. She felt that this emphasized the essential, consistent nature of human beings from all times and all places. In an age such as ours in a pluralistic society which has chosen the noble experiment of a democratic republic, this is a lesson we all need to learn again and again. We are all in this life together, and our chance for success hinges on our ability to see others in ourselves and ourselves in others.

So this humble woman, a cashier in a grocery mart, clearly delineated the value of teaching *Hamlet* to high school seniors. She made her point most emphatically when at the end of her remarks she said that despite her busy schedule as single parent of three boys and cashier she was anxious to have her own son "teach it [the play] to me."

Using your **MDOLC** chart, rate this third response.

Remember: From the dictation, you have made your outline and essay response. Compare the quality of the sample essay and your own. When evaluating both the sample given here and the response you wrote, consider the following questions. Does the sample response clearly and specifically give good evidence from the speech to support the value of teaching *Hamlet* to seniors in English classes? Is there an introduction, a middle which has specific proof, and an end? Is there good transition? Are there sentence structure errors? Do these errors sometimes make the writing confusing?

I would rate this third example as _____.
I will list my reasons under the parts of **MDOLC**.

Quality	Commentary The response:
SESSION ONE, PART A SCORING RUBRIC - **Listening and writing for information and understanding** (see Appendix for complete Scoring Rubric – check evaluation box for each quality scored)	
Meaning: the extent to which the response exhibits sound understanding, interpretation, and analysis of the task and text(s)	
Development: the extent to which ideas are elaborated using specific and relevant evidence from the text(s)	
Organization: the extent to which the response exhibits direction, shape, and coherence	
Language Use: the extent to which the response reveals an awareness of audience and purpose through effective use of words, sentence structure, and sentence variety	
Conventions: the extent to which the response exhibits conventional spelling, punctuation, paragraphing, capitalization, grammar, and usage	

Now share your chart with your writing group.

Good work! Now you are ready to progress to Session One, Part B (the second task).

Now try this Session One, Part B sample question.

☆ CAPSULE – MORE *MDOLC*

Remember that you are being asked to do the following:

M **Meaning**: Read a text and some visuals for information and understanding

D **Develop** a response which uses specific documented references from both the text and the visuals

O **Organize** your response so that your reader can see a focus on the task and a clear transition from one part to another

L Let your **language use** show an awareness of your audience by using appropriate diction and varied sentence structure

C Follow the **conventions** of Standard English in regard to spelling, punctuation, paragraphing, capitalization, grammar, and usage

---

Directions: Read the text and study the chart on the following pages, answer the multiple-choice questions, and write a response based on the *Situation* described below. You may use the margins to take notes as you read. You may use scrap paper to plan your response.

Situation: Your English teacher has assigned each member of your class a grammar topic to research and write about. You were assigned the discussion of the four types of sentences as categorized by structure. To review the essentials of this topic, read the article entitled "Form and Use" by the noted teacher Kevin Francis. Study the chart accompanying the article.

Your Task: Write an essay for presentation in English class regarding the factors determining the four different types of structures of the English sentence. Using relevant information from the text and the chart, discuss how a knowledge of the factors determining sentence structure should affect a careful author's use of the sentence types in his or her writing.

Guidelines:
- Tell the class what they need to know about the four types of English sentences as classified by structure
- Discuss the factors which determine sentence type and the implications of the use of each type
- Use specific, accurate, and relevant information from the text and the chart to develop your discussion
- Use a tone and level of language appropriate for an essay to be presented in English class
- Organize your ideas in a logical and coherent manner
- Be sure to indicate any words taken directly from the article by using quotation marks and referring to the author
- Follow the conventions of written Standard English

"Form and Use" by Kevin Francis

1   The manner in which an object in nature is formed has a great deal to do with the use for which that object exists. The very structure of the human hand, in all its intricacies and with its unique opposable thumb, signals the superior useful nature

5   of that hand above all other pods and paws of the rest of the animal kingdom. Form and use are inextricably tied together. And as in the world of nature, so also in the world of linguistics; form and use reflect each other. In the English language this mutual dependency is nowhere more evident than in the

10   structure and implications for use necessitated by that structure seen in the four types of English sentence structures: simple, compound, complex, and compound-complex.

     The building block of structure in the sentence is the clause: that group of words which includes both a subject and

15   a predicate. By combining the independent clause (the clause which can stand alone) and the dependent clause (the clause which needs completion), the language user is capable of forming four entirely different structures. The simple beauty of this linguistic structure is reminiscent of the natural

20   world in which the same basic forms are found everywhere, but the combination of those forms results in startlingly different things.

     The first and most basic of the types is the simple sentence. This one independent clause is direct and unadorned. A para-

25   graph composed completely of simple sentences would be staccato. A single simple sentence written as a paragraph would command remarkable attention so the author would

have to be very sure that that particular paragraph could sustain all of that importance. The name of the sentence type is
30   misleading when one ponders the possible effect of its use.
Misuse of this type will sound childish, but careful use will add
emphasis and power to one's writing.

The compound sentence eschews incompletion. All of its
elements are complete in themselves. The harmony of the sen-
35   tence comes from this fact. The compound sentence lends itself
to an even-handed perusal of things, a balancing of ideas or a
comparison of concepts. The wise user of this sentence type
respects this natural tendency to show both sides of an issue or
at very least, to balance one value against another.

40   The complex sentence holds within it the dynamic of
incompletion. That part of the sentence which seems weakest
at first is actually the element that provides a powerful tension.
That tension, well used by an author, will propel a paragraph
as the reader seeks to resolve it by learning more. Complexity
is never boring. This sentence type insures that life enters the
writing.

Compound and complex – surely this speaks for itself. With
the compound-complex sentence type, the user will find both
balance and tension. This is the type worthy to explain the intri-
45   cate unions and challenging choices of life.

So the elements are basic and repeated in these sentence
types, but the thoughtful user of the four English sentence
types understands that there is much more. Each of the four
structures implies a power and a use. Choose wisely when you
50   edit and revise, and you will empower your writing to a
remarkable degree.

Structure of the Four English Sentence Types			
Simple Sentence	Compound Sentence	Complex Sentence	Compound-Complex Sentence
only one independent clause (phrases may be used also)	at least two independent clauses (phrases may be used also)	only one independent clause and at least one dependent clause (phrases may be used also)	at least two independent clauses plus at least one dependent clause (phrases may be used also)

Multiple-Choice Questions

Directions: Answer the following questions. The questions may help you think about the ideas and information you might want to use in your essay. You may return to these questions anytime you wish. (Note the chart at the bottom of page 150.)

9 The speaker makes reference to the natural world and in doing so uses
   (1) rhetorical question   (3) hyperbole
   (2) simile   (4) onomatopoeia

10 According to the text, the structure of the English sentence is a good clue to its proper
   (1) spelling   (3) use
   (2) grammar   (4) capitalization

11 The reference to the "basic forms...found everywhere" in line 20, is analogous to which basic building block of the sentence?
   (1) phrase   (3) period
   (2) word   (4) clause

12 According to the text, misuse of which sentence type would result in a childish sound to the writing?
   (1) simple   (3) complex
   (2) compound   (4) compound- complex

13 The text and the information on the chart imply that what element of the sentence has the ability to cause "tension"?
   (1) the phrase   (3) independent clause
   (2) punctuation   (4) dependent clause

14 The proper audience for the remarks of Mr. Francis would apparently be
   (1) new speakers of the language
   (2) those with little or no background in grammar
   (3) writers who wish to improve their skills
   (4) casual speakers of English

15 The chart clearly indicates that all four sentence types must have
   (1) a phrase   (3) a tension
   (2) a dependent clause   (4) an independent clause

16 The chart shows that which element is optional in all sentence types?
   (1) punctuation   (3) dependent clause
   (2) capitalization   (4) the phrase

☆ Capsule – Reviewing and Using *MDOLC*

Your Response: After you have finished answering these questions, review the *Situation*, *Your Task*, and the *Guidelines*. Underline the commands and major constraints of the task.

Your Task: Write an essay for presentation in English class regarding the factors determining the four different types of structures of the English sentence. Using relevant information from the text and the chart, discuss how a knowledge of the factors determining sentence structure should affect a careful author's use of the sentence types in his or her writing.

Decide upon your point of view. Make an assertion and then a thesis on the task.

Simple Assertion using Verb "To Be"
Knowing sentence structure is helpful for writers.

Dynamic Verb Thesis Made from Assertion:
Mr. Francis makes an excellent case for showing how a writer's knowledge of sentence structure could increase the power of that person's writing.

Make an outline now of your response keeping *Your Task* and the *Guidelines* in mind.

After you have finished your rough draft, use the *MDOLC* to revise it:

Meaning: Do you show an understanding of the information in the text and the chart?

Development: Did you make specific, documented reference to the text and the chart?

Organization: Did you use an introduction with a clear thesis, a body which kept the focus on *Your Task*, and a conclusion which succinctly summarized your writing? Did you use clear transitions in all of these sections and between all of these sections?

Language Use: Did you write for your English class and vary your sentence structure for greatest effect?

Conventions: Did you adhere to Standard English rules?

Here are three responses to this task. Since ultimately your response will be graded on a score of #1 to #6, you should try to evaluate this writing by others so that you become more aware of how **MDOLC** is applied. Try to grade each of these three pieces as a #1, #3, or #6.

Session One, Part B – Sample One Response

There are four types of English sentences according to structure. They are very important to writing and every student should know them says teacher Mr. Kevin Francis.

There is the simple sentence which is not really simple if you know what to use it for. It is one independent clause. It can be powerful.

There are three other sentence types which are also important. Simple, compound, complex, and compound-complex. Each of these has a very big influence on writing.

Writers should know the sentence types and use them carefully. This will make for better writing.

I would rate this first example as _____.
I will list my reasons under the parts of **MDOLC**.

SESSION ONE, PART B SCORING RUBRIC - **Reading & writing for information & understanding** (see Appendix for complete Scoring Rubric – check evaluation box for each quality scored)	
Quality	Commentary The response:
Meaning: the extent to which the response exhibits sound understanding, interpretation, and analysis of the task and document(s)	
Development: the extent to which ideas are elaborated using specific and relevant evidence from the document(s)	
Organization: the extent to which the response exhibits direction, shape, and coherence	
Language Use: the extent to which the response reveals an awareness of audience and purpose through effective use of words, sentence structure, and sentence variety	
Conventions: the extent to which the response exhibits conventional spelling, punctuation, paragraphing, capitalization, grammar, and usage	

Now share this chart with your writing group.

Now here is a second response to be rated.

Session One, Part B – Sample Two Response

Mr. Kevin Francis is an English teacher who appreciates nature. He ties together his love for both language and the natural world when he explains the relationship of structure to use both in nature and in the four types of English sentence structures. Mr. Francis explains that the factors determining the English sentence types are simple and repeat from type to type but that the impact of the particular type of sentence is the result of how the basic components are combined. Further, Mr. Francis makes an excellent case for showing how a writer's knowledge of sentence structure could help increase the power of that person's writing.

It just takes a glance at the chart accompanying Mr. Francis' text to see that there are really only two factors which determine sentence structure: the independent and dependent clauses. In the combination of these two factors lies the determination of the kind of sentence and also the possibility that that sentence has for most effective usage.

Mr. Francis points out some of the ways that sentence use flows from the structure. He indicates that the simple sentence with its one independent clause is "simple and unadorned," and then he continues to show that such simplicity allows the sentence to be used to "command remarkable attention." Of the compound sentence, he says that proper use should respect the natural balance of the sentence. The complex sentence he commends for its tension, which provides for excellent usage when one is dealing with an intricate issue. He assigns much of the complexity of the problems of the modern world to the compound-complex sentence, which he says has both the tension balance to handle the job.

Mr. Francis really does make a case for understanding how a sentence is put together in order to better understand how to use that sentence. Writers would be wise to listen to him.

I would rate this second example as _____.
I will list my reasons under the parts of **MDOLC** on the next page.

SESSION ONE, PART B SCORING RUBRIC -
Reading & writing for information & understanding
(see Appendix for complete Scoring Rubric – check evaluation box for each quality scored)

Quality	Commentary The response:
Meaning: the extent to which the response exhibits sound understanding, interpretation, and analysis of the task and document(s)	
Development: the extent to which ideas are elaborated using specific and relevant evidence from the document(s)	
Organization: the extent to which the response exhibits direction, shape, and coherence	
Language Use: the extent to which the response reveals an awareness of audience and purpose through effective use of words, sentence structure, and sentence variety	
Conventions: the extent to which the response exhibits conventional spelling, punctuation, paragraphing, capitalization, grammar, and usage	

Now share your chart with your writing group.

Here is the third response to be rated.

Session One, Part B – Sample Three Response

Nature is beautiful and so is english. Nature like the humen hand has a lot of uses.

There are for kinds of sentences. Simple, compound, complex, and compound-complex. They ar dificult but important.

The chart shows the for kinds.

I would rate this third example as _____.
I will list my reasons under the parts of **MDOLC** on the next page.

SESSION ONE, PART B SCORING RUBRIC -
Reading & writing for information & understanding
(see Appendix for complete Scoring Rubric – check evaluation box for each quality scored)

Quality	Commentary The response:
Meaning: the extent to which the response exhibits sound understanding, interpretation, and analysis of the task and document(s)	
Development: the extent to which ideas are elaborated using specific and relevant evidence from the document(s)	
Organization: the extent to which the response exhibits direction, shape, and coherence	
Language Use: the extent to which the response reveals an awareness of audience and purpose through effective use of words, sentence structure, and sentence variety	
Conventions: the extent to which the response exhibits conventional spelling, punctuation, paragraphing, capitalization, grammar, and usage	

Practice Test B: Session Two, Part A – Sample Question

 Capsule – Literary Response

This question challenges your ability to read and write for literary response. You need to read carefully the two texts and then apply the directions as outlined in *Your Task* and *Guidelines*. Read with a pencil in hand noting any important concepts that seem to reflect the task to which you have to respond. Then follow the writing process by taking some pre-writing notes, webbing, and then making a formal outline. Write a first draft, read it carefully, edit, and revise. Then, keeping *MDOLC* in mind, write a good final draft.

Directions: Read the passages on the following pages (a letter and a poem) and answer the multiple-choice questions. Then write the essay described in *Your Task*. You may use the margins to take notes as you read and scrap paper to plan your response.

Your Task:  After you have read the passages and answered the multiple-choice questions, write a unified essay about the attitudes and effects of prejudice as revealed in the letter and the poem that you have just read. In your essay, use ideas from both passages to show how each author uses tone and effective literary techniques to emphasize that particular point of view.

Guidelines:
- Use ideas from both passages to establish a controlling idea about the effects of prejudice on people as revealed in the passages
- Use specific and relevant evidence from both passages to develop your controlling idea
- Show how each author uses specific literary element (for example, symbolism, irony, figurative language) to portray the effects of prejudice on people
- Organize your ideas in a logical and coherent manner.
- Use language that communicates ideas effectively
- Follow the conventions of written Standard English

Texts: "A Letter from Nancy" by Nancy Enna
"Symbiosis" an essay by Neal Obstat

Passage I: "A Letter from Nancy" by Nancy Enna

1   Dear Delia,

Something happened today that surprised me about me. My morning park walk was interrupted by a radio blaring. That's happened before. This one wasn't blaring music or rap.
5   This one was blaring hate.

As I came down the hill about one-quarter mile from the area where I left my car, I heard a smooth, sure announcer talking about how this country wasn't the same since "they" came. The comments got more crude and always started with
10   the same refrain: "The America I was raised in didn't..." I was really distressed by what I heard. Races were named and stereotypes were spat out with great venom. The trees

absorbed what they could of the prejudice, but even they could tolerate only so much and had to let most of the oily poison permeate the clear summer air.

15

In the past when music has blared, I'd feel my blood pressure rise as I thought how inconsiderate some fool was to think that everybody shared his or her taste in music. "Thinks he's or she's the center of the universe," I'd mutter. But I never did anything about my anger. All those stories about road rage jumped into my head and cooled down my rushing blood long enough for me to get into my car and drive away. After all, a sixty year-old widow is no match for some spoiled little brat who's got a volume control with a lot more power than his or her brain.

20

25

But this time it was different. This was pure hate, no pretense of music, no pretense of beat. And as I rounded the corner, I saw what else was different. The owner of the radio was standing by his car with the door open. He was just standing there, cleaning his ash tray by turning it upside down on the pavement. He was silver haired and quite spruced up. He was a man as old as I; he was standing next to a shiny new car with its radio blaring.

30

He was blaring it on purpose, Delia. So into my head jumped the road rage tales and the "Old, fat woman found near a pile of cigarette trash with her head bashed in by recently cleaned car ash tray" stories, but this time they didn't stop me. This time I figured that I could take the old fool, or if I couldn't, then at least I'd go for a good cause. And anyway, I'm tired of keeping my mouth shut; it's my park too. And it's the park of that young girl who runs every summer morning, and we shouldn't have to hear this.

35

40

"Sir," I said as I got nearer, not near enough to get banged in the head by the ash tray, but nearer.

45

No response, small wonder, what with that radio melting my ear drums.

But on the second, "Sir," he looked up, not startled but curious. He had this shiny face and chubby cheeks. "Sir," I asked, "could you please turn your radio down? I could hear it up on the ridge."

50

He spit out, "OH...COME ON." He screamed this as if trying to look more clearly, stared at me as if I were a closet other-race

person. He couldn't figure it. I'm the same race as he is. And I'm
an old woman. I guess he figured I should either agree with that
55 garbage on the radio or at least not talk back to a man.

He didn't touch the blaring radio.

So, I walked a little closer and said, "The America that I
was brought up in didn't have its radios blaring in quiet parks
and didn't have old men who should know better dumping
60 their dirty old butts on the ground."

Then I got into my car, nice and slowly, as I tried to calm
my shaky hands and surging blood.

Next time, I'm taking on the kids with the blaring radios. Fair
is fair, and there is still life in this old girl yet.

65   Love,
                                Nancy

Passage II: "Symbiosis" by Neal Obstat

1   He beamed his smile at me,
    Big man, fanning the flame of me,
    Warmed by his heart glow,
    I sighed a softer soul and swiftly grew
5   Safer and surer as we.

    He hissed his hate and hurled it at me,
    It struck me at my root,
    Blood surged draining all my me
    Down that same sewer as all his he
10 And we each
    Cold
    Hard
    Alone
    Shriveled

Directions: Answer the following questions. The questions may
                help you think about the ideas you might want to use
                in your essay. You may return to these questions any-
                time you wish.

Multiple-Choice Questions
(Questions 1-6 refer to "A Letter from Nancy," Passage I)

1   The tone of this letter is
    (1) grave   (3) ironic
    (2) sorrowful   (4) objective

2   Line 35 (Old, fat...me) refers to
    (1) Nancy   (3) the man
    (2) Delia   (4) the spoiled kid

3   The woman is surprised to see that the
    (1) owner of the radio is her neighbor
    (2) man owns a car
    (3) owner of the radio is as old as she
    (4) park rangers do not ticket the man

4   The allusion to the young girl who runs (lines 40-41) is meant to show
    that the
    (1) man has an accomplice
    (2) woman is thinking of the affect of the hate words on others
    (3) woman is lonely
    (4) girl is the woman's daughter

5   In line 45 (the radio...), there is an example of
    (1) allusion   (3) simile
    (2) hyperbole   (4) apostrophe

6   The old man seems surprised by
    (1) the race of the woman   (3) the woman's screaming
    (2) the loud radio   (4) the young girl

(Questions 7-9 refer to the "Symbiosis" poem, Passage II)

7   The speaker of the poem is
    (1) not affected by others   (3) definitely a man
    (2) greatly affected by others (4) definitely a woman

8   Lines 11-13 refer to the
    (1) person in the poem other than the speaker
    (2) speaker of the poem
    (3) reader of the poem
    (4) speaker and the person in the poem other than the speaker

9   In lines 4 and 6 there are examples of
    (1) simile   (3) alliteration
    (2) apostrophe   (4) interruption of a line

☆ CAPSULE – ASSERTING A POINT OF VIEW

Your Response: After you have finished answering these questions, review the *Situation*, *Your Task*, and the *Guidelines*. Underline the commands and major constraints of the task.

Your Task: Write an essay about the attitudes and effects of prejudice as revealed in the letter and the poem that you have just read. In your essay, use ideas from both passages to show how each author uses tone and effective literary techniques to emphasize that particular point of view.

Decide upon your point of view. Make an assertion and then a thesis based on the task.

Simple Assertion using Verb "To Be"
The tone and literary techniques of both pieces of writing are ways the authors use to show that prejudice is negative.

Dynamic Verb Thesis Made from Assertion:
Using fine literary elements and techniques, the two texts, "A Letter from Nancy" and "Symbiosis" by Neal Obstat both show that prejudice has a negative affect on the person who practices the prejudice as well as on the object of the prejudice.

Make an outline now of your response keeping *Your Task* and the *Guidelines* in mind. After you have finished your rough draft, use the **MDOLC** to revise it.

Here are sample responses. Before you score these, review **MDOLC**.

Session Two, Part A – Sample One Response

Prejudice is evil and affects you when you get involved with it. Both Obstat and Nancy understood that and wrote about it. They showed that prejudice makes people mean.

In the letter, Nancy talks about the mean man who played the radio loudly and it was a hate radio channel. Nancy shows that the man was bad and expected women to just let him be. Nancy spoke up. She decided not to let prejudice ruin the park. Good for her.

In the poem Obstat shows that people are affected by prejudice by getting smaller and drying up, both the people. He uses rhyme and images like cold and hard. He shows the evils of prejudice on everybody.

Both genres were good in how they taught a lesson about prejudice.

Now fill out the **MDOLC** rubric (on page 162) on this sample and then score the sample. I would rate this sample as a _____.

SESSION TWO, PART A SCORING RUBRIC - Reading & writing for literary response

(see Appendix for complete Scoring Rubric – check evaluation box for each quality scored)

Quality	Commentary The response:
Meaning: the extent to which the response exhibits sound understanding, interpretation, and analysis of the task and text(s)	
Development: the extent to which ideas are elaborated using specific and relevant evidence from the text(s)	
Organization: the extent to which the response exhibits direction, shape, and coherence	
Language Use: the extent to which the response reveals an awareness of audience and purpose through effective use of words, sentence structure, and sentence variety	
Conventions: the extent to which the response exhibits conventional spelling, punctuation, paragraphing, capitalization, grammar, and usage	

Now share your **MDLOC** rubric sheet with your writing group.

Session Two, Part A – Sample Two Response

Hating is bad. The lady in the letter is old but she nos this. The man is mean and trying to mak others just be sad that is just mean. The poem is about some guy who feels good when he is being talked nice to. You should do that becuz peeple feel beter. Then if they talk mean to me I feel like a piece of garbage that is relly lozy. These two have a good point.

Now score this on your **MDOLC** rubric sheet below. I would rate this sample as a _____.

SESSION TWO, PART A SCORING RUBRIC - Reading & writing for literary response

(see Appendix for complete Scoring Rubric – check evaluation box for each quality scored)

Quality	Commentary The response:
Meaning: the extent to which the response exhibits sound understanding, interpretation, and analysis of the task and text(s)	
Development: the extent to which ideas are elaborated using specific and relevant evidence from the text(s)	
Organization: the extent to which the response exhibits direction, shape, and coherence	
Language Use: the extent to which the response reveals an awareness of audience and purpose through effective use of words, sentence structure, and sentence variety	
Conventions: the extent to which the response exhibits conventional spelling, punctuation, paragraphing, capitalization, grammar, and usage	

Now share your **MDOLC** rubric sheet with your writing group.

Session Two, Part A – Sample Three Response

Sometimes it seems that the victim of prejudice is just the person who is the object of the prejudice. However, using fine literary elements and techniques, the two texts, "A Letter from Nancy" and "Symbiosis" by Neal Obstat both show that prejudice has a negative affect on the person who practices the prejudice as well as on the object of the prejudice.

In "A Letter from Nancy," the author uses a humorous conversational tone to emphasize how prejudice is not just a court room issue. The narrator, Nancy, considers herself to be an "old, fat widow," not a national celebrity. The very nature of the prejudice she encounters is fairly insignificant: a mature man has his radio blaring hate messages. But the intensity of Nancy's reaction evidences that her tone is not merely humorous but also ironic. Nancy risks "road rage" to chastise the man for his actions. Hers is not the action of a hero, but the reaction of someone who, even though she is the same race as the prejudiced man, feels that she and others have been violated by having the air of the park filled with such hateful words. The victim, Nancy, undergoes great stress but resolves to confront the offender. Nancy is both hurt and partially healed by her reactions to prejudice. However, the offender is merely hurt. He stares stupidly at Nancy and yells an inane, "Oh... Come on!" There is no healing in him. He does not turn down the radio. But he does lose face when Nancy has the last word, which begins with a phrase she repeats from the spiel of the hate commentator, "In the America I was raised in..."

In "Symbiosis" even the title emphasizes the mutual affect of prejudice on the victim and the victimizer. Mr. Obstat begins his poem with a stanza that images the positive results of treating another well. The diction, "big" and "grew" suggest the magnanimity of such a kind person and the resultant growth of spirit of the recipient of the kindness. Then, the tone changes from joyous to grave. The actor is now a prejudiced person and the recipient is now a victim. The onomatopoeia of "hiss," "hurl," and "struck" are powerful sound images. The "sewer" of line 9 is an ugly but effective reminder of the mutual destruction going on. And the use of end rhyme of the two key words in lines 8 and 9, "me" and "he" draw the two people inextricably together in their plummet to the end, "alone."

The power of the writing of Enna and Obstat delineates the power of prejudice to destroy. Ironically the destruction is not just reserved for the intended victim but for the victimizer as well.

Now rate this sample on your **MDOLC** rubric guide on the next page.

I would rate this sample as a _____.

SESSION TWO, PART A SCORING RUBRIC - Reading & writing for literary response (see Appendix for complete Scoring Rubric – check evaluation box for each quality scored)	
Quality	**Commentary** The response:
Meaning: the extent to which the response exhibits sound understanding, interpretation, and analysis of the task and text(s)	
Development: the extent to which ideas are elaborated using specific and relevant evidence from the text(s)	
Organization: the extent to which the response exhibits direction, shape, and coherence	
Language Use: the extent to which the response reveals an awareness of audience and purpose through effective use of words, sentence structure, and sentence variety	
Conventions: the extent to which the response exhibits conventional spelling, punctuation, paragraphing, capitalization, grammar, and usage	

Now share your rubric chart with your writing group.

PRACTICE TEST B: SESSION TWO, PART B – SAMPLE QUESTION

Your Task: Write a critical essay in which you discuss two works of literature you have read from the particular perspective of the statement that is provided for you in the *Critical Lens*. In your essay, provide a valid interpretation of the statement, agree or disagree with the statement as you have interpreted it, and support your opinion using specific references to appropriate literary elements from the two works. You may use scrap paper to plan your response.

Critical Lens: William Faulkner said, "I believe that man will not merely endure: he will prevail."

Guidelines:
* Provide a valid interpretation of the *Critical Lens* that clearly establishes the criteria for analysis
* Indicate whether you agree or disagree with the statement as you have interpreted it
* Choose two works you have read that you believe best support your opinion
* Use the criteria suggested by the *Critical Lens* to analyze the works you have chosen
* For each work, do not summarize the plot but use specific references to appropriate literary elements (for example, theme, characterization, structure, language, point of view) to develop your analysis
* Organize your ideas in a unified and coherent manner
* Specify the titles and authors of the literature you choose
* Follow the conventions of written Standard English

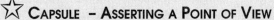

☆ CAPSULE – ASSERTING A POINT OF VIEW

Your Response: After you have finished answering these questions, review the *Situation*, *Your Task*, and the *Guidelines*. Underline the commands and major constraints of the task.

Your Task: Write a critical essay in which you discuss two works of literature you have read from the particular perspective of the statement that is provided for you in the *Critical Lens*. In your essay, provide a valid interpretation of the statement, agree or disagree with the statement as you have interpreted it and support your opinion using specific references to appropriate literary elements from the two works.

Decide upon your point of view. Make an assertion and then a thesis based on the task.

Simple Assertion using Verb "To Be"
Words by Heart by Ouida Sebestyen and *To Kill a Mockingbird* by Harper Lee are books that show the truth of Faulkner's statement.

Dynamic Verb Thesis Made from Assertion:
Using analyzing the two novels, the truth of Faulkner's words becomes clear.

Make an outline now of your response keeping *Your Task* and the *Guidelines* in mind. After you have finished your rough draft, use the **MDOLC** to revise it.

Here are three responses to this task. One is a #1; one is a #3; and one is a #6. Read each and fill out the **MDOLC** rubric sheet for it. Then evaluate it with a #1, #3, or #6. After that, share your evaluation with your writing group.

Session Two, Part B – Sample One Response

Faulkner said that he believed man would not just survive, but also win out against all the forces that try to destroy him. That is a very optimistice outlook. When I think of the two novels <u>Words by Heart</u> and <u>To Kill a Mockingbird</u>, I think Faulkner is probably right about mankind and its future.

<u>Words by Heart</u> is a novel about an African-American family in the early part of the twentieth century. This family has a daughter who has learned many verses of the <u>Bible</u> by heart. Lena is her name. Her dad is a very good man who insists that Lena treat all people fairly, no matter how they treat her. At the end of the story Lena's dad is killed by a racist young boy, but before he dies, he makes Lena understand that she must extend love even to her father's murderer. There is hope for all mankind in the ending when the racist father of the murderer comes to help with the farm work of Lena's deceased father so that Lena's family can get by.

<u>To Kill a Mockingbird</u> by Harper Lee is a great book that shows that mankind will survive even hatred and injustice. The lawyer, Atticus Finch risks his life and that of his family to stand up for an innocent young black man

accused of wraping a white girl. Even though Atticus loses the case and the innocent young man later dies, the town has learned how it allowed hatred to make it an injust place. There is hope that in the future things will be better because the young witness what happened and learn from it. We know this because the narrator was a little girl when the story happened.

Both these books show that despite prejudice and hatred man doesn't just survive, but also learns a lesson.

Now fill out your **MDOLC** rubric sheet (top, next page) on this sample. I would rate this sample as a _____.

SESSION TWO, PART B SCORING RUBRIC - Reading & writing for critical analysis		
(see Appendix for complete Scoring Rubric - check evaluation box for each quality scored)		
Quality	**Commentary** The response:	
Meaning: the extent to which the response exhibits sound understanding, interpretation, and analysis of the task and text(s)		
Development: the extent to which ideas are elaborated using specific and relevant evidence from the text(s)		
Organization: the extent to which the response exhibits direction, shape, and coherence		
Language Use: the extent to which the response reveals an awareness of audience and purpose through effective use of words, sentence structure, and sentence variety		
Conventions: the extent to which the response exhibits conventional spelling, punctuation, paragraphing, capitalization, grammar, and usage		

Share this sheet with your peer writing group.

Here is a second example of that same task. Read it and evaluate it. I would rate this sample as a _____.

Session Two, Part B – Sample Two Response

Man willnot just endur but will prefer. That is tru becaus man don't just put up with things but prefers one thing and not another thing. Lots of storys show this like Zoro. So it is a good idea. Zoro and Letal Wepin.

Now fill out this **MDOLC** rubric sheet (at the top of page 167) for this sample.

Now share this sheet with your writing peer group.

SESSION TWO, PART B SCORING RUBRIC - Reading & writing for critical analysis
(see Appendix for complete Scoring Rubric – check evaluation box for each quality scored)

Quality	Commentary The response:
Meaning: the extent to which the response exhibits sound understanding, interpretation, and analysis of the task and text(s)	
Development: the extent to which ideas are elaborated using specific and relevant evidence from the text(s)	
Organization: the extent to which the response exhibits direction, shape, and coherence	
Language Use: the extent to which the response reveals an awareness of audience and purpose through effective use of words, sentence structure, and sentence variety	
Conventions: the extent to which the response exhibits conventional spelling, punctuation, paragraphing, capitalization, grammar, and usage	

Now here is the third and final sample to be evaluated.

Session Two, Part B – Sample Three Response

William Faulkner believed in a better future for mankind. He showed this when he said, "Man will not merely endure: he will prevail." This statement evidenced Faulkner's belief that humanity is not destined to just survive but rather to overcome those forces which thwart the progress of the human race. By analyzing two novels, Words by Heart by Oudia Sebestyen and To Kill a Mockingbird by Harper Lee, the truth of his words becomes clear.

Ms. Sebestyen's novel deals with the ability of love to overcome both ignorance and prejudice. The protagonist, Lena, is a young African-American girl at the beginning of the twentieth century in America. Lena strives to live according to her father's gentle guidance and strict set of principles, but this is difficult for her. As the title of the work foreshadows, the words of both the Biblical excerpts that Lena memorizes and the wisdom of the father she reveres must be learned by her by heart. The omniscient point of view of narration allows the reader to understand the difficulty that Lena has in learning to live by the words of love and forgiveness her religion and her father mandate. When Lena's father is murdered by a young racist, Lena faces her ultimate test. In this test is the lesson for us all because the character of Lena was never presented as a saint: she is a kind of Everyman, flawed in her humanity, willing to steal and return hate for hate. So when Lena overcomes her natural desire for vengeance, there is a victory for us all. Truly through the character of Lena, Ms. Sebestyen evidences Faulkner's belief: humanity will not merely survive but will vanquish the forces of destruction such as prejudice.

To Kill a Mockingbird by Harper Lee is a novel which presents a story of the triumph of humanity over the negative forces in the world. The story is told from the first person narration of the daughter of a white lawyer in Macomb, Alabama, years before the Civil Rights Movement brought equality to African-Americans. Scout, the narrator is a real child: she fights, complains, dreams, and fears. Her father, Atticus Finch, unintentionally brings her and her older brother into the center of a battle for justice when Atticus carries on a valid defense of a young African-American man unjustly charges with raping a white woman. The title image of a bird becomes a central symbol as the the lawyer, Finch, decries the need to kill any songbird which exists freely without harming anyone around it. That symbol seems sufficient to represent the innocent African-American, the Finch family, and a much maligned recluse who also lives in the town.

But the songbirds do not merely survive; symbolically, they carry the day. Through the sympathetic characters who are the victims of prejudice, Ms. Lee shows us the ability of good people to withstand hardship and hate and ultimately show Maycomb that prejudice is unclean and unworthy of any decent person. Ms. Lee brings Faulkner's point home to the reader. Man does not merely put up with evil; he is capable of overcoming it.

Both these works bring the hope implicit in Faulkner's message to life. Both show that humanity has the power not merely to continue in the face of destructive forces, but also to prevail.

Now rate this on your **MDOLC** rubric score sheet. I would rate this sample as a _____.

SESSION TWO, PART B SCORING RUBRIC - Reading & writing for critical analysis	
(see Appendix for complete Scoring Rubric - check evaluation box for each quality scored)	
Quality	Commentary The response:
Meaning: the extent to which the response exhibits sound understanding, interpretation, and analysis of the task and text(s)	
Development: the extent to which ideas are elaborated using specific and relevant evidence from the text(s)	
Organization: the extent to which the response exhibits direction, shape, and coherence	
Language Use: the extent to which the response reveals an awareness of audience and purpose through effective use of words, sentence structure, and sentence variety	
Conventions: the extent to which the response exhibits conventional spelling, punctuation, paragraphing, capitalization, grammar, and usage	

Now share your score sheet with your writing peer group.

End of Practice English Test B

Practice English Test C follows. Now that you have completed Practice Tests A and B, you should be able to apply what you have learned on them. You will do more of the work yourself on this next practice exam. The Session One and Session Two, Parts A and B Scoring Rubrics have not been filled out for you. You will evaluate each of the sample responses based on the Rubric Qualities (**MDOLC**).

Now try a third Practice Test, C, Session One, Part A question.

☆ CAPSULE – ADJECTIVES

Again, you are being asked to do the following:

M Listen for **meaning**, take notes on the meaning, and write a response which clearly evidences that you understand and can communicate the meaning of what you have heard.

D **Develop** with specific and relevant evidence the specifics of what you have heard and then write a well developed, precise response.

O **Organize** your notes based on the organization of the listening passage and then organize your writing well so that your reader may clearly follow your presentation.

L Use your **language** to show an awareness of your audience by using good diction and effective and varied sentence structure.

C Follow the **conventions** of Standard English in regard to spelling, punctuation, paragraphing, capitalization, grammar, and usage.

Reminder: When taking notes on this English Practice Test Session One, Part A, use the webbing form described on page 100-101.

Overview: For this part of the test, you listen to a speech about being an election inspector during a time of change, answer some multiple-choice questions, and write a response based on the situation described. You will hear the speech twice. You may take notes anytime you wish during the readings.

Situation: In social studies class you have studied the irregularities of the 2000 national election. Your teacher asked each member of the class to decide whether current voting practices should undergo any change and then to write a letter to the editor of your local paper in which you defend your point of view. In preparation for writing your report on the voting practices, you have decided to listen to a speech delivered by Lincoln Roosevelt, a retired teacher and a current inspector who is attempting to bring change to the way in which people vote. Then you will use relevant information from the speech to write your response.

Your Task: Write a letter to the editor of your local paper in which you state whether or not there should be some change in the way people in the United States vote.

Guidelines: In your letter be sure to do the following:
- Tell the editor your opinion as to whether there should be a change in voting practices
- Use specific, accurate, and relevant information from the speech to support your argument
- Use a tone and level of language appropriate for a letter to the editor of a newspaper
- Organize your ideas in a logical and coherent manner
- Indicate any words taken directly from the speech by using quotation marks and referring to the speaker
- Follow the conventions of written Standard English

Directions: The following is the text to be read aloud. Try to have a classmate or instructor read this to you without allowing you to see it first. Ask him or her to read it slowly, clearly, and carefully two times aloud.

Homeland Security: Step One – Vote
by Lincoln Roosevelt

People in this country have had a very difficult twenty-first century, and we have yet to live past the single digit part of the 2000's. Terrorism, fear, war, and confusion have dominated our headlines and all but obliterated other important issues. One issue which we cannot afford to neglect is a practice at the heart of this democratic republic: voting. Waving flags may signify patriotism to many, but voting in every election is what guarantees a citizen a voice in the government and an opportunity to affect the direction which the elected officials take. According to the Federal Election Commission web site, in the 2000 general election, less than 52% of the voting age population actually voted. Based on a report from the Cal Tech/MIT Voting Technology Project, approximately four to six million of those who voted did not have their votes counted as a result of errors and inefficient procedures ranging from voter and machine error to limited hours at the polls. Of the entire voting age population, only 78% are registered to vote. These statistics are unworthy of a technological and democratic world leader. So why are so many in the voting age population not voting? Well, there are some who fall within this group of people who are extremely ill or in some other way not able to vote. But when almost 49% of the voting population stays home for a Presidential election, there must be more happening, and that is what we need to address.

Let's talk consistency, sameness, nationwide. North Dakota as of this moment does not require any voter registration.

Wisconsin permits voters to register at the polls on election day. Our state requires weeks in advance registration. Some states allow voters to write in candidates, and some do not. The voting hours among states differ, and even within states there is often a major discrepancy in polling times. Some states require identification papers at the polls, and some do not.

Some states use paper ballots (remember Florida in 2000 and the infamous chads?) while other states use machines. Within the same state paper ballots and lever machines are used in different areas. States rights are a Constitutional guarantee, and no one is suggesting that these rights be ignored. However, when Congress passed the *Help America Vote Act* in 2002, the possibility for ending these differences and making voting more attractive and efficient became real. What has been lacking since the signing of that bill is an intense media and political discussion of the bill's implications. Should there not, at the very least, be national discussion about these voting issues? Is not the state of U.S. voting practice at least as important as the state of voting practices beyond our borders? Or is not the health of our voting practice at least as important as the latest transient relationship of one of this year's celebrities or reality show "stars"?

How important is voting to our society? Is voting important enough to close businesses and schools for a whole or half day? Some states have a holiday on election day and close the schools, thus freeing many polling places to focus only on the election and not have to worry about where to put school students, staff, and the influx of voters and their cars. Some states have business as usual on election day and pit voters and voting inspectors against school personnel who need to continue to work around a major distraction. Voting becomes easier if one does not have to fit it in a day already cluttered with commuting and working nine hours. If we care about voting, let us make it a priority! We can easily have our Veterans' Day holiday truly honor the veterans by making it election day, a day when all adult U.S. citizens actually do something to ensure the health and welfare of their society. This would be a fitting tribute to those who fought and died to enable the democracy to thrive.

What about doing a better job of informing voters regarding issues and how the candidates stand on these issues? The airwaves are public; the Federal Communications Commission regulates interstate communications by radio, television, wire, satellite, and cable. This commission has jurisdiction over all fifty states. The commission consists of five persons each appointed by the President and confirmed by the Senate to serve for a five year term. This group issues licenses to those who use the airways. It is conceivable that this group could mandate that all radio, cable, and television stations offer hours of prime time to any candidates running for any office or only to those candidates who qualify based on the number of names on their nominating petitions.

Several proposals of this nature have been suggested over the years, but other than the current meager rules requiring equal time for candidates to respond to an editorial support-ing their opponents, there has really been no progress in employing the air waves to enhance the voting process. Check the Federal Communications Commission web site at www.fcc.gov and become familiar with what the law is and what the current practice is regarding these publicly owned airways. If we want more information before we vote, we have to make our voices heard. If we want more voices telling us how to interpret the news and what news we will hear, we have to make our voices heard. This web site does have a place for public reaction. Start here to try to make a change.

I am an election inspector, and I work with some very com-petent people. Most of these people are retired because in my state election days are also school and work days. Also in my county, the inspector must work the full day from 6:00 a.m. to 9:00 p.m.; therefore, only those who can leave their homes, jobs, and family for fifteen hours need apply. This is not a wise policy. The more people who can get involved in aspects of the voting process, the more probable the process will work well and remain healthy. Further, most humans tend to tire at a job after ten hours. In the case of elections, this is just about the time when most voters appear to cast their ballots. Again, if voting is really at the heart of our democratic republic, we had better do some rethinking about how, when, where, and who votes for what and why.

I'm the grandson of immigrants who had no voting privi-leges in their native land. They taught by example: they voted in every election; it really is the least a person can do. I applaud your coming here to listen. Listening is a first step. Visit the FCC web site. Call your political party and ask about the conditions at the polls in your area. Study the Help America Vote Act of 2002 and question how it is being implemented in your area. Write some e-mail, fax some opinions, call some Congress people, and make a difference. Your country needs you, and your vote is probably the most important thing you can do to ensure its security.

After the second reading, jot down notes in the format of speech beginning, speech middle, and speech end. Then you will know what to list as the main idea of the speech. Repetition of ideas and extensive use of specifics will allow you to see those ideas as being of major importance.

After you finish your notes and before you write, you will read and respond to the short answer multiple-choice questions about this speech because the questions themselves might well give you some more information about the speech or help you to check that you have received the correct impression from the text.

Multiple -Choice Questions

Directions: Use your notes to answer the following questions about the passage read to you. Write your answers to these questions on the answer sheet. The questions may help you think about ideas and information you might use in your writing. You may return to these questions anytime you wish.

1   According to the speaker, waving a flag is
    (1) essential to the democratic republic
    (2) not important
    (3) not a guarantee that the citizen will have a voice in the government
    (4) a symbol of patriotism practiced only in the United States

2   The speaker
    (1) has no respect for any voter who did not vote
    (2) understands that some who did not vote were not capable of doing so
    (3) is impressed that so many voter aged persons did register even if they did not vote
    (4) believes that the problem of low voter turn out cannot be solved

3   The speaker relies heavily on evidence from
    (1) his experience as a member of the Federal Communications Commission
    (2) his days as a teacher
    (3) recent books on the problem of low voter turnout
    (4) government agency web sites

4   The state which the speaker says has no registration requirement is
    (1) New York   (3) North Dakota
    (2) Florida   (4) Wisconsin

5   The speaker suggests using the current November Veterans' Day Holiday as
    (1) a day to hold forums about the Help American Vote Act
    (2) election day
    (3) a time to write the Federal Communications Commission
    (4) as a day to also honor those who work at the polls

6 The speaker says that the airwaves are owned by
   (1) five people appointed by the President
   (2) radio, television, and cable stations
   (3) the American people as a whole
   (4) about ten very wealthy people

7 The speaker seems to think that election inspectors
   (1) should be paid more
   (2) should be jobs which are open to more citizens rather than just a few
   (3) are all incompetent
   (4) should not have to work at the polls on election day

8 The speaker says that for most of his listeners, the most important thing they can do to ensure the security of this country is
   (1) pay taxes   (3) spy
   (2) join the armed forces (4) vote

☆ CAPSULE – REVIEWING AND OUTLINING

Your Response: After you have finished answering these questions, review the *Situation*, *Your Task*, and the *Guidelines*. Underline the commands and major constraints of the task.

Your Task: Write a letter to the editor of your local paper in which you state whether or not there should be some change in the way people in the United States vote.

Now refer to your notes, which are your brainstorming for this task. Decide upon your point of view. Make an assertion and then a thesis based on the task.

Simple Assertion Using Verb "To Be"
There is a need to change the way people in the United States vote.

Dynamic Verb Thesis Made from Assertion:
The need to change the way people in the United States vote arises from the importance of the voting process and current inconsistent and ineffective voting practices.

Now pull out the major ideas that you listed in the Middle section of your notes. Use these ideas as notes for the body of your own letter to the editor. Group and delete from your notes. When this is done to your satisfaction, make an outline. In your outline include the introductory and concluding elements of your letter. Try to begin your introduction segment with a good attention grabber, a motivator.

I. Introductory segment:
    A. Motivator: After September 11, 2001 almost everybody wants to be as patriotic and secure as possible.
    B. Thesis:

☆ CAPSULE CONTINUES ON NEXT PAGE

II. Body paragraphs
   A. Problem: fewer than 52% of the voting age population voted in the last Presidential election
   B. Why, since voting is key to the success of this country?
   C. Voting practice problems
      1. Inconsistent
      2. Ineffective in turning out the vote

III. Conclusion
   A. Use other words to restate thesis
   B. Close with quotation from Roosevelt's speech

Now you are ready to follow your outline and write your rough draft. Once your rough draft is complete, proofread, edit, and revise it. But before you do so, you must check *Your Task* and *Guidelines* and see that you have fulfilled all of the requirements. Be sure you have

- Told the editor your opinion as to whether there should be a change in voting practices
- Used specific, accurate, and relevant information from the speech to support your argument
- Used a tone and level of language appropriate for a letter to the editor of a newspaper
- Organized your ideas in a logical and coherent manner
- Indicated any words taken directly from the speech by using quotation marks and referring to the speaker
- Followed the conventions of written Standard English

Once you have finished proofreading, editing, and revising you will write your final draft.

Now write your final draft remembering **MDOLC**.

****

Here is the first response. Evaluate it as a #6 (very good), a #3 (writing in need of work), or a #1 (very poor).

Session One, Part A: Sample Response One

September 11, 2001, changed so many things in the United States. Suddenly the nation became preoccupied with security and terrorism. These topics understandably dominated the news to the exclusion of many other critical issues, one of the most important of which was the need to improve the United States voting process in an effort to increase voter turnout and thus insure the best possible government, essential for national security. The need to change the way people in the United States vote arises from the importance of the voting process and current inconsistent and ineffective voting practices.

I hadn't realized how few people actually vote until I heard retired teacher, elections inspector Lincoln Roosevelt speak to a group of concerned citizens at the civic center last Thursday evening. Mr. Roosevelt said that according to statistics from the Federal Elections Commission, in the Presidential election of 2000, less than 52% of the voter age population in the United States voted. This election was very close, so close that the result remained contested until the United States Supreme Court intervened. What would have happened if even 5% more of the population voted? No one knows, but this speculation itself demonstrates just how important each person's right to vote actually is.

Mr. Roosevelt posed the question as to why, if the public vote is key to the security of this country, do so few people vote? Mr. Roosevelt suggests that there are two key reasons for poor voter turnout: inconsistent and ineffective voting practices.

Although all Americans are taught that their votes are of equal value, not all states or even all counties in the same state necessarily have the same rules regarding who can vote and when.

In South Dakota, Mr. Roosevelt said, no one has to register before voting. In Wisconsin people may register when they come to vote. In our state, people must register weeks before voting.

Further, Mr. Roosevelt said that poll times vary in some states from county to county. I looked into this, and he is right. In my county on primary day, the polls are open from noon to nine at night, but if I lived two counties to the south, I could vote from six in the morning until nine at night. Don't I deserve the same longer voting day as my fellow citizens in those southern counties?

Mr. Roosevelt also said that not all states allow citizens to write in candidates not on the ballot. Some states, he said, have holidays so people can vote more easily while other states like ours expect voters to just fit votng into hectic work and family schedules. He pointed to the 2000 Presidential election and the Florida chad problem to underscore the problem of having some people vote by paper while others vote on machines. There are just too many inconsistencies in our voting practices.

Also there are some very inefficient voting practices. Although Mr. Roosevelt said that the airwaves belong to the public and there is even a Federal Communications Commission to safeguard the public interest, the media does not do a very good job keeping the public informed about election issues. Mr. Roosevelt said that there have been attempts to have radio, television, and cable stations give free, prime air time to candidates, but that these proposals have not been taken seriously. Mr. Roosevelt suggested that we voters e-mail, fax, or phone our representatives and tell them that since voting is the key to a secure nation, we want to use our air waves to have issues aired before elections.

As an election inspector himself, Mr. Roosevelt sees first hand the ineffective use of these personnel. He makes the case that because inspectors now must spend full days at the polls only those citizens whose jobs and family don't need them on election day can afford to be inspectors. Mr. Roosevelt suggests using shifts of voting inspectors to increase the number of citizens who can get involved and also to ensure the maximum efficiency and focus of the inspectors.

Having heard Mr. Roosevelt speak, I began to seriously question how the media can spend so much time discussing the voting procedures of other countries and the strength of democracy outside our borders when we have much to do here to improve the basis of our democracy: our voting practices. Truly Mr. Roosevelt was correct when he said, "Your vote is probably the most important thing you can do" to ensure the security of this country.

Now rate this essay using the **MDOLC** chart.

I would rate this example as _____.
I will list my reasons under the parts of **MDOLC**.

SESSION ONE, PART A SCORING RUBRIC - Listening and writing for information and understanding (see Appendix for complete Scoring Rubric – check evaluation box for each quality scored)	
Quality	**Commentary** The response:
Meaning: the extent to which the response exhibits sound understanding, interpretation, and analysis of the task and text(s)	
Development: the extent to which ideas are elaborated using specific and relevant evidence from the text(s)	
Organization: the extent to which the response exhibits direction, shape, and coherence	
Language Use: the extent to which the response reveals an awareness of audience and purpose through effective use of words, sentence structure, and sentence variety	
Conventions: the extent to which the response exhibits conventional spelling, punctuation, paragraphing, capitalization, grammar, and usage	

Now share your chart with your writing group.

Session One, Part A – Sample Response Two

Security sure is a big problem, and I think probably we shold due something about it.

Voting is a good idea to. I am going to tell you in this letter why we should vote.

Voting is something people die to due in other countries. We should not just think we can vote whenever ,voting is a reel privleg so change your ways and vote.

You could vote late or early but you should vote ofen and you shold vote for somebody who carries a flag and wants more peple voting, this guy Lincoln sad so in his speech. Lots of times you hear people talk about not voting and how stupit the guy are who are trying to get elected. This doesn't help security. Chads and 9/11 are horrible and should be stoped. Five men the president wanted help him get peple vote. Writting to them is good or to call them on the telephone to or on the computer.

This was my reasons for voting, you should to.

Now rate this response using the **MDOLC** chart.

I would rate this example as _____.
I will list my reasons under the parts of **MDOLC**.

SESSION ONE, PART A SCORING RUBRIC - Listening and writing for information and understanding (see Appendix for complete Scoring Rubric – check evaluation box for each quality scored)	
Quality	**Commentary** The response:
Meaning: the extent to which the response exhibits sound understanding, interpretation, and analysis of the task and text(s)	
Development: the extent to which ideas are elaborated using specific and relevant evidence from the text(s)	
Organization: the extent to which the response exhibits direction, shape, and coherence	
Language Use: the extent to which the response reveals an awareness of audience and purpose through effective use of words, sentence structure, and sentence variety	
Conventions: the extent to which the response exhibits conventional spelling, punctuation, paragraphing, capitalization, grammar, and usage	

Now share your chart with your writing group.

Session One, Part A, Sample Response Three

I went to hear Mr. Lincoln Roosevelt talk about voting in the U.S. He spoke very good and did a nice job. I was glad to hear him and about his idea about voting. In this letter I will tell you why you should vote and how you should change the voting in the United States today. I will quote form Lincoln.

Lincoln said that he is an election inspector and a retried member of the Federal Elections Commission. He said that voting is a way to secure the U.S. and that not too many people vote, like only a little over fifty-one % in the 2000 Presidential election. I was really surprised. Even together both guys running could barely get a majority of all voters. That really stinks.

He said lots of states do things differently and people in one state like Wisconsin get a better break about registering than in other states like ours. Voting hours are all different from state to state, and some states even get election day as a holiday so people can vote better. Also he said people are not well enough informed about the issues even though we own the air waves.

He made alot of sense to me. My brother had to go and risk his life in the army and some people don't even vote. Actualy my dad doesn't cause he works weird hours down in the city. So, we should make voting more important and help people get to the polls. I don't want my brother to go fight somebody because people don't vote or can't vote. "Voting is at the heart of this democratic republic."

Now rate this essay using the **MDOLC** chart.

I would rate this third example as _____.
I will list my reasons under the parts of **MDOLC** (on the next page).

SESSION ONE, PART A SCORING RUBRIC -
Listening and writing for information and understanding
(see Appendix for complete Scoring Rubric – check evaluation box for each quality scored)

Quality	Commentary The response:
Meaning: the extent to which the response exhibits sound understanding, interpretation, and analysis of the task and text(s)	
Development: the extent to which ideas are elaborated using specific and relevant evidence from the text(s)	
Organization: the extent to which the response exhibits direction, shape, and coherence	
Language Use: the extent to which the response reveals an awareness of audience and purpose through effective use of words, sentence structure, and sentence variety	
Conventions: the extent to which the response exhibits conventional spelling, punctuation, paragraphing, capitalization, grammar, and usage	

Now share your chart with your writing group.

Directions: Read the text and study the graph that follows, answer the multiple-choice questions, and write a response based on the situation described below. You may use the margins to take notes as you read and scrap paper to plan your writing.

Situation: Your Politics in Government class has been studying responsible use of public air waves. You and four hundred ninety-nine of your peers and those in the class ahead of you took a survey about their viewing habits. Your assignment was to compare past government aspirations regarding television programming and contemporary viewing patterns. You chose to analyze the survey results. You wish to see how the consumption of television shows and the enjoyment by you and your peers reflect the 1961 opinions of President John F. Kennedy's Federal Communications Commission Chairman, Newton N. Minow.

Your Task: Using relevant information from all the documents, write a persuasive essay for your teacher in which you either agree or disagree with the idea that contemporary television remains a "vast wasteland" which does not fully understand or appreciate the taste of the viewing public.

Guidelines:
- Tell your audience exactly what Mr. Minow meant by "a vast wasteland" and the absence of appreciation or understanding of public taste evident in television programming
- Use specific, accurate, and relevant information from the reading and graphs to support your argument
- Use a tone and level of language appropriate for persuading your classroom teacher
- Indicate any words taken directly form the readings by using quotation marks and by referring to the author
- Follow the conventions of written Standard English

Excerpt from Mr. Minow's Speech
to the 39th Annual Convention of Broadcasters

1   "When television is good, nothing-- not the theater, not the magazines or newspapers--nothing is better.

But when television is bad, nothing is worse. I invite you to sit down in front of your television set when your station goes on
5   the air and stay there without a book, magazine, newspaper, profit and loss sheet, or rating book to distract you-- and keep your eyes glued to that set until the station signs off. I can assure you that you will observe a vast wasteland.

You will see a procession of game shows, violence,
10 audience-participation shows, formula comedies about totally unbelievable families, blood and thunder, mayhem, violence, sadism, murder, western bad men, western good men, private eyes, gangsters, more violence, and cartoons. And endless commercials – many screaming, cajoling, and offending. And
15 most of all, boredom. True, you will see a few things you will enjoy. But they will be very, very few. And if you think I exaggerate, try it...

Why is so much of television bad? I have heard many answers: demands of your advertisers; competition for higher
20 ratings; the need to always attract a mass audience; the high cost of television programs; the insatiable appetite for programming material-- these are some of them.

I do not accept the idea that the present overall programming is aimed accurately at the public taste. The ratings
25 tell us only that some people have their television sets turned on and of that number, so many are tuned to one channel and so many to another. They don't tell us what the public might watch if they were offered half a dozen additional choices. A rating, at best, is an indication of how many people
30 saw what you gave them. Unfortunately, it does not reveal the depth of the penetration, or the intensity of reaction, and it never reveals what acceptance would have been if what you gave them had been better-- if all the forces of art and creativity and daring and imagination had been unleashed. I
35 believe in the people's good sense and good taste and I am not convinced that the people's taste is as low as some of you assume."

Here are the results of your survey reduced to the following graphs:

Pie Graph A:
Student Hours Per Week
Spent Watching T.V.

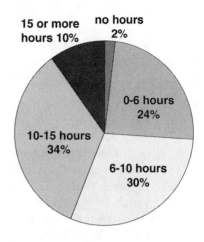

15 or more hours 10%

no hours 2%

0-6 hours 24%

10-15 hours 34%

6-10 hours 30%

Bar Graph B
Television Time Spent on
Various Program Formats

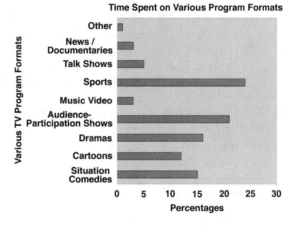

Time Spent on Various Program Formats

Various TV Program Formats

- Other
- News / Documentaries
- Talk Shows
- Sports
- Music Video
- Audience-Participation Shows
- Dramas
- Cartoons
- Situation Comedies

Percentages

Bar Graph C
Percentages of Students
Rating Television
Viewing Time
as Worthwhile or
Entertaining

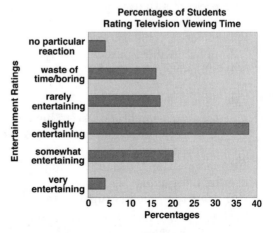

Percentages of Students
Rating Television Viewing Time

Entertainment Ratings

- no particular reaction
- waste of time/boring
- rarely entertaining
- slightly entertaining
- somewhat entertaining
- very entertaining

Percentages

Multiple-Choice Questions

Directions: (9-17): Write your answers to these questions on an answer sheet. The questions may help you think about ideas for your own response. You may refer to these questions at any point from now to the end of this section of the exam.

9   What test does Mr. Minow suggest people try in order to test his theory about the quality of television?
   (1) get a good book and sit before the television from the start to the end of the broadcast day
   (2) write to their Congress people and see if these representatives respond
   (3) watch television for a week
   (4) sit without distraction and watch television from the start to the end of the broadcast day

10 The strategy of Mr. Minow's first comment reveals an attempt to
   (1) show the importance of other mass media and entertainment forms
   (2) irritate his audience
   (3) present his respect for the medium which he is criticizing
   (4) indicate that he never expects television to be good

11 "The vast wasteland" of which Mr. Minow speaks is what figure of speech?
   (1) allegory
   (2) simile
   (3) personification
   (4) metaphor

12 Mr. Minow says that the viewer of an entire day's broadcasting will see programs that, more than anything else will depict
   (1) boredom
   (2) violence
   (3) unbelievable families
   (4) offensive behavior

13 Mr. Minow believes that
   (1) the television broadcasters have no real problems
   (2) television broadcasters have not tried hard enough to solve their problems
   (3) competition for higher ratings is actually an incentive to present higher quality
   (4) most television is superior to most magazine reporting

14 Mr. Minow says that
  (1) he has faith in the good taste of the public
  (2) ratings are the result of dishonest statistics
  (3) ratings mean absolutely nothing
  (4) people have so many programming choices that they become confused

15 Graph A (see page 183) shows that
  (1) all the students surveyed watched at least some television during the week
  (2) nearly 75% of those surveyed watched more than six hours of television per week
  (3) the 10% who watch more than fifteen hours of television per week have no jobs or after school activities
  (4) 2% of those taking the survey lied about their television viewing

16 Graph B (see page 183) makes clear that
  (1) audience participation shows and sports are most popular with the group surveyed
  (2) the dramas have too much violence
  (3) cartoons have replaced human actors on 50% of the programs
  (4) cooking shows seem to be replacing music videos

17 Graph C (see page 183) supports the idea that
  (1) television has a small audience
  (2) approximately 75 % of the people who took the survey find fault with what they watch
  (3) nobody really enjoys television
  (4) the movies are attracting those who would normally be watching television

☆ Capsule – Reviewing and Outlining

Your Response

After you have finished answering these questions, review *The Situation*, *Your Task*, and the *Guidelines*. Underline the commands and major constraints of the task.

Your Task: Using relevant information from all the documents, write a persuasive essay for your teacher in which you either agree or disagree with the idea that contemporary television remains a "vast wasteland" which does not fully understand or appreciate the taste of the viewing public.

Now refer to the text, graphs, and short answer questions which comprise a type of brainstorming for this question. Having reached an opinion about the question, write a simple assertion which you will tighten to construct a thesis for your response.

Simple Assertion Using Verb "To Be":

Contemporary television is still the "vast wasteland" that Mr. Minow described in 1961 because the broadcasters do not value the taste of the American television audience.

Dynamic Verb Thesis Made from Assertion:

The continued existence of the "vast wasteland" that Mr. Minow described as television broadcasting in 1961 survives today because broadcasters still do not truly value the taste of the American television audience.

Now pull out the major ideas that by underlining the topic sentence of each paragraph, checking the graphs, and rereading the short answer questions. Use these ideas as notes for the body of your essay. Group and delete your ideas until your emerging outline seems workable and you are sure that each outline point defends your thesis statement. When this is done to your satisfaction, make a final outline. In your outline include the introductory and concluding elements of your essay. Try to begin your introduction segment with a good attention grabber, a motivator.

☆ Capsule CONTINUES ON NEXT PAGE

I.   Introductory segment:
    A. Motivator: My grandmother remembers growing up with television.

    B. Thesis: The continued existence of the "vast wasteland" that Mr. Minow described as television broadcasting in 1961 survives today because broadcasters still do not truly value the taste of the American television audience.

II. Body paragraphs
    A. Mr. Minow's insights in 1961

    B. Graph information and how things have not changed essentially

    C. Hope is Mr. Minow's "unleashing" idea

III. Conclusion
    A. Use other words to restate thesis

    B. Close with quotation from student who took survey

Now you are ready to follow your outline and write your rough draft. Once your rough draft is complete, proofread, edit, and revise it. But before you do so, you must check *Your Task* and *Guidelines* and see that you have fulfilled all of the requirements. Have you remembered to:

Guidelines:
- Tell your audience exactly what Mr. Minow meant by "a vast wasteland" and the absence of appreciation or understanding of public taste evident in television programming
- Use specific, accurate, and relevant information from the reading and graphs to support your argument
- Use a tone and level of language appropriate for persuading your classroom teacher
- Indicate any words taken directly form the readings by using quotation marks and by referring to the reading
- Follow the conventions of written Standard English

Once you have finished proofreading, editing, and revising you will write your final draft.

****

Read these sample responses (on the following pages) which were evaluated as a #6 (the highest score), a #3 (a mid-range score), and a #1 (a poor score). Decide which score you would give and complete the **MDOLC** rubric (on the next page) for each after you have read the sample.

Session One, Part B: Sample One Response

Television is either really good or very bad. This was said in 1961 by President John Kennedy's man, Mr. Minow. He said mostly television was really boring because programmers of television shows just don't get that people have minds and want interesting and different shows on t.v. He's right, and a survey that I took proves that he is still right even today.

So, my teacher gave this survey to four hundred juniors and seniors. They were either sixteen or seventeen years old and had to agree to take the survey and answer all the questions honestly. The survey showed that kids don't really enjoy what they watch, and a few don't even watch television. Graph "C" shows that almost three-quarters of the kids who answered didn't like the shows they watched. That is what Mr. Minow said about ratings not showing how much better people would have liked television if "what you gave them had been better."

People are still not happy with the television even if they do watch it, some of them more than fifteen hours during a school week. Its to bad that things aren't improved by now. Mr. Minow sure had a crystal ball when he made his speech in '61.

Now rate this essay using the **MDOLC** that follows.

I would rate this example as _____.

I will list my reasons under the parts of **MDOLC**.

<table>
<tr><td colspan="2" align="center">SESSION ONE, PART B SCORING RUBRIC -
Reading and writing for information and understanding
(see Appendix for complete Scoring Rubric – check evaluation box for each quality scored)</td></tr>
<tr><td align="center">Quality</td><td>Commentary
The response:</td></tr>
<tr><td>Meaning: the extent to which the response exhibits sound understanding, interpretation, and analysis of the task and text(s)</td><td></td></tr>
<tr><td>Development: the extent to which ideas are elaborated using specific and relevant evidence from the text(s)</td><td></td></tr>
<tr><td>Organization: the extent to which the response exhibits direction, shape, and coherence</td><td></td></tr>
<tr><td>Language Use: the extent to which the response reveals an awareness of audience and purpose through effective use of words, sentence structure, and sentence variety</td><td></td></tr>
<tr><td>Conventions: the extent to which the response exhibits conventional spelling, punctuation, paragraphing, capitalization, grammar, and usage</td><td></td></tr>
</table>

Now share your chart with your writing group.

Session One, Part B, Sample Two Response

When my grandmother was very young, so was television. Her memories of early telvision are fond, but she says that by the time she was thirteen, there was very little new on television and much of the programming was boring. She says she thought there would be more creativity as the years went by, but basically, with few exceptions, she just sees show after show about the same thing. She was in her late teens when Mr. Minow, President John F. Kennedy's Chairman of the Federal Communications Commission, spoke in 1961. She agreed with him then, and she thinks that what he says still applies today. I think she is right. The continued existence of the"vast wasteland" that Mr. Minow described as television broadcasting in 1961 survives today because broadcasters still do not truly value the taste of the American television audience.

Mr. Minow believed in the potential of television. He said in his speech to the 39th annual convention of broadcasters, "When television is good nothing...nothing is better." What bothered Mr. Minow was how little telvision broadcasters in general seemed to care about captivating their audience with challenging ideas and innovative programs. Mr. Minow said that even ratings did not prove what would happen if what broadcasters gave the audience "had been better-- if all the forces of art and creativity and daring and imagination had been unleashed."

The recent survey of five hundred students that I and my peers took about our viewing habits and our reaction to what we viewed showed that Mr. Minow's observations are still correct today in the twenty-first century. Graph "A" constructed from the results of this survey show that approximately 75% of those surveyed watch more than six hours of television each week. Since this survey was taken during school time among people many of whom work part time jobs, this is a significant amount of television. But Graph "B," also assembled based on the survey results, shows that most of the television time was spent watching a combination of audience participation shows and sports. Both these categories by definition are more spontaneous than scripted shows. It would be fair to surmise that the viewing audience prefers the unexpected to the traditional scripts. This desire for the unexpected, even if some of these shows are "reality" formats, seems to indicate that the audience is just plain bored with the rest of television. Finally, Graph "C" shows that 75% of those who watch television are not satisfied with much of their experience.

Mr. Minow's analysis of the problem seems to hold true in the light of the survey. People want spontaneity, challenge, risk, and imagination, and to the degree that television supplies that, they watch television in significant numbers. But even these viewers want more. They want what Mr. Minow wanted, respect from the broadcasters and a true appreciation of the taste of the American viewing public.

The hope seems to be there in Mr. Minow's own words. We must push the broadcasters until all the potential of good television is "unleashed."

Now rate this essay using the **MDOLC** that follows.

I would rate this example as _____.
I will list my reasons under the parts of **MDOLC**.

SESSION ONE, PART B SCORING RUBRIC - Reading and writing for information and understanding (see Appendix for complete Scoring Rubric – check evaluation box for each quality scored)	
Quality	**Commentary** The response:
Meaning: the extent to which the response exhibits sound understanding, interpretation, and analysis of the task and text(s)	
Development: the extent to which ideas are elaborated using specific and relevant evidence from the text(s)	
Organization: the extent to which the response exhibits direction, shape, and coherence	
Language Use: the extent to which the response reveals an awareness of audience and purpose through effective use of words, sentence structure, and sentence variety	
Conventions: the extent to which the response exhibits conventional spelling, punctuation, paragraphing, capitalization, grammar, and usage	

Now share your chart with your writing group.

Session One, Part B, Sample Three Response

Mr. Minow spoke in 1961 to peple about tv. He though that tv wasnt good. He wanted tv to be better, today we do to. Why cant tv be more fun. Sometimes you just put it on and walk away and your mother sez why dont you turn of the tv cause you not watching it. Its like a radio only no so good. So this guy Minow is right and he should force them to make better tv. I hope you agree.

Now rate this essay using the **MDOLC** that follows.

I would rate this third example as _____.
I will list my reasons under the parts of **MDOLC**.

<table>
<tr><td colspan="2">SESSION ONE, PART B SCORING RUBRIC -
Reading and writing for information and understanding
(see Appendix for complete Scoring Rubric – check evaluation box for each quality scored)</td></tr>
<tr><td>Quality</td><td>Commentary
The response:</td></tr>
<tr><td>Meaning: the extent to which the response exhibits sound understanding, interpretation, and analysis of the task and text(s)</td><td></td></tr>
<tr><td>Development: the extent to which ideas are elaborated using specific and relevant evidence from the text(s)</td><td></td></tr>
<tr><td>Organization: the extent to which the response exhibits direction, shape, and coherence</td><td></td></tr>
<tr><td>Language Use: the extent to which the response reveals an awareness of audience and purpose through effective use of words, sentence structure, and sentence variety</td><td></td></tr>
<tr><td>Conventions: the extent to which the response exhibits conventional spelling, punctuation, paragraphing, capitalization, grammar, and usage</td><td></td></tr>
</table>

Now share your chart with your writing group.

Directions: Read the poem "Finally" by S. Matrose and the journal entries by Yvonne Aritewell and answer the multiple-choice questions. Then write the essay described in Your Task. You may use the margins to take notes as you read and scrap paper to plan your response.

Your Task: After you have read the passages and answered the multiple-choice questions, write a unified essay about the feelings one has after attaining long awaited experiences, as revealed in the poem and the journal. In your essay, use ideas from both passages to establish a controlling idea about the feelings that accompany long awaited experiences. Using evidence from each passage, develop your controlling idea and show how the author uses specific literary elements or techniques to convey that idea.

Guidelines:
- Use ideas from both passages to establish a controlling idea about feelings that accompany attaining long awaited goals
- Use specific and relevant evidence from each passage to develop your idea
- Show how each author uses literary elements (such as theme, characterization, structure, point of view) or techniques (such as symbolism, irony, figurative language) to evidence the controlling idea
- Organize your ideas logically and coherently
- Use appropriate language
- Follow the rules of written Standard English

Texts: "Finally" by S. Matrose, "Journal Entries" by Yvonne Aritewell

Passage I: Finally

1   Rehydrated with Spring
    the crabapple outside my window
    finally looks more like a tree
    than kindling.
5   One sturdy branch of camouflage
    shoots toward my open window
    as if I am the sun
    and bursts into a single pink bloom
    just for me.

10   Framed in my window pane,
        it mocks the look of photographs.
        But even Georgia O'Keefe's *
        would lose their brilliance
        when combined with germination
15   and pollination.
        Sneeze whiplash
        and mushrooming pressure
        behind my oozing eyes
        kill the beauty of this
20   allergen outside my closed window.

                                    —S. Matrose

* A 20th century American artist famed for her imitative realism in many
of her paintings of flowers.

Passage II

May 15, 2004

1   So, she gets all like snotty and says to the class, "Well, if
        you are not going to do any of the homework I assign and you
        don't show up half the time and when you do show up all you
5   want to do is chat and sleep, I've got a suggestion." And then
        she says, "How about you pick up your books and pocket-
        books and cell phones and earphones, and I'll get my
        bag, and we all meet at the cemetery and just wait."

        We all just like looked at each other. This old lady has
10   really snapped. What does she mean wait at the cemetery.
        For what?

        Does she like mean we should wait to die? Well not me,
        girl. I've got things to do. The prom is fourteen days away, and
        it is definitely something worth living for. My parents can just
15   relax about the homework stuff. I am a senior and this is my
        time. I'll get by okay, and nobody is cutting in on my senior
        year. Me and Rico and the prom!!!!! Mary Kate, Tomiko, Sheila,
        Tanya, and Kyeisha and I are taking Thursday off to get our
        nails done and make sure the limo, flowers, and party stuff is all
20   done...right! Who would leave all those details to those guys?
        And Friday we'll do a late brunch at the diner and then our
        hair. Pictures start at Rico's place at 5:30. He and his cousin
        Richie and Richie's girl Candy and I are gonna stop time that
        weekend. Rico says he's got plans and it's gonna be a sur-
25   prise!!!! Just two more weeks to crawl through. I don't know
        how I'm gonna sit through those classes. Blah, blah, blah.........

June 13, 2004

So I told Rico that was it. Over. Who needs that jerk anyway? I knew right after the prom weekend he was finished.
30 What a waste going with him!! Let her have him. Big, she's-all-that Candy, well they deserve each other big time. He is as finished as yesterday's pizza crusts staring at me from the trash. It's just fourteen days until this high school stuff is all over. I'm crossing each one off the calendar in big red marker.

35 I have to do that report for Scagwaller or I don't get out of here. So, I'll do it; I'll blah, blah, blah and soon this school is history......

June 30, 2004

Mom says I've got to get a full time job now and start
40 paying my share. She's worried about my medical insurance because as of September I can't be on her policy. Also my car is probably history because I can't pay the insurance by myself and the car payments too, and the brakes are going.
45 Mary Kate and Tayeisha leave for college in a month because they have to get there early to train with their teams. There's no time for anything now but work. I thought I might try a course at the community college but I couldn't place high enough on the tests, so if I take a course it will be remedial and
50 no credit, but I still have to pay for it. Rico called and wants to hang out. He's such a jerk, but everyone else is going away or back to school. I can't wait till everybody gets together at homecoming this fall. I marked it on the calendar. It's only fourteen weeks away.

Directions: Answer the following questions. The questions may help you think about ideas you may want to use in your essay. You may come back to these questions any time you wish.

Multiple-Choice Questions
Passage I (the poem) 1-5

1 The window in the poem changes from "open" to " closed" to suggest
  (1) a change of seasons
  (2) a coming storm
  (3) discomfort with the coming of spring
  (4) fear of the unknown

2 "As if I am the sun" is
  (1) personification   (3) end rime
  (2) a simile   (4) a pun

3 In line 8, "bursts" is an example of
  (1) simile   (3) personification
  (2) onomatopoeia   (4) repetition

4 The speaker of the poem changes his or her regard for the "pink bloom" based on
  (1) Georgia O'Keefe's paintings
  (2) the closing of the window
  (3) an allergic reaction to the bloom
  (4) a car accident

5 The reference in line 12 to Georgia O'Keefe is an example of :
  (1) metaphor   (3) hyperbole
  (2) allusion   (4) personification

Passage II (the essay) 6-10

6 The author of these journal entries is a
  (1) girl who cannot wait to graduate
  (2) teacher who wants to take her students on a field trip to the cemetery
  (3) mother looking back to her youth
  (4) man named Rico

7 During the time gap from the May 15 journal entry to the June 13 journal entry what has occurred?
  (1) graduation
  (2) homecoming
  (3) the prom
  (4) a new friendship has begun between Candy and the author

8 In line 32, " he is as finished as yesterday's pizza crusts" is an example of:
  (1) personification   (3) a pun
  (2) simile   (4) rhetorical question

9 The persona of the journals is
   (1) unable to see the present time as being important in itself
   (2) rewarded for waiting by having a great time at the prom
   (3) not sociable
   (4) going away to college

10 One image that shows the journal persona's impatience with the present is
   (1) the car brakes
   (2) having her nails done
   (3) the crossing out of the dates with a red marker
   (4) the "limo"

☆ CAPSULE – REVIEWING AND OUTLINING
Your Response
After you have finished answering these questions, review *Your Task* and the *Guidelines*. Underline the commands and major constraints of the task.

Your Task: After you have read the passages and answered the multiple-choice questions, write a unified essay about the feelings one has after attaining long awaited experiences, as revealed in the poem and the journal that you have just read. In your essay, use ideas from **both** passages to establish a controlling idea about the feelings that accompany experiences long awaited. Using evidence from **each** passage, develop your controlling idea and show how the author uses specific literary elements or techniques to convey that idea.

Now refer to the passages which comprise a type of brainstorming for this question. Having formed a point of view about how both passages make a point about the feelings one has after experiencing something long awaited, write a simple assertion which you will tighten to construct a thesis for your response.

Simple Assertion Using Verb "To Be":

Both pieces are reminders that what we long for cannot be perfect in the experience.

☆ CAPSULE CONTINUES ON NEXT PAGE

Dynamic Verb Thesis Made from Assertion:

Both pieces remind us that the lack of perfection in experiencing long awaited events results from the difference between thought and reality.

In proofreading this statement, realize that the guidelines mandate that you discuss how the authors used literary devices to convey this idea. Some mention of that should be made in the thesis. Revise the thesis to read this way:

Using literary devices, both authors remind us that the lack of perfection in experiencing long awaited events results from the difference between thought and reality.

With this as your thesis, you are ready to write. Pull out the major ideas that you gather from the readings by underlining the topic sentence of each paragraph, rereading each stanza, and checking the short answer questions. Use these ideas as notes for the body of your essay. Group and delete from your ideas until your emerging outline seems workable and you are sure that each outline point defends your thesis statement. When this goal is accomplished to your satisfaction, make a final outline. In your outline, include the introductory and concluding elements of your essay. Try to begin your introduction segment with a good attention grabber, a motivator.

I.   Introductory segment:
     A.   Motivator: Voices of the personae in literature are created to be as different as the speakers.
     B.   Thesis: Using literary devices, both authors remind us that the lack of perfection in experiencing long awaited events results from the difference between thought and reality.

II. Body paragraphs
     A.   Poem's use of images, voice, and simile to emphasize difference between thought and reality
     B.   Journal's use of images, voice, and repetition to emphasize difference between thought and reality

III. Conclusion
     A.   Use other words to restate thesis
     B.   Close with reminder about how difficult the craft of writing is

Now you are ready to follow your outline and write your rough draft. Once your rough draft is complete, proofread, edit, and revise it. But before you do so, you must check *Your Task* and *Guidelines* and see that you have fulfilled all of the requirements.

Guidelines: (*MDOLC*)

- Use ideas from both passages to establish a controlling idea about feelings that accompany attaining long awaited goals
- Use specific and relevant evidence from each passage to develop your idea
- Show how each author uses literary elements (such as theme, characterization, structure, point of view) or techniques (such as symbolism, irony, figurative language) to evidence the controlling idea
- Organize your ideas logically and coherently
- Use appropriate language
- Follow the rules of written Standard English

Once you have finished proofreading, editing, and revising you will write your final draft.

****

When you have completed your essay, read these sample responses which were evaluated as a #6 (the highest score), a #3 (a mid-range score), and a #1 (a poor score). Decide which score you would give and complete the *MDOLC* rubric for each after you have read it.

Session Two, Part A : Sample One Response

Voices of the personae in literature are created to be as different as the speakers. The persona in S. Matrose's "Finally" and the persona in Yvonne Aritewell's journal entries are very different people in many ways; the speaker of the poem is very aware of nature, very impressed by natural beauty, and willing to relax and enjoy a moment of purely visual beauty.

The writer of the journal is willing to ignore the present and concentrate entirely on an upcoming event. People seem to preoccupy the journal writer who says nothing at all about nature. How different each persona is, yet there is a common thread. Using literary devices, both authors remind us that the lack of perfection in experiencing long awaited events results from the difference between thought and reality.

The problem of the speaker of the poem is essentially one of the speaker's imagining that the bloom is sheer perfection: a perfect symbol of spring. The image of the single pink bloom that has grown from a piece of "kindling" rehydrated by spring is the author's way to paint for us the beauty of this flower. The simile "as if I am the sun" evidences the effect of the bloom on the speaker: the flower makes the speaker feel like the center of the universe. All this euphoria is destroyed when the speaker has a very real allergic reaction to the bloom. At that point the calm and appreciative voice of the speaker changes and begins to use hyperbole to emphasize the death of the imagined beauty at the hands of the real allergen.

The writer of the journals imagines that the coming event will be far superior to any present reality. The images of the teacher's ironic invitation to wait at the cemetery, the crossed off calendar dates, and the future "hanging out" with Rico just to pass time all evidence the journal writer's inability to seize the real present rather than wait for the supposedly perfect future. This voice is unhappy, likely to grow even more unhappy in the future. The repetition of fourteen as the writer's key to the magic happy, ideal future also emphasizes the sad state of the writer.

Although Matrose's piece is a poem and Aritewell's piece is a group of journal entries, both authors have emphasized that people become frustrated because the perfect image they construct mentally can never match the imperfect reality. Long awaited experiences can never be as perfect as we imagine they will be. This unpleasant life lesson is shown to us by two skillful authors who understand how to use literary devices to underscore their points.

Now rate this essay using the **MDOLC** chart.

I would rate this example as _____.

I will list my reasons under the parts of **MDOLC**.

SESSION TWO PART A SCORING RUBRIC - Reading and writing for literary response (see Appendix for complete Scoring Rubric - check evaluation box for each quality scored)	
Quality	Commentary The response:
Meaning: the extent to which the response exhibits sound understanding, interpretation, and analysis of the task and text(s)	
Development: the extent to which ideas are elaborated using specific and relevant evidence from the text(s)	
Organization: the extent to which the response exhibits direction, shape, and coherence	
Language Use: the extent to which the response reveals an awareness of audience and purpose through effective use of words, sentence structure, and sentence variety	
Conventions: the extent to which the response exhibits conventional spelling, punctuation, paragraphing, capitalization, grammar, and usage	

Now share your chart with your writing group.

Session Two, Part A, Sample Two Response

Both of these writings show that life is not what you want. You need to be happy with what you have, take the good and the bad. The poem says this, and the journal entries really show how true this is.

"Finally" is about a person who is really happy about spring and a bloom on a tree, then the person starts sneezing and it is all over. The tree is the bad guy then. The author uses onopatomea to show this with "whiplash." Also the author exaggerates and says the pressure "kills" the beauty of spring. A bit much, kill.

The journals are about how miserable this girl is that she can't just be doing great stuff all the time and has to wait. She wishes her life away and is miserable like her "stale crusts of pizza." She keeps saying 14 days or weeks and everything will be perfect. She doesn't get that there is no perfect in this life.

These are pretty good pieces. They tell you about how life is life and dreams are dreams.

Now rate this essay using the **MDOLC** that follows.

I would rate this example as _____.
I will list my reasons under the parts of **MDOLC**.

SESSION TWO PART A SCORING RUBRIC - Reading and writing for literary response (see Appendix for complete Scoring Rubric – check evaluation box for each quality scored)	
Quality	**Commentary** The response:
Meaning: the extent to which the response exhibits sound understanding, interpretation, and analysis of the task and text(s)	
Development: the extent to which ideas are elaborated using specific and relevant evidence from the text(s)	
Organization: the extent to which the response exhibits direction, shape, and coherence	
Language Use: the extent to which the response reveals an awareness of audience and purpose through effective use of words, sentence structure, and sentence variety	
Conventions: the extent to which the response exhibits conventional spelling, punctuation, paragraphing, capitalization, grammar, and usage	

Now share your chart with your writing group.

Session Two, Part A, Sample Three Response

The poem and the journal were about two people who had bad luck. The poem was about a person who loved flowers and then was in a car accident and got whiplashed and her friend Al was killed. The journal was about a girl whose boyfriend did her dirt with his best friend's girl Candy. This was sad. The journal girl was so mad and hated Candy and might not even get back together with Rico. So they show life is sad and not to get to excited about stuff.

Now rate this essay using the **MDOLC** that follows.

I would rate this third example as _____.
I will list my reasons under the parts of **MDOLC**.

Quality	Commentary The response:
SESSION TWO, PART A SCORING RUBRIC - **Reading and writing for literary response** (see Appendix for complete Scoring Rubric - check evaluation box for each quality scored)	
Meaning: the extent to which the response exhibits sound understanding, interpretation, and analysis of the task and text(s)	
Development: the extent to which ideas are elaborated using specific and relevant evidence from the text(s)	
Organization: the extent to which the response exhibits direction, shape, and coherence	
Language Use: the extent to which the response reveals an awareness of audience and purpose through effective use of words, sentence structure, and sentence variety	
Conventions: the extent to which the response exhibits conventional spelling, punctuation, paragraphing, capitalization, grammar, and usage	

Now share your chart with your writing group.

Your Task: Write a critical essay in which you discuss two works of literature you have read from the particular perspective of the statement that is provided for you in the Critical Lens. In your essay, provide a valid interpretation of the statement, agree or disagree with the statement as you have interpreted it, and support your opinion using specific references to appropriate literary elements from the two works. You may use scrap paper to plan your response.

Critical Lens: "The test of literature is, I suppose, whether we ourselves live more intensely for the reading of it." Elizabeth Drew

Guidelines:
- Provide a valid interpretation of the *Critical Lens* that clearly establishes the criteria for analysis
- Indicate whether you agree or disagree with the statement as you have interpreted it
- Choose two works you have read that you believe best support your opinion
- Use the criteria suggested by the *Critical Lens* to analyze the works you have chosen
- For each work, do not summarize the plot but use specific references to appropriate literary elements (for example, theme, characterization, structure, language, point of view) to develop your analysis
- Organize your ideas in a unified and coherent manner
- Specify the titles and authors of the literature you choose
- Follow the conventions of written Standard English

Once again these task *Guidelines* provide you with a review of **MDOLC**. Now begin your writing.

☆ **CAPSULE – REVIEWING AND OUTLINING**

First paraphrase the quotation; put Ms. Drew's meaning into your words. This will allow you to interpret what she is saying. Drew speaks of an evaluation of literature. She states that the essence of this "test" is whether the reader will "live" or exist more "intensely," on a deeper plane.

Now that you have paraphrased Drew, decide whether or not you agree with her. You must also think of two works of literature which you have read which you will use as evidence of your opinion about Ms. Drew's comment.

☆ CAPSULE CONTINUES ON NEXT PAGE

You know that there have been some pieces of literature that have caused you to feel deeply and think on a level much deeper than usual for you. You believe that this is what Ms. Drew is talking about, so you decide to agree with her statement and choose two of these pieces to discuss. You choose Shakespeare's *Macbeth* and Pearl S. Buck's *The Good Earth*.

These books present a type of brainstorm for you in their content. What you must do is extract those memorable parts of the book which moved you deeply and made you think. Take note of the following outline of a response using these novels.

On your own now, review the *Task* and the *Guidelines*. Then write an assertion, which you will next revise to be a thesis. Have confidence.

I. Introduction
   A. Paraphrase and explain Drew's idea
   B. State my agreement with it and how literary devices helped me see her point

II. Discuss William Shakespeare's tragedy <u>Macbeth</u>
   A. Feel deeply: ruin of a good man through ambition
   B. Think about
      1. Macbeth's great reputation at beginning and later: images
      2. Macbeth's being manipulated by Duncan, witches, and wife: characterization
      3. Macbeth's loss of everything by end of play: theme

III. Discuss Pearl S. Buck's novel <u>The Good Earth</u>
   A. Feel deeply the pain of Olan and her hard life
   B. Think about
      1. Olan's embarrassment over her normal sized feet: image
      2. Betrayal by Wang Lung: characterization
      3. The land endures even after people die: theme

IV. Conclusion

Now you are ready to follow your outline and write your rough draft. Once your rough draft is complete, proofread, edit, and revise it. But before you do so, you must check *Your Task* and *Guidelines* and see that you have fulfilled all of the requirements.

Once you have finished proofreading, editing, and revision you will write your final draft.

When you have completed your essay, read these sample responses which were evaluated as a #6 (the highest score), a #3 (a mid-range score), and a #1 (a poor score). Decide which score you would give and complete the **MDLOC** rubric for each after you have read it.

Session Two, Part B: Sample One Response

When Elizabeth Drew stated that literature was "good" if it made the reader live more deeply, she put into words a feeling I have long had. Two works which make me feel strongly and think deeply are William Shakespeare's tragedy *Macbeth* and Pearl S. Buck's novel, *The Good Earth*. Both these works use powerful images, strong characterization, and provocative themes to cause the reader to "live intensely."

Macbeth, a tragic play about how extreme ambition causes the downfall of once heroic man, uses potent images to make the reader see. The characters are strong and reminiscent of real people, and the theme that excessive ambition destroys lives reminds us of current events as well as of people from history such as Benedict Arnold.

At first we see Macbeth hailed as a hero by his peers, his soldiers, and his king. This is impressive and may help the reader to think of those times when he or she has been praised. Then we see Macbeth plotting with criminals and lying to his peers. This is sickening because we had seen him when he was both decent and well loved. This juxtaposition of images might well cause us to see ourselves when we give in to our own ambition and push others aside or connive in order to win or look good.

The characters in this play are strong and remind us of flesh and blood people we know, as well as of ourselves at our worst. King Duncan, the witches, and Lady Macbeth all manipulate Macbeth by playing with his ego. King Duncan lavishes praise on the battle field general Macbeth and leads Macbeth to believe he might be selected by Duncan to succeed as king. This does not happen, and Macbeth then is of a mind to seek revenge for his private humiliation. The witches manipulate Macbeth by stroking his ego and promising him greatness. They do this through partial truths and praise. Again, Macbeth falls because he allows himself to be taken in. And finally, his own wife manipulates him by praising his manhood when he agrees to murder. Macbeth is a ruined man because he allows his ambition and his ego to make him vulnerable to flattery and false promises. These strong characters are very like the real people we meet who flatter us and lead us astray. The characters make us feel our own weaknesses and reflect on how we can guard against falling victim to our foibles and such temptors.

The theme of this play is that inordinate ambition is destructive. We see this in the ruin of Macbeth and the upheaval he causes in his country. This destructive ambition and the havoc it causes occurs in our own lives too. *The Good Earth* by Pearl Buck is a novel about a Chinese farmer who values his land more than any other thing. The images, characters, and theme of this piece also affect the reader deeply and cause him or her to think about life on a profound level.

The image of the farmer's wife, Olan, trying to make herself less visible because of her normal sized feet is a disturbing picture. At this time it was a sign of beauty to have bound, practically useless feet, and Olan's self-image is ruined because she has natural rather than mutated feet. This image may well cause the reader to think about the mutilation our society practices in the form of self-starvation and piercing for the sake of cosmetics.

The character of the farmer, Wang Lung, is disturbing in his single-mindedness. Although love of the land is admirable, Wang Lung places this love above all else, his wife, his children, and even his own welfare. When Wang Lung chooses to leave his farm during a famine rather than sell the place in exchange for at least a modicum of security, he endangers not just his family but himself as they flee without any assurance of continued survival. Such a character makes us reflect on our own tunnel vision and those times when we refuse to recognize the short-sightedness of our own decisions.

The theme of *The Good Earth* is also thought-provoking: the land does survive us all. This may cause us to consider what we do with the relatively little time we have here and the way we treat this earth while we are on it. These are questions worth asking, and the answers will help us to live more deeply.

This play and this novel allow us to see the horrifying results of unbridled ambition and obsessive single-mindedness. Such life lessons, learned through reacting to literature and reflecting on it, are relatively painless ways for readers to become deeper people who live " more intensely."

Now rate this essay using the **MDOLC** chart.

I would rate this example as _____.
I will list my reasons under the parts of **MDOLC**.

SESSION TWO PART B SCORING RUBRIC - Reading and writing for critical analysis (see Appendix for complete Scoring Rubric – check evaluation box for each quality scored)		
Quality	The response:	Commentary
Meaning: the extent to which the response exhibits sound understanding, interpretation, and analysis of the task and text(s)		
Development: the extent to which ideas are elaborated using specific and relevant evidence from the text(s)		
Organization: the extent to which the response exhibits direction, shape, and coherence		
Language Use: the extent to which the response reveals an awareness of audience and purpose through effective use of words, sentence structure, and sentence variety		
Conventions: the extent to which the response exhibits conventional spelling, punctuation, paragraphing, capitalization, grammar, and usage		

Now share your chart with your writing group.

Session Two, Part B, Sample Two Response

I read two pieces that were good. *Macbeth* by Shakespeare and *The Good Earth* by Pearl Buck. They were really good.

Macbeth was about a general who becomes king. He is a good guy, then he murders. His wife is not a good guy. She makes him murder because she threatens to call him a wimp.

The Good Earth is in China about how a man wants to own his farm and marries and then has mistresses and then his kids turn into bums and want to sell his land. He gets rich along the way and dies.

These are both good books that I read.

Now rate this essay using the **MDOLC** chart (on page 207).

I would rate this example as _____.
I will list my reasons under the parts of **MDOLC**.

SESSION TWO PART B SCORING RUBRIC -
Reading and writing for critical analysis
(see Appendix for complete Scoring Rubric – check evaluation box for each quality scored)

Quality	Commentary The response:
Meaning: the extent to which the response exhibits sound understanding, interpretation, and analysis of the task and text(s)	
Development: the extent to which ideas are elaborated using specific and relevant evidence from the text(s)	
Organization: the extent to which the response exhibits direction, shape, and coherence	
Language Use: the extent to which the response reveals an awareness of audience and purpose through effective use of words, sentence structure, and sentence variety	
Conventions: the extent to which the response exhibits conventional spelling, punctuation, paragraphing, capitalization, grammar, and usage	

Now share your chart with your writing group.

Session Two, Part B, Sample Three Response

Elizabeth Drew said, "The test of literature is, I suppose, whether we ourselves live more intensely for the reading of it." She was right. I know this because I read two books that show this, "Macbeth" by William Shakespeare and "The Good Earth" by Pearl Buck.

"Macbeth" was about a general who becomes a king because he murders the king. This Macbeth is very ambitious. To be that ambitious can get you in trouble. You start to listen to rumors like the witches tell Macbeth and then you begin to lie to your friends and cheat. It makes you think.

"The Good Earth" makes you think too about how little respect a person gets makes that person think they don't deserve respect. Like Olan the wife. She gets no respect from her husband and then she begins to think she is nothing and says not very much when he takes a mistress and lets him take the earrings she has and give them to her. This makes the reader think about how people can affect other people and should be careful.

So Ms. Drew had it straight. Good books make you think and thinking makes you intense.

Now rate this essay using the **MDOLC** chart.

I would rate this third example as _____.

I will list my reasons under the parts of **MDOLC**.

SESSION TWO PART B SCORING RUBRIC - Reading and writing for critical analysis (see Appendix for complete Scoring Rubric – check evaluation box for each quality scored)	
Quality	Commentary The response:
Meaning: the extent to which the response exhibits sound understanding, interpretation, and analysis of the task and text(s)	
Development: the extent to which ideas are elaborated using specific and relevant evidence from the text(s)	
Organization: the extent to which the response exhibits direction, shape, and coherence	
Language Use: the extent to which the response reveals an awareness of audience and purpose through effective use of words, sentence structure, and sentence variety	
Conventions: the extent to which the response exhibits conventional spelling, punctuation, paragraphing, capitalization, grammar, and usage	

Now share your chart with your writing group.

End of Practice English Test C

UNIT SIX
APPENDICES

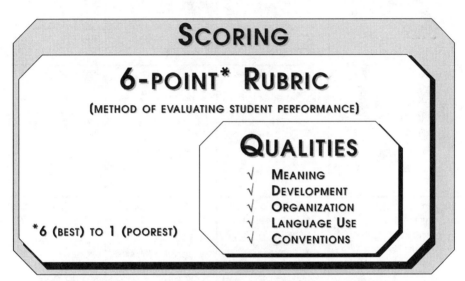

SCORING

6-POINT* RUBRIC

(METHOD OF EVALUATING STUDENT PERFORMANCE)

QUALITIES

√ MEANING
√ DEVELOPMENT
√ ORGANIZATION
√ LANGUAGE USE
√ CONVENTIONS

*6 (BEST) TO 1 (POOREST)

The five qualities of the rubrics (identified above) can be remembered by the initials: **MDOLC** (*pronounced "em-dolk"*).

A helpful mnemonic for **MDOLC** is

Mature Drivers Obey Legal Constraints

Mature (Meaning)	=	**M**
Drivers (Development)	=	**D**
Observe (Organization)	=	**O**
Legal (Language Use)	=	**L**
Constraints (Conventions)	=	**C**

The four rubrics on the following pages are the complete rubrics for evaluating all four parts of the English Test:

SESSION ONE, PART A – Listening and writing for information and understanding
SESSION ONE, PART B – Reading and writing for information and understanding
SESSION TWO, PART A – Reading and writing for literary response
SESSION TWO, PART B – Reading and writing for critical analysis

SESSION ONE, PART A SCORING RUBRIC -
Listening and writing for information and understanding
(Revised Regents Comprehensive Examination in English, Spring 1998, NYS Education Department)

Quality	6 Responses at this level:	5 Responses at this level:	4 Responses at this level:
Meaning: the extent to which the response exhibits sound understanding, interpretation, and analysis of the task and text(s)	– reveal an in-depth analysis of the text – make insightful connections between information and ideas in the text and the assigned task	– convey a thorough under-standing of the text – make clear and explicit connections between information and ideas in the text and the assigned task	– convey a basic understanding of the text – make explicit connections between information and ideas in the text and the assigned task
Development: the extent to which ideas are elaborated using specific and relevant evidence from the text(s)	– develop ideas clearly and fully, making effective use of a wide range of relevant and specific details from the text	– develop ideas clearly and consistently, using relevant and specific details from the text	– develop some ideas more fully than others, using relevant and specific details from the text
Organization: the extent to which the response exhibits direction, shape, and coherence	– maintain a clear and appropriate focus – exhibit a logical and coherent structure through skillful use of appropriate devices and transitions	– maintain a clear and appropriate focus – exhibit a logical sequence of ideas through use of appropriate devices and transitions	– maintain a clear and appropriate focus – exhibit a logical sequence of ideas but may lack internal consistency
Language Use: the extent to which the response reveals an awareness of audi-ence and purpose through effective use of words, sentence structure, and sen-tence variety	– are stylistically sophis-ticated, using lan-guage that is precise and engaging, with a notable sense of voice and awareness of audience and pur-pose – vary structure and length of sentences to enhance meaning	– use language that is fluent and original, with evident awareness of audience and purpose – vary structure and length of sentences to control rhythm and pacing	– use appropriate language with some awareness of audience and purpose – occasionally make effective use of sentence structure or length
Conventions: the extent to which the response exhibits conventional spelling, punctuation, paragraphing, capitalization, grammar, and usage	– demonstrate control of the conventions with essentially no errors, even with sophisticated language	– demonstrate control of the conventions, exhibiting occasional errors only when using sophisticated language	– demonstrate partial control of the conventions, exhibiting occasional errors that do not hinder comprehension

Session One, Part A

3 Responses at this level:	2 Responses at this level:	1 Responses at this level:
– convey a basic understanding of the text – make few or superficial connections between information and ideas in the text and the assigned task	– convey a confused or inaccurate understanding of the text – allude to the text but make unclear or unwarranted connections to the assigned task	– provide no evidence of textual understanding – make no connections between information in the text and the assigned task
– develop some ideas briefly, using some details from the text	– are incomplete or largely undeveloped, hinting at ideas, but references to the text are vague, irrelevant, repetitive, or unjustified	– are minimal, with no evidence of development
– establish, but fail to maintain an appropriate focus – exhibit rudimentary structure but may include some inconsistencies or irrelevancies	– lack an appropriate focus but suggest some organization, or suggest a focus but lack organization	– show no focus or organization
– rely on language from the text or basic vocabulary, with little awareness of audience or purpose – exhibit some attempt to vary sentence structure or length for effect, but with uneven success	– use language that is imprecise or unsuitable for the audience or purpose – reveal little awareness of how to use sentences to achieve an effect	– are minimal – use language that is incoherent or inappropriate
– demonstrate emerging control of the conventions, exhibiting occasional errors that hinder comprehension	– demonstrate a lack of control of the conventions, exhibiting frequent errors that make comprehension difficult	– are minimal, making assessment of conventions unreliable – may be illegible or not recognizable as English

SESSION ONE, PART B SCORING RUBRIC -
Reading and writing for information and understanding
(Revised Regents Comprehensive Examination in English, Spring 1998, NYS Education Department)

Quality	6 Responses at this level:	5 Responses at this level:	4 Responses at this level:
Meaning: the extent to which the response exhibits sound understanding, interpretation, and analysis of the task and document(s)	– reveal an in-depth analysis of the documents – make insightful connections between information and ideas in the documents and the assigned task	– convey a thorough understanding of the documents – make clear and explicit connections between information and ideas in the documents and the assigned task	– convey a basic understanding of the documents – make explicit connections between information and ideas in the documents and the assigned task
Development: the extent to which ideas are elaborated using specific and relevant evidence from the document(s)	– develop ideas clearly and fully, making effective use of a wide range of relevant and specific details from the documents	– develop ideas clearly and consistently, using relevant and specific details from the documents	– develop some ideas more fully than others, using relevant and specific details from the documents
Organization: the extent to which the response exhibits direction, shape, and coherence	– maintain a clear and appropriate focus – exhibit a logical and coherent structure through skillful use of appropriate devices and transitions	– maintain a clear and appropriate focus – exhibit a logical sequence of ideas through use of appropriate devices and transitions	– maintain a clear and appropriate focus – exhibit a logical sequence of ideas but may lack internal consistency
Language Use: the extent to which the response reveals an awareness of audience and purpose through effective use of words, sentence structure, and sentence variety	– are stylistically sophisticated, using language that is precise and engaging, with a notable sense of voice and awareness of audience and purpose – vary structure and length of sentences to enhance meaning	– use language that is fluent and original, with evident awareness of audience and purpose – vary structure and length of sentences to control rhythm and pacing	– use appropriate language with some awareness of audience and purpose – occasionally make effective use of sentence structure or length
Conventions: the extent to which the response exhibits conventional spelling, punctuation, paragraphing, capitalization, grammar, and usage	– demonstrate control of the conventions with essentially no errors, even with sophisticated language	– demonstrate control of the conventions, exhibiting occasional errors only when using sophisticated language	– demonstrate partial control of the conventions, exhibiting occasional errors that do not hinder comprehension

SESSION ONE, PART B SCORING RUBRIC - continued		
3 Responses at this level:	**2** Responses at this level:	**1** Responses at this level:
– convey a basic understanding of the documents* – make few or superficial connections between information and ideas in the documents and the assigned task	– convey a confused or inaccurate understanding of the documents – allude to the documents but make unclear or unwarranted connections to the assigned task	– provide no evidence of textual understanding – make no connections between information in the documents and the assigned task
– develop some ideas briefly, using some details from the documents	– are incomplete or largely undeveloped, hinting at ideas, but references to the documents are vague, irrelevant, repetitive, or unjustified	– are minimal, with no evidence of development
– establish, but fail to maintain an appropriate focus – exhibit rudimentary structure but may include some inconsistencies or irrelevancies	– lack an appropriate focus but suggest some organization, or suggest a focus but lack organization	– show no focus or organization
– rely on language from the documents or basic vocabulary, with little awareness of audience or purpose – exhibit some attempt to vary sentence structure or length for effect, but with uneven success	– use language that is imprecise or unsuitable for the audience or purpose – reveal little awareness of how to use sentences to achieve an effect	– are minimal – use language that is incoherent or inappropriate
– demonstrate emerging control of the conventions, exhibiting occasional errors that hinder comprehension	– demonstrate a lack of control of the conventions, exhibiting frequent errors that make comprehension difficult	– are minimal, making assessment of conventions unreliable – may be illegible or not recognizable as English

READING & WRITING
STOP
FOR INFORMATION & UNDERSTANDING

Session

One,

Part B

* If the student addresses only one document, the response can be scored no higher than a 3

Quality	6 Responses at this level:	5 Responses at this level:	4 Responses at this level:
Meaning: the extent to which the response exhibits sound understanding, interpretation, and analysis of the task and text(s)	– establish a controlling idea that reveals an in-depth analysis of both texts – make insightful connections between the controlling idea, the ideas in each text, and the elements or techniques used to convey those ideas	– establish a controlling idea that reveals a thorough understanding of both texts – make clear and explicit connections between the controlling idea, the ideas in each text, and the elements or techniques used to convey those ideas	– establish a controlling idea that shows a basic understanding of both texts – make explicit connections between the controlling idea, the ideas in each text, and the elements or techniques used to convey those ideas
Development: the extent to which ideas are elaborated using specific and relevant evidence from the text(s)	– develop ideas clearly and fully, making effective use of a wide range of relevant and specific details from both texts	– develop ideas clearly and consistently, using relevant and specific details from both texts	– develop some ideas more fully than others, using relevant and specific details from both texts
Organization: the extent to which the response exhibits direction, shape, and coherence	– maintain the focus established by the controlling ideas – exhibit a logical and coherent structure through skillful use of appropriate devices and transitions	– maintain the focus established by the controlling idea – exhibit a logical sequence of ideas through use of appropriate devices and transitions	– maintain a clear and appropriate focus – exhibit a logical sequence of ideas but may lack internal consistency
Language Use: the extent to which the response reveals an awareness of audience and purpose through effective use of words, sentence structure, and sentence variety	– are stylistically sophisticated, using language that is precise and engaging, with a notable sense of voice and awareness of audience and purpose – vary structure and length of sentences to enhance meaning	– use language that is fluent and original, with evident awareness of audience and purpose – vary structure and length of sentences to control rhythm and pacing	– use appropriate language, with some awareness of audience and purpose – occasionally make effective use of sentence structure or length
Conventions: the extent to which the response exhibits conventional spelling, punctuation, paragraphing, capitalization, grammar, and usage	– demonstrate control of the conventions with essentially no errors, even with sophisticated language	– demonstrate control of the conventions, exhibiting occasional errors only when using sophisticated language	– demonstrate partial control of the conventions, exhibiting occasional errors that do not hinder comprehension

Session Two, Part A

3 Responses at this level:	2 Responses at this level:	1 Responses at this level:
– establish a controlling idea that shows a basic understanding of the texts* – make few or superficial connections between the controlling idea, the ideas in the texts, and the elements or techniques used to convey those ideas	– convey a confused or inaccurate understanding of the texts – fail to establish a controlling idea – allude to the texts but give no examples of literary elements or techniques	– provide minimal evidence of textual understanding – make no connections between the ideas in the texts and literary elements or techniques
– develop ideas briefly, using some details from the texts	– are incomplete or largely undeveloped, hinting at ideas, but references to the text are vague, irrelevant, repetitive, or unjustified	– are minimal, with no evidence of development
– establish, but fail to maintain an appropriate focus – exhibit rudimentary structure but may include some inconsistencies or irrelevancies	– lack an appropriate focus but suggest some organization, or suggest a focus but lack organization	– show no focus or organization
– rely on language from the texts or basic vocabulary, with little awareness of audience or purpose – exhibit some attempt to vary sentence structure or length for effect, but with uneven success	– use language that is imprecise or unsuitable for the audience or purpose – reveal little awareness of how to use sentences to achieve an effect	– are minimal – use language that is incoherent or inappropriate
– demonstrate emerging control of the conventions, exhibiting occasional errors that hinder comprehension	– demonstrate a lack of control of the conventions, exhibiting frequent errors that make comprehension difficult	– are minimal, making assessment of conventions unreliable – may be illegible or not recognizable as English

* If the student addresses only one text, the response can be scored no higher than a 3

SESSION TWO, PART IB SCORING RUBRIC - Reading and writing for critical analysis
(Revised Regents Comprehensive Examination in English, Spring 1998, NYS Education Department)

Quality	6 Responses at this level:	5 Responses at this level:	4 Responses at this level:
Meaning: the extent to which the response exhibits sound understanding, interpretation, and analysis of the task and text(s)	– provide an interpretation of the "critical lens" that is faithful to the complexity of the statement and clearly establishes the criteria for analysis – use the criteria to make an insightful analysis of the chosen texts	– provide a thoughtful interpretation of the "critical lens" that establishes the criteria for analysis – make implicit connections between the criteria and the chosen texts	– provide a reasonable interpretation of the "critical lens" that establishes the criteria for analysis – make implicit connections between the criteria and the chosen texts
Development: the extent to which ideas are elaborated using specific and relevant evidence from the text(s)	– develop ideas clearly and fully, making effective use of a wide range of relevant and specific evidence and appropriate literary elements from both texts	– develop ideas clearly and consistently, with reference to relevant and specific evidence and appropriate literary elements from both texts	– develop some ideas more fully than others, with reference to relevant and specific evidence and appropriate literary elements from both texts
Organization: the extent to which the response exhibits direction, shape, and coherence	– maintain the focus established by the critical lens – exhibit a logical and coherent structure through skillful use of appropriate devices and transitions	– maintain the focus established by the critical lens – exhibit a logical sequence of ideas through use of appropriate devices and transitions	– maintain a clear and appropriate focus – exhibit a logical sequence of ideas but may lack internal consistency
Language Use: the extent to which the response reveals an awareness of audience and purpose through effective use of words, sentence structure, and sentence variety	– are stylistically sophisticated, using language that is precise and engaging, with a notable sense of voice and awareness of audience and purpose – vary structure and length of sentences to enhance meaning	– use language that is fluent and original, with evident awareness of audience and purpose – vary structure and length of sentences to control rhythm and pacing	– use appropriate language, with some awareness of audience and purpose – occasionally make effective use of sentence structure or length
Conventions: the extent to which the response exhibits conventional spelling, punctuation, paragraphing, capitalization, grammar, and usage	– demonstrate control of the conventions with essentially no errors, even with sophisticated language	– demonstrate control of the conventions, exhibiting occasional errors only when using sophisticated language	– demonstrate partial control of the conventions, exhibiting occasional errors that do not hinder comprehension

Session Two, Part B

3 Responses at this level:	2 Responses at this level:	1 Responses at this level:
– provide a simple interpretation of the "critical lens" that suggests some criteria for analysis – make superficial connections between the criteria and the chosen texts*	– provide a confused or incomplete interpretation of the "critical lens" – may allude to the "critical lens" but do not use it to analyze the chosen texts	– do not refer to the "critical lens" – reflect minimal analysis of the chosen texts or omit mention of texts
– develop ideas briefly, using some evidence from the texts	– are incomplete or largely undeveloped, hinting at ideas, but references to the text are vague, irrelevant, repetitive, or unjustified	– are minimal, with no evidence of development
– establish, but fail to maintain an appropriate focus – exhibit rudimentary structure but may include some inconsistencies or irrelevancies	– lack an appropriate focus but suggest some organization, or suggest a focus but lack organization	– show no focus or organization
– rely on basic vocabulary, with little awareness of audience or purpose – exhibit some attempt to vary sentence structure or length for effect, but with uneven success	– use language that is imprecise or unsuitable for the audience or purpose – reveal little awareness of how to use sentences to achieve an effect	– are minimal – use language that is incoherent or inappropriate
– demonstrate emerging control of the conventions, exhibiting occasional errors that hinder comprehension	– demonstrate a lack of control of the conventions, exhibiting frequent errors that make comprehension difficult	– are minimal, making assessment of conventions unreliable – may be illegible or not recognizable as English

* If the student addresses only one text, the response can be scored no higher than a 3

clause, independent (sentence all by itself; because requires a subject and a predicate and the stating of a complete concept, it can stand on its own), 78

climax (n., a moment of great or culminating intensity in a narrative or drama, especially the conclusion of a crisis; the turning point in a plot or dramatic action), 130

coherent (adj., marked by orderly and logical unity), 86

collective nouns (refer to group), 17

colon (punctuation mark [:] used after a word introducing a quotation, an explanation, an example, or a series), 95

comma-splice run-ons (writing error of connecting clauses indefinitely with the use of inappropriately placed commas), 92

comma (punctuation mark [,] used to indicate a separation of ideas or of elements within the structure of a sentence), 71, 90-93, 94

common noun (identifies one or all of the members of a type, class, or category), 14

comparative degree (adjective or adverb form used to estimate similarities and differences between two items), 25

complement (n., word or words used after a verb to complete a predicate construction), 92

complete predicate (main action of a group of words or a way of existing that state something about the subject), 76-77

complex sentence (see sentence types), 80-81, 82, 149-156

compound noun (noun composed of two or more words), 15-16

compound sentence (see sentence types), 80, 82, 92, 149-156

compound-complex sentence (see sentence types), 80, 81, 82, 92, 149-156

conclusion (n., end part of composition; restates the basic thesis and conveys a judgment reached after discussion of facts and ideas in the body), 74, 101, 107, 126, 132, 142, 175, 186-187, 197, 203

conjugate (v., to inflect (a verb) in its forms for distinctions such as number, person, voice, mood, and tense), 5-14

conjunction (part of speech – such as *as, and, but, because* – that serves to connect words, phrases, clauses, or sentences), 20, 29-30

conjunctive adverb (words that join two independent clauses such as *also, besides, for example, however, nevertheless, in addition, instead, meanwhile, then,* and *therefore*), 30, 94

connotation (n., general sense of a word in addition to its precise, literal meaning), 84

consistent (adj., uniform, in agreement), 86

consonant (n., letter or character representing a speech sound produced by a partial or complete obstruction of the air stream), 16, 26, 27

controlling idea (see thesis), 157, 192, 196, 198

convention (n., a widely used and accepted device or technique; standard rubric quality evaluating a piece of writing on grammar, usage, punctuation, paragraphing, or spelling), 59, 63, 83, 89, 90-97, 102, 108, 109, 110, 111, 113, 119-121, 122, 127-129, 131, 134-136, 137, 138, 143, 144, 145, 147, 148, 149, 152, 153-156, 157, 162, 164, 166-168, 169, 170, 175, 177, 178, 180, 181, 187, 188, 190, 191, 199-201, 202, 206-208, 209-217

coordinating conjunction (words that join clauses including *and, but, or, nor, for, yet,* and *so*), 29, 80, 92

correlative conjunction (indicative of complementary relationship; used in pairs such as *either...or*), 29

criteria (n., basis for judgment), 87, 117, 131, 143, 164, 202

critical analysis & evaluation (writing to appraise or judge material from an intellectual opinion as required on final tests), 89, 130-137, 164-165, 202-207

critical lens (quotation used as a basis for analysis and interpretation as as required on final tests), 89, 130-136, 164-165, 202-207

criticize (v., to judge the merits and faults of; analyze and evaluate), 88

degree of comparison (modification or inflection of an adjective or adverb used to estimate similarities and differences), 25 (chart)

delete (v., to remove by striking out or canceling), 39

delineate (v., to clearly picture), 88

denotation (n., dictionary meaning of a word), 84

denouement (n., final resolution or clarification of a dramatic or narrative plot; the events following the climax of a drama or novel in which such a resolution or clarification takes place; the outcome of a sequence of events), 130

dependency word (subordinating conjunction), 78

dependent clause (see clause), 78, 80-81, 92

describe (v., to convey an idea or impression of; characterize), 38 develop (v., to present fully), 88, 122, 137, 148, 169

development (standard rubric quality evaluating a piece of writing on the extent of elaboration of ideas by using specific evidence), 59, 63, 70, 71-73, 75, 109-111, 119-121, 127-129, 134-136, 143, 144, 145, 147, 148, 152, 153, 155, 156, 162, 164, 166-168, 169, 177, 178, 180, 188, 190, 191, 199-201, 206-028, 209-218

dictation (n., material read aloud for analysis), 89, 101, 107, 143, 145, 147

diction (n., choice and use of words in writing), 65, 68, 84, 126, 137

discuss (v., to present and explain fully), 88

distinction (n., distinguishing factor, attribute, or characteristic), 87

dominant (adj., outstanding), 86

edit (v., to prepare written material for publication or presentation, as by correcting, revising, or adapting), 108, 156, 175, 187, 197, 198, 203

element (n., part), 87

English Learning Standards (the degree or level of requirement, excellence, or attainment set in English language arts), 60-63, 74, 97

essay (n., a personal viewpoint), 48, 89, 102, 108, 111, 122, 124, 126, 128, 129, 131, 137, 141, 142, 148, 151, 156, 157, 159, 161, 164, 165, 181, 186, 188, 190, 191, 192, 194, 196, 198, 199, 200, 201, 202, 204, 206, 208

evidence (v., to provide facts), 88

explanation (n., an account of an event designed to clarify its causes), 67

explicate (v. to fully explain or decipher), 67, 88

factor (n., element), 87

Faulkner, William (1897-1962, American author; best known for novels such as *The Sound and the Fury*, 1929 and *The Unvanquished*, 1938; explored the decay of traditional Southern values), 164, 165, 167-168

feature article (special piece of writing in a newspaper or magazine), 89

figurative language (language which says more than or other than what the meaning of the words alone indicate), 65, 83, 122, 157, 192, 198

figuratively (adj., based on or making use of figures of speech; metaphorical; see figurative language), 65

fluent (adj., flowing effortlessly, polished), 86

fragments (incomplete sentences; parts missing), 77

FRDSS (initials signifying the tone techniques used in order to convince a reader such as *repetition, rhyme, arrangement of words in sentence, explanations,* and *interruptions* [pronounced *ferds*]), 65, 68-70

Frost, Robert (1874-1963, American poet whose deceptively simple works, often set in rural New England, explore the relationships between individuals and between people and nature), 97

future tense (verb relating to action yet to come), 6

future perfect tense (verb relating to action that will be finished before a certain time in the future), 7

genre (n., a category of artistic composition; kind or type of literature as in novel, short story, poem, etc.), 83, 122

gerund (verbal noun ending in *-ing*), 44

grammar (n., study of how words and their component parts combine to form sentences), 36, 90

graph (n., visual device used to present some numerical concept), 89, 112, 115, 117, 181, 183, 186, 187

guidelines (n., procedures by which to determine a course of action), 102, 107-108, 112-113, 117, 122, 125 131, 138, 149, 152, 156, 157, 161, 164, 165, 170, 174, 175, 181, 186, 187, 192, 196, 197, 198, 202, 203

Hamlet (classic stage play *The Tragical History of Hamlet Prince of Denmark* [1603] by William Shakespeare dealing with murder, revenge, the nature of existence, and human relationships), 72, 137-147

Hersey, John Richard (1914-1993, American writer whose novels [*Hiroshima*, 1946] and essays examined the moral implications of contemporary political and historical events), 131-136

How to Succeed in Business Without Really Trying (Frank Loesser's 1961 Broadway musical poking fun at corporate culture), 115, 118

Humphrey, Hubert Horatio (1911-1978; U.S. Senator [MN, 1949-1965] and 38th Vice President of the U.S. under Lyndon Johnson; presidential candidate, 1968), 56-57

hyperbole (n., a figure of speech in which exaggeration is used for emphasis or effect), 66, 84

Icon (n., image; a representation; symbol), 62

illustrate (v., to clarify, as by use of examples or comparisons), 88

imperative mood (relating to the mood of a verb that expresses a command or request), 5

independent clause (see clause), 78, 80-81, 94, 95

indicative mood (relating to the mood of a verb used in ordinary objective statements), 5

infinitive (verb form that functions as a substantive while retaining certain verbal characteristics, such as modification by adverbs, and that may be preceded by *to*), 6, 8, 9-11

inflection (alternation of the form of a word by changing the form of a base that indicates grammatical features such as number, person, mood, or tense), 8

interjection (part of speech expressing emotion and capable of standing alone), 30

interpret (v., to explain the meaning of), 88

interpretation (n., explanation or a conceptualization by a critic of a work of literature), 87

interruption (n., a break in the sentence), 67, 93

introduction [introductory segement] (n., beginning part of composition), 107, 125, 132, 142, 174, 186, 197, 203

irony (n., the difference between what is and what is expected or between what is and what seems to be), 84, 122, 157, 192, 198

irregular verb (verb form departs from the usual pattern of inflection, derivation, or word formation), 8-13

Jefferson, Thomas (1743-1826; 3rd President of the United States [1801-1809]; drafted the *Declaration of Independence* [1776]), 57

Key Terms List, Group #1 (phrases having to do with writing), 83

Key Terms List, Group #2 (words describing people, places, things, or ideas), 86

Key Terms List, Group #3 (words naming concepts), 87

Key Terms List, Group #4 (actions or command words), 88

Key Terms List, Group #5 (phrases naming various writing forms), 89

language use (standards rubric quality evaluating a piece of writing by the awareness of audience and purpose through effective use of words, sentence structure, and sentence variety), 59, 63, 76-89, 109, 110, 111, 113, 122, 127, 128, 129, 134, 135, 136, 137, 138, 143, 144, 145, 147, 148, 152, 153, 155, 156, 157, 162, 164, 166, 168, 169, 170, 175, 177, 178, 180, 181, 187, 188, 190, 191, 199, 200, 201206, 207, 208, 209-217

Learning Standards, English (acknowledged measure of comparison for quantitative or qualitative value; criterion of education used by an authority), 61-70, 74, 97

Lee, Harper (1926, American author, *To Kill a Mockingbird*, 1961), 165-168

level of language (difficulty and/or appropriate formality of diction and sentence structure), 83, 102, 108, 113, 138, 149, 170, 175, 181

linking verb (verb that expresses a way of being, or relating to the senses, or a condition), 5

literally (adv., in a literal manner; word for word; in a strict sense), 65

literal language (n., language which says exactly what the words mean), 83

literary (adj., having to do with books), 65, 83

literary devices (techniques such as repetition, rhyme, arrangement of words in sentence, explanations, and interruptions used in order to convince a reader), 65, 197, 197, 198

literary response and expression, 61

logical (adj., evidencing reason based on earlier or otherwise known statements, events, or conditions), 86

MacBeth (classic stage play *The Tragedy of Macbeth,* written c. 1605 by William
    Shakespeare, concerns the king of Scotland [1040-1057] who ascended the throne after
    killing his cousin King Duncan in battle; psychological portrait of a villain-hero who feels
    his own guilt acutely, but eventually loses all moral sensitivity), 203-207
metaphor (n., an identification between two essentially different things), 50, 66, 83
MDOLC (initials signifying the scoring rubric qualities [pronounced *em-dolk*]), 63, 109-111,
    112, 117, 119-121, 122, 126-129, 131, 134-136, 137, 143-147, 148, 152-156, 161-164, 165-
    168, 169, 175, 177-180, 187, 188-191, 198, 199-201, 202, 204, 206-208, 209-217
meaning (n., standard rubric quality evaluating a piece of writing by the degree of
    understanding, interpretation, and analysis), 59, 63, 65-70, 73, 75, 109-111, 112, 117,
    119-121, 122, 126-129, 131, 134-136, 137, 143-147, 148, 152-156, 161-164, 165-168, 169,
    175, 177-180, 187, 188-191, 198, 199-201, 202, 204, 206-208, 209-217
mind's eye (inherent mental ability to imagine or remember scenes; the imagination), 38
Minow, Newton N. (1926- ; Chairman of the Federal Communications Commission, 1960s;
    critical of television programming), 55-56, 181-182, 186-191
mention (v., to state without explaining), 88
metaphor (n., figure of speech in which a word or phrase that ordinarily designates one thing
    is used to designate another, thus making an implicit comparison), 50, 57, 69, 83
mnemonic (adj., device, such as a formula or rhyme, used as an aid in remembering), 63
modifier (n., word, phrase, or clause that limits or qualifies the sense of another word or word
    group; adjectives, adverbs), 24
motivating segment (see motivator concept), 37
motivator concept (n., word or phrase – incentive or reason to move to action; used in an
    introduction to impel reader to continue), 37, 47, 48, 74, 101, 107, 125, 142, 174, 186, 197
multi-paragraph (adj., more than one distinct division of written or printed matter that
    begins on a new, usually indented line), 45, 74, 117, 122

nominative (belonging to a case of the subject of a finite verb and of words identified with
    the subject), 21, 22
noun (n., word used to name a person, place, thing, quality, or action and can function as the
    subject or object of a verb, the object of a preposition, or an appositive), 14-19, 24, 28, 91
number (n., pronouns must agree with the noun for which they form a substitute [antecedent]
    – be either singular or plural), 18

Object (n., noun that receives or is affected by the action of a verb within a sentence), 22
objective (adj., the case of a noun or pronoun that serves as the object of a verb; relating to a
    noun or pronoun used in this case), 21, 22
Oedipus the King (*Oedipus Rex,* more properly called *Oedipus Tyrannus,* Sophocles' [497-406
    BC] Greek tragedy written c. 429 BC on the power of fate and the tragic destiny of those
    who fail to exercise moral self-restraint), 115-120
Oliver ! (1960's British musical loosely based on Charles Dickens 1837 novel, *Oliver Twist*),
    115-120
omniscient (adj., having total knowledge), 84
onomatopoeia (n., a literary device in which the sound of the words imitates the meaning of
    the words), 67, 84
organization (n., standard rubric quality evaluating a piece of writing by the extent of
    direction, shape and coherence), 59, 63, 73, 74-75, 102, 108, 109-111, 112, 117, 119-121,
    122, 126-129, 131, 134-136, 137, 143-147, 148, 152-156, 161-164, 165-168, 169, 175, 177-
    180, 187, 188-191, 198, 199-201, 202, 204, 206-208, 209-217
organize (v., to arrange in a coherent form), 45-52, 59, 63, 73, 74-75, 102, 108, 109-111, 112,
    117, 119-121, 122, 126-129, 131, 134-136, 137, 143-147, 148, 152-156, 161-164, 165-168,
    169, 175, 177-180, 187, 188-191, 198, 199-201, 202, 204, 206-208, 209-217
Orwell, George (1903-1950, pen name of Eric Arthur Blair; British writer of nonfiction and
    imaginative fiction attacked totalitarianism and reflected his concern with social justice;
    works include *Animal Farm* [1945] and *1984* [1949]), 50
outline (n., a general description covering the main points of a text of a written work or
    speech, usually analyzed in headings and sub-headings), 14, 100-101, 107, 117, 122, 125-
    126, 132, 142, 174-175, 186-187, 197, 203
overview (n., broad, comprehensive view; a survey of a situation), 87, 100
Owen, Wilfred, (1893-1918 British poet hadability to transmute the experience of war into
    poetry), 132, 133, 135

Palette (n., a board, typically with a hole for the thumb, which an artist can hold while painting and on which the artist mixes colors; the range of colors used in a particular painting; the range of qualities inherent in literature), 36, 42, 44, 48

paragraph (n., distinct division of written or printed matter that begins on a new, usually indented line; consists of one or more sentences, and typically deals with a single thought or topic or quotes a speaker's continuous words), 96, 45, 96, 74, 117, 122, 137

paraphrase (n., restatement of a text or passage in another form or other words, often to clarify meaning), 53-58, 71, 72, 132, 203

parenthesis, pl. parentheses (the upright curved lines "( )" used to mark off explanatory or qualifying remarks in writing), 72-73

parenthetical (adj., using a parenthesis to enclose the author, title of the work, and/or page numbers of some paraphrased idea or quotation used), 72-73

participle (n., form of a verb that can function independently as an adjective and is used with an auxiliary verb to indicate tense, aspect, or voice), 7, 9-11, 24, 91

part of speech (one of a group of traditional classifications of words according to their functions in context, including the noun, pronoun, verb, adjective, adverb, preposition, conjunction, and interjection), 5-33

passive voice (property of verbs indicating the predicate is receiving the action expressed by the verb), 5

past participle (see participle)

past perfect tense (verb relating to action begun before another action), 7

past tense (verb relating to action occurring at an earlier time), 6

perceive (v., to become aware of directly through any of the senses, especially sight or hearing), 66

personal pronoun (pronoun designating the person speaking [*I, me, we, us*], the person spoken to [*you*], or the person or thing spoken about [*he, she, it, they, him, her, them*]), 21, 23

personification (n., giving the qualities of a person to a non-person), 66, 83

perspective (n., point of view), 87

Pirates of Penzance (satirical operetta by British composers Gilbert and Sullivan in 1879), 114-120

plot (n., a literary or dramatic story line), 132

plural forms of nouns and verbs, 16-17, 20-21

poetry (n., piece of literature written in meter; verse, that which is not prose), 43

phrase (n., group of words that does not include both a subject and a predicate), 76, 77

point of view (n., angle from which the story is told as in first person, third person, or omniscient), 84, 165, 202

possessive case (pronoun case that indicates ownership), 15, 21-22

possessive noun (noun that indicates ownership), 15

predicate (see complex predicate and simple predicate)

preposition (n., fairly short words: *at, by, in, to, from, with*, which tie a noun or a pronoun to the rest of the sentence), 28-29, 30, 91

prepositional phrase (group of words anchored to a preposition that modify something else in a sentence), 28-29, 91

present tense (verb relating to action occurring at that precise moment), 6

present perfect tense (verb relating to action begun in the past and continuing to that moment), 7

prewriting (n., creation and arrangement of ideas preliminary to writing: brainstorming, jotting notes, etc.), 44

process (n., series of actions, changes, or functions bringing about a result), 35, 38, 39, 72, 100, 107-108

pronoun (n., a class of words that function as substitutes for nouns or noun phrases [antecedents] and designate persons or things asked for, previously specified, or understood from the context), 14, 18-24, 28, 77, 91

proofread (v., to read a piece of writing in order to improve it by finding errors and marking corrections), 30-33, 62, 74, 197, 202, 203, 204

proper noun (belonging to the class of words used as names for unique individuals, events, or places and usually having few possibilities for modification), 14

propose (v., to suggest), 88

punctuation marks (standard signs in writing and printing used to separate words into sentences, clauses, and phrases in order to clarify meaning: comma, period, colon, semicolon, question mark, exclamation mark), 90-97

purpose (n., reason for doing, intent), 87

quotation (n., explicit reference to words of another author), 71-73, 91, 95, 202
quotation marks (punctuation signs ["..."] which indicate that the exact words of a speaker are being used), 71-72, 83

relative (adj., having a connection to another), 86
relevant (adj., having a connection to the matter or topic at hand), 86, 175
repetition (n., act of doing or saying again), 67, 87, 140
revise / revision (v., to change or improve), 37, 50-51, 74, 108, 175, 187, 197, 198, 203, 204
rhetorical (adj., using language effectively and persuasively), 65
rhetorical devices (n., tools of persuasion used by good language users), 65, 67, 83
rhetorical question (a question asked for dramatic effect and not intended to evoke a response), 83
Richter Scale (logarithmic scale used to express the total amount of energy released by an earthquake), 70
rhyme, or rime (n., repetition of similar or exact sounds), 67
rough draft (first full writing attempt on a task; must be edited, refined, and polished into an acceptable final writing piece), 37, 48-49, 107, 117, 152, 161, 165, 175, 187, 197, 203
rubric (n., grid method of evaluation providing short commentary or explanation of a quality of work), 59, 62-64, 65, 71, 74, 75, 76, 90, 109-111, 112, 117, 119-121, 122, 126-129, 131, 134-136, 137, 143-147, 148, 152-156, 161-164, 165-168, 169, 175, 177-180, 187, 188-191, 198, 199-201, 202, 204, 206-208, 209-217
run-ons (sentences that are appended or added without a proper break from punctuation), 76

Salient (adj., outstanding, dominant), 86
satiric (adj., relating to, or characterized by satire – attacking folly, vice, or stupidity), 65
segment (n., part into which something can be divided), 37, 47, 107, 142, 174, 187, 197
selection of detail (what facts a writer chooses to include), 65, 68
semicolon (punctuation mark [;] used to connect independent clauses and indicating a closer relationship between the clauses than a period does), 30, 94
sentence (n., grammatical unit that is independent and has a subject that is expressed or understood and a predicate that contains at least one finite verb), 76-82
sentence structure (arrangement of clauses used to express a complete thought; selection of a variety of the four kinds of structure: simple, compound, complex, compound-complex), 65, 68, 76-89, 137, 148, 149-156
sentence types (simple – has only one independent clause; compound – has at least two independent clauses; complex – includes only one independent clause and one dependent clause; compound-complex – includes at least one dependent and at least two independent clauses), 80, 137, 148, 149-156
sexism (n., attitudes, conditions, or behaviors that promote stereotyping of social roles based on gender), 19
Shakespeare, William (1564-1616; English playwright and poet whose body of works is considered the greatest in English literature), 137-141, 142-143, 146, 203-205, 206, 207
signify (v., to indicate), 88
simile (n., a comparison made between two essentially different things), 66, 83, 197
simple predicate (also see verb; main action of a group of words or a way of existing), 5, 21, 22, 54, 55, 56, 76-77, 78, 92
simple sentence (see sentence types), 80-82, 151, 153-155
singular forms of nouns and verbs, 16-17, 20-21
situation (n. set of circumstances), 87, 101, 102, 105, 112, 137, 140, 148, 169, 174, 181, 186
social interaction (relating within society through various communication, including listening, speaking, and writing), 60-61
specific (adj., precise, exact), 86
specify (v., to state explicitly or in detail), 88
staccato effect (adj., marking by abrupt, disconnected parts), 82
Standard English (conventions; proper rules of the English language spoken and written by most respected speakers of English), 63, 82, 83, 89, 103, 108, 113, 122, 131, 137, 138, 149, 152, 157, 164, 169, 170, 175, 181, 187, 192, 198, 202
Standards, English Learning (the degree or level of requirement, excellence, or attainment set in English language arts), 60-63, 74, 97
stanza (n., one of the divisions of a poem, composed of two or more lines usually characterized by a common pattern of meter, rhyme, and number of lines), 197

Steinbeck, John (1902-1968, American author; best known for his novels, including the *Grapes of Wrath*, *Of Mice and Men*, and *East of Eden*), 132, 133

state (v., to set forth in words), 88

stereotyping (v., to impart a conventional, formulaic, and oversimplified conception, opinion, or image), 19

subject (noun, noun phrase, or pronoun in a sentence or clause that denotes the doer of the action or what is described by the predicate), 22, 28, 29, 77, 92

subordinating conjunction (word signalling a clause determined, influenced, or controlled by another), 29, 78

subjunctive mood (relating to a mood of a verb used for hypothetical action, action viewed subjectively), 5

superlative degree (adjective or adverb form used to estimate similarities and differences between three or more items), 25

symbolism (n., attributing representational meanings or significance to objects, events, or relationships), 122, 157, 192, 198

sympathetic (adj., expressing, feeling, or resulting from sympathy), 63

synonym (n., word having the same or nearly the same meaning as another word or other words in a language), 42-44

task (n., job; piece of work assigned or done as part of one's duties), 35-36, 38-42, 48, 62, 74-75, 82, 87, 99, 102, 107, 112, 122, 125, 131, 137, 142, 143, 148, 152, 157, 161, 164, 165, 169, 174, 181, 186, 192, 196, 202

TASK-AUDIENCE formula (an acronym for a systematic design to enhance proofreading), 35-37, 59, 75

technique (n., method), 83

tendency (n. inclination), 87

tense (n., any of the inflected forms in the conjugation of a verb that indicates the time, such as past, present, or future, as well as the continuance or completion of action), 6-14

tension (n., interplay of conflicting elements in a piece of writing), 46

text (n., body of a written work), 89

thesaurus (n., book of synonyms, often including related and contrasting words and antonyms), 43, 44

thesis (n., proposition statement advancing an original point of view; in writing, a controlling idea), 37, 45-46, 47, 72, 74, 100, 101, 107, 125-126, 142, 152, 161, 165, 174, 186-187, 197

thesis / support paper (n., research paper presenting a point of view and documented proof to support that point of view), 89

tone (n., author's attitude toward his or her work), 41-42, 47, 48, 65-69, 83, 102, 108, 113, 122, 132, 138, 149, 170, 175, 181, 187

topic sentence (sentence within a paragraph or discourse that states the main thought, often placed at the beginning), 45, 197

transition (n., word, phrase, sentence, or series of sentences connecting one part of a discourse to another),18, 36, 37, 62

Valid (adj., Containing premises from which the conclusion may logically be derived; convincing), 86

verb (part of speech that expresses existence, action, or occurrence), 5-14, 42, 43, 44, 46, 76, 78, 95

visual (n., capable of being seen), 87

vowel (n., letter, such as *a, e, i, o, u,* and sometimes *y* forming the most prominent and central sound of a syllable), 16, 26

Washington, George (1732-1799; American military leader and 1st President of the United States [1789-1797]), 54

writing process (series of actions to bring forth a piece of writing from conception, through planning, to the rough and final drafts), 38-52, 74, 99-101, 107-108, 122

web, webbing (v., connecting the elements of a structure or arrangement), 36, 100-101, 102, 105, 122, 137 (*example* 140), 169

☆ **CAPSULE – LISTENING PASSAGES**

Note: The following instructions and passages are separated intentionally from the tests as a reminder that the passages must be read aloud to the test-taker by a person other than the test-taker (himself or herself).

COMPREHENSIVE EXAMINATION IN ENGLISH
January 2003

1 Before the start of the examination period, say:

> **Do not open the examination booklet until you are instructed to do so.**

2 Distribute one examination booklet and one essay booklet to each student.

3 After each student has received an examination booklet and an essay booklet, say:

> **Tear off the answer sheet, which is the last page of the examination booklet, and fill in its heading. Now circle "Session One" and fill in the heading on each page of your essay booklet.**

4 After the students have filled in all headings on their answer sheets and essay booklets, say:

> Look at page 2 of your examination booklet and follow along while I read the Overview and The Situation.
>
> *Overview*:
> For this part of the test, you will listen to a speech about the struggle of women to obtain voting rights in England, answer some multiple-choice questions, and write a response based on the situation described below. You will hear the speech twice. You may take notes on the next page anytime you wish during the readings.
>
> *Situation*:
> For a social studies unit on the history of voting rights, your teacher has asked each student to prepare a report on an issue related to the struggle for voting rights in another country. You have decided to do your report on the social conditions that led women in England to seek the right to vote. In preparation for writing your report, listen to a speech delivered in 1908 by Emmeline Pankhurst. Then use relevant information from the speech to write your report.
>
> Now I will read the passage aloud to you for the first time.

5 Now read the passage aloud with appropriate expression, but without added comment.

Listening Passage – January 2003

...What, then, is this vote that we are hearing so much about just now [in 1908], so much more than people have heard in discussion at least, for a great many years? I think we may give the vote a threefold description. We may describe the vote as, first of all, a symbol, secondly, a safeguard, and thirdly, an instrument. It is a symbol of freedom, a symbol of citizenship, a symbol of liberty. It is a safeguard of all those liberties which it symbolizes. And in these later days it has come to be regarded more than anything else as an instrument, something with which you can get a great many more things than our forefathers who fought for the vote ever realized as possible to get with it. It seems to me that such a thing is worth fighting for, and women today are fighting very strenuously in order to get it....

In the first place, it is important that women should have the vote in order that in the government of the country the women's point of view should be put forward....

First of all, let us take the marriage laws. They are made by men for women. Let us consider whether they are equal, whether they are just, whether they are wise. What security of maintenance has the married woman? Many a married woman having given up her economic independence in order to marry, how is she compensated for that loss? What security does she get in that marriage for which she gave up economic independence? Take the case of a woman who has been earning a good income. She is told that she ought to give up her employment when she becomes a wife and mother. What does she get in return? All that a married man is obliged by law to do for his wife is to provide for her shelter of some kind, food of some kind, and clothing of some kind. It is left to his good pleasure to decide what the shelter shall be, what the food shall be, what the clothing shall be. It is left to him to decide what money shall be spent on the home, and how it shall be spent; the wife has no voice legally in deciding any of these things. She has no legal claim upon any definite portion of his income. If he is a good man, a conscientious man, he does the right thing. If he is not, if he chooses almost to starve his wife, she has no remedy. What he thinks sufficient is what she has to be content with.

I quite agree, in all these illustrations, that the majority of men are considerably better than the law compels them to be, so the majority of women do not suffer as much as they might suffer if men were all as bad as they might be, but since there are some bad men, some unjust men, don't you agree with me that the law ought to be altered so that those men could be dealt with?

Take what happens to the woman if her husband dies and leaves her a widow, sometimes with little children. If a man is so insensible to his duties as a husband and father when he makes his will, as to leave all his property away from his wife and children, the law allows him to do it. That will is a valid one. So you see that the married woman's position is not a very secure one. It depends entirely on her getting a good ticket in the lottery. If she has a good husband, well and good: if she has a bad one, she has to suffer, and she has no remedy. That is her position as a wife, and it is far from satisfactory....

Let us consider her position as a mother. We have repeated this so often at our meetings that I think the echo of what we have said must have reached many. By English law no married woman exists as the mother of the child she brings into the world. In the eyes of the law she is not the parent of her child. The child, according to our marriage laws, has only one parent, who can decide the future of the child, who can decide where it shall live, how it shall live, how much shall be spent upon it, how much it shall be educated, and what religion it shall profess. That parent is the father....

Now let me say something on another point. Among those here are some professional women. You know what a long and a weary struggle it has been for women to get into the professions, some of which are now open to women. But you all know that the position of women in those professions is not what it ought to be, and is certainly not what it will be when women get the franchise. How difficult it is for women to get posts after they have qualified for them. I know this from practical experience on a public body. Every time we had applications from women for posts open to them, we had applications also from men. Usually the standing of the women was very much higher than that of the men. And yet the women did not get those appointments. The men got them. That would all be altered if we got political equality. It is the political key that is needed to unlock the door....

Almost everywhere the well-paid posts are given to men. Take the College of Arts. Women art students do quite as well as the men students. And yet after their training is over, women never get any of the posts. All the professorships, all the well-paid posts in the colleges and Universities are given to men. I knew the Head of one of the training colleges in one of our great cities. She said to me: "It makes me feel quite sad to see bright young girls expecting to get their living, and finding after their training is over that they can get nothing to do." The Parliamentary vote will settle that. There is no department of life that you can think of in which the possession of the Parliamentary vote will not make things easier for women than they are to-day....

I hope that there may be a few men and women here who will go away determined at least to give this question more consideration then they have in the past. They will see that we women who are doing so much to get the vote, want it because we realize how much good we can do with it when we have got it. We do not want it in order to boast of how much we have got. We do not want it because we want to imitate men or to be like men. We want it because without it we cannot do that work which it is necessary and right and proper that every man and woman should be ready and willing to undertake in the interests of the community of which they form a part. It has always been the business of women to care for these things, to think of these home questions. I assure you that no woman who enters into this agitation need feel that she has got to give up a single one of her woman's duties in the home. She learns to feel that she is attaching a larger meaning to those duties which have been woman's duties since the race began, and will be till the race has ceased to be. After all, home is a very, very big thing indeed. It is not just your own little home, with its four walls, and your own little private and personal interests that are looked after there. The home is the home of everybody of the nation. No nation can have a proper home unless women as well as men give their best to its building up and to making it what a home ought to be, a place where every single child born into it shall have a fair chance of growing up to be a fit, and a happy, and a useful member of the community.

— excerpted from "The Importance of the Vote,"
An Historical Anthology of Select British Speeches

6   After reading the passage aloud once, say:

> You may take a few minutes to look over The Situation and your notes. (Pause) Now I will read the passage aloud a second time.

7   Read the passage a second time.

8   After the second reading, say:

> Now turn to page 4 of your examination booklet, read the directions, and answer the multiple-choice questions. Be sure to follow all the directions given in your examination booklet and your essay booklet. You may now begin.

☆ **CAPSULE – LISTENING PASSAGES**

Note: The following instructions and passages are separated intentionally from the tests as a reminder that the passages must be read aloud to the test-taker by a person other than the test-taker (himself or herself).

COMPREHENSIVE EXAMINATION IN ENGLISH
June 2003

1   Before the start of the examination period, say:

> **Do not open the examination booklet until you are instructed to do so.**

2   Distribute one examination booklet and one essay booklet to each student.

3   After each student has received an examination booklet and an essay booklet, say:

> **Tear off the answer sheet, which is the last page of the examination booklet, and fill in its heading. Now circle "Session One" and fill in the heading on each page of your essay booklet.**

4   After the students have filled in all headings on their answer sheets and essay booklets, say:

> Look at page 2 of your examination booklet and follow along while I read the **Overview** and **The Situation**.
>
> *Overview*:
> For this part of the test, you will listen to a speech about effective speech writing, answer some multiple-choice questions, and write a response based on the situation described below. You will hear the speech twice. You may take notes on the next page anytime you wish during the readings.
>
> *Situation*:
> Your English class intends to publish a handbook for incoming freshmen, advising them on skills needed for high school. Your assignment is to write an article on techniques for effective speechwriting. In preparation for writing your article, listen to a speech by Jane Tully, a professional speechwriter. Then use relevant information from the speech to write your article.
>
> Now I will read the passage aloud to you for the first time.

5   Now read the passage aloud with appropriate expression, but without added comment.

...You see, I have a theory that giving a speech is a lot like giving a party. You, the audience, are the invited guests. As the speaker, I am the host–at least for the moment. The speech I am delivering to you is like a meal. I want it to be nourishing food for thought - full of substance, with interesting ideas for you to chew on. I want to present it in a way that's appealing, so you'll be eager to take in my ideas. And like a good meal, I want my speech to be appropriate for this particular occasion.

If you think of a speech that way, then where does the speechwriter fit in? Actually, I like to think of myself as a kind of verbal caterer. You call on professionals like me when you don't have the time or expertise to do the job yourself, or when you have a special occasion and you want that extra something that will really make your speech stand out....

So in my role as caterer, I'd like to take this opportunity to share my basic recipe for a successful presentation. Follow this easy three-step recipe and you can't go wrong:

- Know who's coming to the party,

- Use only the best ingredients, and

- Focus on the main course.

First, know who's coming....

What do we need to know about audiences? Size, for one thing. This is important because smaller audiences pay closer attention. When a group is small, the speaker can easily maintain eye contact and hold people's attention. The larger the audience, the easier it is for listeners to feel anonymous and to drift off, so a speaker has to offer more entertainment value. With large convention-sized audiences of hundreds, or even thousands of people, this is essential: bring in audiovisual support whenever you can; add stories and humor. Keep it moving, and keep it short, or you'll lose them.

To the extent that it's possible, speechwriters also want to know the age range of the audience. Will it be a group of seniors, or young professionals, or students—or a mixed group? This affects the kinds of stories, humor, and other support material we will choose to make the speaker's points. Because so much of humor comes out of life experience, the jokes Grandma enjoys may fall completely flat with your teenage son. If your audience includes a wide range of ages, you need to find humor that has a very broad appeal.

This is also true for any examples from history. A number of years ago, a friend of mine was once asked to speak to a church youth group on the subject of war and whether or not it is ever justified. He started by telling about how he had felt, as a senior in college at the height of the Vietnam War, when his draft notice arrived in the mail. A young man in the group interrupted him to say, "Oh, yeah, Vietnam. We read about that in history last week."

My friend was barely 30 at the time, and he said he had never felt so old in all his life! But it was an important lesson for him as a speaker: never assume that your audience shares your experience or knowledge of history, and be sure to give your illustrations the historical context they need–especially if you are speaking to a younger audience.

Speechwriters also want to know what the gender mix of an audience will be. Will there be more men than women, or vice versa? Again, this information affects the kinds of illustrations we choose. One of my clients, a product sales manager at Citibank, recently gave a speech to pump up a group of brokers who were being asked to meet some new revenue goals. We used a story featuring the retired Notre Dame coach Lou Holtz. The story ends with a great one-liner about a quarterback who runs 85 yards to score a winning goal. The speaker delivered it beautifully, and he got a big laugh--the vast majority of his listeners were men. It was perfect for that group, but if the audience had been more mixed, I probably would have used something different.

For the speech I'm delivering to you, I actually had to think twice about my food image. At first I thought the comparison might be a little too domestic for an audience of professional women. But after giving it some thought, I decided that since so many of the world's great chefs are men, and since we all have to eat, this image can work for both male and female audiences. My point is that it was important for me to go through the process of thinking about the gender of this audience and how that could affect the way you receive my ideas....

So...know who's coming to the party.

Second, use only the best ingredients. When I give a dinner party, I like to experiment with recipes that have an exotic twist–like a special ingredient I can't get down the street–maybe something I'll only find at Balducci's [gourmet food store] or the green market. The shopping is fun and interesting, and the new ingredient gives a special flavor to the whole meal.

The same is true with researching a speech. It's fun because I'm always learning something new. I have learned that it's worth going out of my way to find a little known fact or two that can help make the speech memorable. A National Geographic Society executive was once asked to accept an award on behalf of the Society from the Leukemia Society of America. In researching his remarks, I learned about a small periwinkle that grows in the tropical rainforest. This little flower is the source of the medication that saves the lives of 95 percent of the children who contract childhood leukemia. With that fact, the speaker was able to relate National Geographic's interest in saving the environment to the life-saving work of the Leukemia Society. The extra effort it took to find that little tidbit of information was really worth it.

Once you have the information you need for a speech, spice it up! A speech writing guide called *American Speaker* points out that "Good quotes in a speech, like good seasoning in a stew, are meant to add zest without detracting from the essential nature of the dish and its basic ingredients." That's true not only of quotes, but of anecdotes and humor as well. These elements must add something to the speech, not detract from it. I think most audiences are impatient with speakers who start out with a belly laugh, then take off in an entirely different direction.

Not only is this annoying, but what a waste of a good story! The whole reason for telling stories in your speech is to help people pay closer attention and remember your ideas. So make sure your illustrations relate to your message, and make the connection clear for the audience....

Your audience will enjoy the story, but more than that, they'll enjoy the way you use it to reinforce your message.

So...know who's coming to the party, use only the best ingredients, and third, focus on the main course. Every great meal has a great main course, a pièce de résistance. And every successful speech has a main focus, a central idea that listeners can take home. This is the concept that pulls the whole speech together and helps your audience remember your supporting points....

At the beginning of the speech writing process, many speakers aren't sure how to focus their messages. At this stage, it's important to ask, "If your audience remembered only one thing, what would you want it to be?" The answer is often a range of choices....

Having a focus not only helps tie the speech together, it helps answer what I consider to be the most important question in speech writing: "What should I leave out?" Usually the answer is, "Much - even most of the material I've found." If the idea or example doesn't support your main point in some way, drop it, no matter how fascinating it is. Save it for another speech.

This will help you keep the speech to 20 minutes or so. That's important, because most audiences begin losing concentration after that amount of time. If you're asked to speak for longer than that, find ways to break it up, perhaps with Q&A, slides, a video, or some kind of interactive exercise. Remember: a speech is like a meal. We can only eat so much at one sitting, and we can only hear so much at one sitting. Mark Twain said that few sinners are saved after the first 20 minutes of a sermon. That's true of just about any oral presentation. So keep it short.

Then you can think of the Q&A as a kind of dessert. Leave room for it, and time. You don't want your listeners to feel like that grand old lady who died during dinner. She was the sister of an 18th century French writer named Brillat-Savarin, and she expired at the table one night just before her 100th birthday. Her last words were, "Bring on the dessert. I think I'm about to die."

— excerpted from "Speeches That Satisfy"
Executive Speeches, June/July 1997

6   After reading the passage aloud once, say:

> You may take a few minutes to look over **The Situation** and your notes. (Pause) Now I will read the passage aloud a second time.

7   Read the passage a second time.

8   After the second reading, say:

> Now turn to page 4 of your examination booklet, read the directions, and answer the multiple-choice questions. Be sure to follow all the directions given in your examination booklet and your essay booklet. You may now begin.

SESSION ONE
PART A

Note: The actual Listening Passage referred to below is to be read aloud by a proctor (not to be read by the student taking the test). It is located on pages 227-230.

Overview: For this part of the test, you will listen to a speech about the struggle of women to obtain voting rights in England, answer some multiple-choice questions, and write a response based on the situation described below. You will hear the speech twice. You may take notes on separate paper anytime you wish during the readings.

> **The Situation:** For a social studies unit on the history of voting rights, your teacher has asked each student to prepare a report on an issue related to the struggle for voting rights in another country. You have decided to do your report on the social conditions that led women in England to seek the right to vote. In preparation for writing your report, listen to a speech delivered in 1908 by Emmeline Pankhurst. Then use relevant information from the speech to write your report.

Your Task: Write a report for your social studies class, in which you discuss the social conditions in England that led women there to seek the right to vote.

Guidelines:

Be sure to

- Tell your audience what they need to know about the social conditions in England that led women there to seek the right to vote

- Use specific, accurate, and relevant information from the speech to support your discussion

- Use a tone and level of language appropriate for a report for a social studies class

- Organize your ideas in a logical and coherent manner

- Indicate any words taken directly from the speech by using quotation marks and referring to the speaker

- Follow the conventions of standard written English

Multiple-Choice Questions

Directions (1–6): Use your notes to answer the following questions about the passage read to you. Select the best suggested answer and write its number in the space provided on the answer sheet. The questions may help you think about ideas and information you might use in your writing. You may return to these questions anytime you wish.

1   The speaker refers to "our forefathers who fought for the vote" in order to emphasize the
   (1) freedom of her ancestors
   (2) peaceful nature of women
   (3) value of the vote
   (4) responsibilities of citizens

2   The speaker suggests that, due to the marriage laws, married women lacked
   (1) emotional maturity   (3) intellectual challenge
   (2) financial security   (4) social acceptance

3   The speaker implies that, when a working woman married, she was expected to
   (1) choose a home   (3) design a budget
   (2) support her parents   (4) quit her job

4   When the speaker says, "the married woman's position is not a very secure one" and "no married woman exists as the mother of the child she brings into the world," the speaker is emphasizing the
   (1) limitations on women's rights
   (2) injustice of married men
   (3) scarcity of unmarried men
   (4) burdens of childless women

5   The quotation about "bright young girls expecting to get their living, and finding after their training is over that they can get nothing to do" is used to illustrate the
   (1) high rate of unemployment
   (2) unfairness of the marriage laws
   (3) poor quality of women's educations
   (4) inequity in hiring practices

6   According to the speaker, how is voting related to women's traditional duties in the home?
   (1) Voting should come second to those duties.
   (2) Voting requires sacrificing some of those duties.
   (3) Voting is an extension of those duties.
   (4) Voting will eventually eliminate those duties.

After you have finished these questions, review **The Situation** and read **Your Task** and the **Guidelines**. Use scrap paper to plan your response. Then write your response to Part A. After you finish your response for Part A, complete Part B.

PART B

Directions: Read the text and study the graphic on the following pages, answer the multiple-choice questions, and write a response based on the situation described below. You may use the margins to take notes as you read and scrap paper to plan your response.

> **The Situation:** As part of a schoolwide project on significant events of the 20th century, your environmental science class is publishing a class book on significant natural disasters that occurred during that period. For your contribution to the book, you have decided to write an essay about Hurricane Mitch and the conditions and effects that made that hurricane a significant natural disaster of the 20th century.

Your Task: Using relevant information from **both** documents, write an essay for a class book on natural disasters of the 20th century in which you describe the conditions and effects that made Hurricane Mitch a significant natural disaster of the 20th century.

Guidelines:

Be sure to

- Tell your audience what they need to know about the conditions and effects that made Hurricane Mitch a significant natural disaster of the 20th century

- Use specific, accurate, and relevant information from the article **and** the graphic to develop your essay

- Use a tone and level of language appropriate for an essay in a class book on significant natural disasters of the 20th century

- Organize your ideas in a logical and coherent manner

- Indicate any words taken directly from the text by using quotation marks or referring to the authors

- Follow the conventions of standard written English

Hurricane Mitch

On the morning of October 20, 1998, satellite images showed unorganized thunderstorm clusters developing over the southern Caribbean and northern Venezuela, which were associated with a weak tropical wave. As the clusters skirted the coast and headed west, meteorologists kept a vigilant eye. It was
5 late in the hurricane season, when the atmosphere-ocean system is primed for hurricane development over the southern Caribbean from tropical downpour-makers just like the ones drenching the South American coast that morning.

Thirty-six hours later, by the early morning of October 22, the clusters had become organized into a tropical depression. Before the day was out, Tropical
10 Storm Mitch was born, the 13th named storm of the season. Number 13 would be more than just unlucky for much of Central America—it was destined to become one of the strongest Atlantic hurricanes ever and one of the Western Hemisphere's greatest natural disasters of the 20th century....

The Monster's Path

Mitch intensified as it drifted north on the 23rd and 24th, slowed by an upper
15 level ridge of high pressure. A turn to the west on the 25th signaled a change: In the next 34 hours Mitch's central pressure would fall 1.77 inches (60 mb)[1], bottoming out at 26.73 inches (905 mb) and tying Hurricane Camille for the fourth-lowest central pressure ever recorded in an Atlantic hurricane. It reached Category 5 intensity at 7:00 am on October 26—and maintained that strength for
20 an amazing 33 hours....

For two days Mitch paralleled the north coast of Honduras as it continued to move slowly to the west. Feeder bands of thunderstorms repeatedly raked the coast and moved inland, dumping incredible amounts of rain over Honduras and Nicaragua. Onshore flow along the north coast of Honduras created waves 40 to
25 50 feet high. The already-torrential rain was enhanced as air was forced upwards by the highlands covering much of Honduras and Nicaragua.

Once onshore, Mitch meandered through the mountains of Honduras and continued to unload extreme amounts of rainfall. The water then cascaded down the steep slopes and was funneled into the narrow valleys, creating
30 unprecedented flooding. When the torrents exited the valleys along the north coast, mud-laden water spread over a wide area. In several locations banana plantation workers waited for two weeks on rooftops for the water to recede.

According to the National Climatic Data Center, estimated maximum total rainfall amounts over Honduras and Nicaragua ranged from 50 to 75 inches—and
35 in one report an incredible 25 inches fell in six hours! Most of the rain gauges were washed away so satellite data will have to be studied to fine-tune the estimates.

To make a desperate situation even worse, much of the steep terrain of Honduras and Nicaragua is covered with poorly consolidated volcanic soil.
40 Mudflows and landslides in this environment are deadly. In northwest Nicaragua, a mudslide traveled 13 miles down the slope of the Casitas Volcano, burying 10 communities. The death toll in this sparsely populated remote area is expected to reach 2,000....

---

[1]mb – millibars – a unit of atmospheric pressure

The Making of a Disaster

What turned Mitch into such a monster?

45   The most important ingredient in Mitch's recipe was very warm ocean water. The intense October sunshine made plenty available by heating most of the surface of the southern Caribbean Sea to nearly 86°F. The warm water quickly evaporated, yielding an unlimited supply of water vapor (high-octane hurricane fuel) to the atmosphere.

50   A second ingredient was a pre-existing surface disturbance that lifted this warm, moistened air, and, as the water vapor cooled and condensed, the energy captured from the sun was made available to the developing storm....

High above the evolving storm was a sprawling area of high pressure that provided two additional ingredients necessary for a monster hurricane: light
55 winds that allowed energy to be concentrated in the region and outflow aloft which supported the lift of the initial disturbance.

As Mitch rapidly strengthened north of Venezuela, a hurricane of epic proportions was born, which matured quickly and went on its deadly rampage.

Economic Impact

During the 1990s, the economies of many Central American countries were
60 finally getting on their feet after the civil unrest of the 1980s. At this critical stage, even a minor disturbance could cause an infant economic recovery to stumble and fall. Mitch would prove to be a powerful giant for both Honduras and Nicaragua to wrestle with, however, leaving each nation's economic system in ruins.

65   In Honduras, agriculture (mostly coffee and bananas) makes up 80 percent of all exports; as well, 60 percent of all jobs are due to agriculture. The figures are similar in Nicaragua. Banana growers estimate damage to the current crop is in the hundreds of millions of dollars and even worse, many of the young trees have been killed, making future yields questionable and putting jobs in jeopardy.
70 When the many Honduran "jornaleros" (day laborers) look out over the chaotic tangle of dead vegetation embedded in vast expanses of mud—which were once the productive north coast banana plantations—they have little hope of work in the near future.

Fortunately, the coffee crop was relatively unharmed. This was because cof-
75 fee grows high on the slopes, well above the elevation where hundreds of small streams combined to concentrate four days of extreme rainfall into killer rivers. However, the "beneficios" (coffee processing plants) are nearly idle, because many mountain roads have disappeared, making it practically impossible to transport the harvest....

80   Nicaragua offers an example of the magnitude of the economic problem. Gross Domestic Product (GDP) is the total value of goods and services that a country produces. Preliminary figures place the total damage in Nicaragua at $1.36 bil-

lion, or 67 percent of the GDP—a monumental figure for a weak economy to overcome. If a natural disaster in the United States caused damage amounting to 67
85 percent of our GDP, the bill would be a staggering $4.3 trillion. That is equivalent to 170 hurricane landfalls the magnitude of Andrew, the costliest natural disaster in United States history.

...[Mitch] brought Honduras and Nicaragua to a standstill, now wholly dependent on the generosity of the world for survival and eventual recovery.
90 Honduras estimates that Mitch wiped out 50 years of progress in four days. In the words of Edna Amador, general editor of La Prensa, San Pedro Sula, Honduras, "As you can see, the tragedy is bigger than anyone can imagine. No Honduran ever expected this to happen and now we are in God's hands."

— Mace Bentley and Steve Horstmeyer
excerpted from "Monstrous Mitch,"
Weatherwise, March/April 1999

GRAPHIC

Chart A			
Deadliest Atlantic Hurricanes			
Year	**Storm**	**Areas Hit**	**Deaths**
1780	"The Great Hurricane"	Martinique St. Eustatius Barbados	22,000
1998	Mitch	Honduras Nicaragua	9,000+
1900	"Great Galveston Hurricane"	Galveston Island	8,000
1974	Fifi	Honduras	8,000
1930	Number 2	Dominican Republic	8,000

Source: National Climatic Data Center

Chart B			
Most Intense Atlantic Hurricanes			
By Lowest Pressure			
Year	**Storm**	**Pressure**	**Duration of Category 5 Status**
1988	Gilbert	26.23"	18 hrs
1935	Florida Keys	26.34"	less than 6 hrs
1980	Allen	26.55"	24 hrs
1969	Camille	26.73"	24 hrs
1998	Mitch	26.73"	33 hrs
By Wind Speed			
Year	**Storm**	**Wind**	**Duration of Maximum Wind**
1969	Camille	195 mph	6 hrs
1980	Allen	195 mph	less than 6 hrs
1988	Gilbert	185 mph	12 hrs
1950	Dog	185 mph	12 hrs
1998	Mitch	180 mph	15 hrs

(adapted)

Multiple-Choice Questions

Directions (7–16): Select the best suggested answer to each question and write its number in the space provided on the answer sheet. The questions may help you think about ideas and information you might want to use in your writing. You may return to these questions anytime you wish.

7 According to the passage, the increase in severity of Tropical Storm Mitch was signaled by a movement from

   (1) low to high ocean waves
   (2) unclear to clear satellite images
   (3) unorganized to organized storm clusters
   (4) high to low atmospheric temperatures

8 Lines 14 through 20 suggest that one measure of a hurricane's strength is a decrease in

   (1) angle of direction
   (2) speed of wind
   (3) distance from the Equator
   (4) pressure at the center

9 Accurate measures of rainfall from the hurricane were difficult to determine due to the

   (1) lack of personnel
   (2) loss of equipment
   (3) time of day
   (4) position of satellites

10 In line 39, the phrase "poorly consolidated volcanic soil" refers to soil that is

   (1) loose   (3) fertile
   (2) wet   (4) gritty

11 In lines 48 and 49, "high-octane hurricane fuel" refers to

   (1) strong solar gases
   (2) complex surface disturbances
   (3) intense October sunshine
   (4) evaporated ocean water

12 Before Hurricane Mitch, the economy in Nicaragua and Honduras could best be described as

   (1) thriving   (3) chaotic
   (2) fragile   (4) fluctuating

13 In Honduras, coffee exports were reduced because the hurricane destroyed the

   (1) factories   (3) crops
   (2) ports   (4) roads

14 The information in Chart A implies that hurricanes are defined as "deadliest" in terms of

   (1) location of impact
   (2) year of occurrence
   (3) number of fatalities
   (4) frequency of occurrence

15 According to Chart A, what was the second deadliest hurricane on record?

   (1) Hurricane Mitch
   (2) the "Great Galveston Hurricane"
   (3) Hurricane Fifi
   (4) Hurricane Number 2

16 According to the information in Chart B, of the five most intense Atlantic hurricanes, Hurricane Mitch can be described as

   (1) having the fastest wind speed
   (2) maintaining Category 5 status the longest
   (3) having the highest pressure
   (4) lasting the shortest period of time

After you have finished these questions, review **The Situation** and read **Your Task** and the **Guidelines**. Use scrap paper to plan your response; then write your response in Part B.

HIGH SCHOOL EXAMINATION

COMPREHENSIVE EXAMINATION IN ENGLISH

SESSION ONE

January 2003

ANSWER SHEET

Session One – Essay A _____
Essay B _____

Session Two – Essay A _____
Essay B _____

Total Essay Score

Session One –
A–Multiple Choice _____
B–Multiple Choice _____

Session Two –
A–Multiple Choice _____

Total Multiple Choice

Final Score

Student . . . . Sex: ☐ Male ☐ Female

School . . . . Grade . . . . . . Teacher . . . .

Write your answers to the multiple-choice questions for Part A and Part B on this answer sheet.

Part A   ### Part B

1 _____   7 _____   12 _____
2 _____   8 _____   13 _____
3 _____   9 _____   14 _____
4 _____   10 _____   15 _____
5 _____   11 _____   16 _____
6 _____

HAND IN THIS ANSWER SHEET WITH YOUR ESSAY BOOKLET, SCRAP PAPER, AND EXAMINATION BOOKLET.

Your essay responses for Part A and Part B should be written in the essay booklet.

I do hereby affirm, at the close of this examination, that I had no unlawful knowledge of the questions or answers prior to the examination and that I have neither given nor received assistance in answering any of the questions during the examination.

_____
Signature

Session Two
Part A

Directions: Read the passages on the following pages (a poem and a myth). Write the number of the answer to each multiple-choice question on your answer sheet. Then write the essay as described in **Your Task**. You may use the margins to take notes as you read and scrap paper to plan your response.

Your Task:

> After you have read the passages and answered the multiple-choice questions, write a unified essay about the power of true friendship as revealed in the passages. In your essay, use ideas from **both** passages to establish a controlling idea about the power of true friendship. Using evidence from **each** passage, develop your controlling idea and show how the author uses specific literary elements or techniques to convey that idea.

Guidelines:
Be sure to

- Use ideas from **both** passages to establish a controlling idea about the power of true friendship

- Use specific and relevant evidence from **each** passage to develop your controlling idea

- Show how each author uses specific literary elements (for example: theme, characterization, structure, point of view) or techniques (for example: symbolism, irony, figurative language) to convey the controlling idea

- Organize your ideas in a logical and coherent manner

- Use language that communicates ideas effectively

- Follow the conventions of standard written English

Passage I

Ah, friend, let us be true
To one another! For the world which seems
To lie before us like a land of dreams,
So various, so beautiful, so new,
5   Hath really neither joy, nor love, nor light,
Nor certitude, nor peace, nor help for pain;
And we are here as on a darkling plain
Swept with confused alarms of struggle and flight,
Where ignorant armies clash by night.

— Matthew Arnold
from *The Book of Friendship*

Passage II

Damon and Pythias were two noble young men who lived on the island of Sicily in a city called Syracuse. They were such close companions and were so devoted to each other that all the people of the city admired them as the highest examples of true friendship. Each trusted the other so completely that nobody
5   could ever have persuaded one that the other had been unfaithful or dishonest, even if that had been the case.

Now it happened that Syracuse was, at that time, ruled by a famous tyrant named Dionysius, who had gained the throne for himself through treachery, and who from then on flaunted his power by behaving cruelly to his own subjects and
10   to all strangers and enemies who were so unfortunate as to fall into his clutches. This tyrant, Dionysius, was so unjustly cruel that once, when he awoke from a restless sleep during which he dreamt that a certain man in the town had attempted to kill him, he immediately had that man put to death.

It happened that Pythias had, quite unjustly, been accused by Dionysius of
15   trying to overthrow him, and for this supposed crime of treason Pythias was sentenced by the king to die. Try as he might, Pythias could not prove his innocence to the king's satisfaction, and so, all hope now lost, the noble youth asked only for a few days' freedom so that he could settle his business affairs and see to it that his relatives would be cared for after he was executed. Dionysius, the
20   hardhearted tyrant, however, would not believe Pythias's promise to return and would not allow him to leave unless he left behind him a hostage, someone who would be put to death in his place if he should fail to return within the stated time.

Pythias immediately thought of his friend Damon, and he unhesitatingly
25   sent for him in this hour of dire necessity, never thinking for a moment that his trusty companion would refuse his request. Nor did he, for Damon hastened straightaway to the palace—much to the amazement of King Dionysius—and gladly offered to be held hostage for his friend, in spite of the dangerous condition that had been attached to this favor. Therefore, Pythias was permitted to
30   settle his earthly affairs before departing to the Land of the Shades,[1] while Damon remained behind in the dungeon, the captive of the tyrant Dionysius.

After Pythias had been released, Dionysius asked Damon if he did not feel afraid, for Pythias might very well take advantage of the opportunity he had been given and simply not return at all, and then he, Damon, would be executed in his
35   place. But Damon replied at once with a willing smile: "There is no need for me to feel afraid, O King, since I have perfect faith in the word of my true friend, and I know that he will certainly return before the appointed time—unless, of course, he dies or is held captive by some evil force. Even so, even should the noble Pythias be captured and held against his will, it would be an honor for me to die
40   in his place."

Such devotion and perfect faith as this was unheard of to the friendless tyrant; still, though he could not help admiring the true nobility of his captive, he

---

1 **Land of the Shades:** Mythical place where people go when they die.

nevertheless determined that Damon should certainly be put to death should Pythias not return by the appointed time.

45 And, as the Fates would have it, by a strange turn of events, Pythias was detained far longer in his task than he had imagined. Though he never for a single minute intended to evade the sentence of death to which he had been so unjustly committed, Pythias met with several accidents and unavoidable delays. Now his time was running out and he had yet to overcome the many impediments that
50 had been placed in his path. At last he succeeded in clearing away all the hindrances, and he sped back the many miles to the palace of the king, his heart almost bursting with grief and fear that he might arrive too late.

Meanwhile, when the last day of the allotted time arrived, Dionysius commanded that the place of execution should be readied at once, since he was still
55 ruthlessly determined that if one of his victims escaped him, the other should not. And so, entering the chamber in which Damon was confined, he began to utter words of sarcastic pity for the "foolish faith," as he termed it, that the young man of Syracuse had in his friend.

In reply, however, Damon merely smiled, since, in spite of the fact that the
60 eleventh hour had already arrived, he still believed that his lifelong companion would not fail him. Even when, a short time later, he was actually led out to the site of his execution, his serenity remained the same.

Great excitement stirred the crowd that had gathered to witness the execution, for all the people had heard of the bargain that had been struck
65 between the two friends. There was much sobbing and cries of sympathy were heard all around as the captive was brought out, though he himself somehow retained complete composure even at this moment of darkest danger.

Presently the excitement grew more intense still as a swift runner could be seen approaching the palace courtyard at an astonishing speed, and wild shrieks
70 of relief and joy went up as Pythias, breathless and exhausted, rushed headlong through the crowd and flung himself into the arms of his beloved friend, sobbing with relief that he had, by the grace of the gods, arrived in time to save Damon's life.

This final exhibition of devoted love and faithfulness was more than even the
75 stony heart of Dionysius, the tyrant, could resist. As the throng of spectators melted into tears at the companions' embrace, the king approached the pair and declared that Pythias was hereby pardoned and his death sentence canceled. In addition, he begged the pair to allow him to become their friend, to try to be as much a friend to them both as they had shown each other to be.

80 Thus did the two friends of Syracuse, by the faithful love they bore to each other, conquer the hard heart of a tyrant king, and in the annals of true friendship there are no more honored names than those of Damon and Pythias—for no person can do more than be willing to lay down his life for the sake of his friend.

— retold by William F. Russell

Multiple-Choice Questions

Directions (1–10): Select the best suggested answer to each question and write its number in the space provided on the answer sheet. The questions may help you think about the ideas and information you might want to use in your essay. You may return to these questions anytime you wish.

Passage I (the poem) — Questions 1–4 refer to Passage I.

1 Which statement best expresses the idea found in lines 2 through 6?
(1) The world honors those who share love and light.
(2) The world is a beautiful and happy place.
(3) The world should guarantee peace to everyone.
(4) The world that promises so much has little to offer.

2 The "darkling plain" (line 7) most likely refers to a
(1) meadow (3) night sky
(2) battlefield (4) sports arena

3 In line 9, the narrator describes the armies as "ignorant" because
(1) the armies are composed of unskilled men
(2) the armies do not have an effective battle plan
(3) people have not learned to live together in peace
(4) people are uninformed about the effects of war

4 The tone of the poem can best be described as
(1) somber (3) bewildered
(2) hopeful (4) lively

Passage II (the myth) — Questions 5–10 refer to Passage II.

5 According to lines 1 through 6, the people of Syracuse viewed Damon and Pythias as
(1) saints (3) stereotypes
(2) kings (4) models

6 Which word from the text most accurately describes a tyrant?
(1) "famous" (line 7) (3) "cruel" (line 11)
(2) "unfortunate" (line 10) (4) "restless" (line 12)

7 According to the text, what was the cause of Dionysius' "amazement" (line 27)?
(1) Damon's refusal (3) Pythias' promise
(2) Damon's arrival (4) Pythias' innocence

8 According to lines 35 through 40, Damon considered dying for his friend to be an act of
(1) respect (3) desperation
(2) justice (4) foolishness

9 That which Dionysius called "foolish faith" (line 57), Damon would probably have called
(1) religion (3) uselessness
(2) loyalty (4) mischievousness

10 Dionysius was so impressed by "This final exhibition" (line 74) that he
(1) offered to die in Pythias's place
(2) burst into tears
(3) issued a proclamation
(4) released Pythias from captivity

After you have finished these questions, review **Your Task** and the **Guidelines**. Use scrap paper to plan your response. Then write your response to Part A. After you finish your response for Part A, complete Part B.

Part B

Your Task:

Write a critical essay in which you discuss *two* works of literature you have read from the particular perspective of the statement that is provided for you in the **Critical Lens**. In your essay, provide a valid interpretation of the statement, agree *or* disagree with the statement as you have interpreted it, and support your opinion using specific references to appropriate literary elements from the two works. You may use scrap paper to plan your response.

Critical Lens:

> All literature shows us the power of emotion. It is emotion, not reason, that motivates characters in literature.
>
> — paraphrased from an interview with Duff Brenna

Guidelines:

Be sure to

- Provide a valid interpretation of the critical lens that clearly establishes the criteria for analysis

- Indicate whether you agree *or* disagree with the statement as you have interpreted it

- Choose *two* works you have read that you believe best support your opinion

- Use the criteria suggested by the critical lens to analyze the works you have chosen

- Avoid plot summary. Instead, use specific references to appropriate literary elements (for example: theme, characterization, setting, point of view) to develop your analysis

- Organize your ideas in a unified and coherent manner

- Specify the titles and authors of the literature you choose

- Follow the conventions of standard written English

COMPREHENSIVE EXAMINATION IN ENGLISH

SESSION TWO

January 2003

ANSWER SHEET

Student . . . . Sex: Male   Female

School . . . . Grade . . . . . Teacher . . . .

Write your answers to the multiple-choice questions for Part A and Part B on this answer sheet.

Part A

1 _____   6 _____
2 _____   7 _____
3 _____   8 _____
4 _____   9 _____
5 _____   10 _____

HAND IN THIS ANSWER SHEET WITH YOUR ESSAY BOOKLET, SCRAP PAPER, AND EXAMINATION BOOKLET.

Your essay responses for Part A and Part B should be written in the essay booklet.

I do hereby affirm, at the close of this examination, that I had no unlawful knowledge of the questions or answers prior to the examination and that I have neither given nor received assistance in answering any of the questions during the examination.

_____

Signature

SESSION ONE – PART A

Note: The actual Listening Passage referred to below is to be read aloud by a proctor (not to be read by the student taking the test). It is located on pages 231-235.

Overview: For this part of the test, you will listen to a speech about effective speech writing, answer some multiple-choice questions, and write a response based on the situation described below. You will hear the speech twice. You may take notes on separate paper anytime you wish during the readings.

> **The Situation:** Your English class intends to publish a handbook for incoming freshmen, advising them on skills needed for high school. Your assignment is to write an article on techniques for effective speechwriting. In preparation for writing your article, listen to a speech by Jane Tully, a professional speechwriter. Then use relevant information from the speech to write your article.

Your Task: Write an article for a handbook for incoming freshmen in which you discuss techniques for effective speechwriting.

Guidelines:

Be sure to

- Tell your audience what they need to know about techniques for effective speechwriting

- Use specific, accurate, and relevant information from the speech to support your discussion

- Use a tone and level of language appropriate for an article for high school freshmen

- Organize your ideas in a logical and coherent manner

- Indicate any words taken directly from the speech by using quotation marks or referring to the speaker

- Follow the conventions of standard written English

Multiple-Choice Questions

Directions (1–6): Use your notes to answer the following questions about the passage read to you. Select the best suggested answer and write its number in the space provided on the answer sheet. The questions may help you think about ideas and information you might use in your writing. You may return to these questions anytime you wish.

1   According to the speaker, keeping listeners' attention is more difficult with a large audience than with a small audience because people in large groups
   (1) feel pressured by peers
   (2) feel unnoticed
   (3) cannot hear the speaker clearly
   (4) cannot see the speaker

2   According to the speaker, knowing the age range of the audience would be helpful to a speechwriter in
   (1) selecting support materials
   (2) finding a topic
   (3) choosing a setting
   (4) predicting the number of participants

3   The speaker expresses concern about the use of the "food image" to illustrate the importance of choosing stories according to an audience's
   (1) size   (3) gender
   (2) location   (4) age

4   As an example of her advice to speechwriters to "use only the best ingredients," the speaker recommends that speeches include
   (1) sophisticated vocabulary
   (2) an unusual fact
   (3) foreign phrases
   (4) a generally accepted theory

5   According to the speaker, the speechwriter's main purpose in using appealing quotations and stories is to
   (1) add historical accuracy
   (2) provide comic relief
   (3) improve the speaker's credibility
   (4) help the audience remember ideas

6   By asking the question, "If your audience remembered only one thing, what would you want it to be?" a speechwriter can establish
   (1) an intriguing opening
   (2) a strong ending
   (3) a main idea
   (4) an organizing principle

After you have finished these questions, review **The Situation** and read **Your Task** and the **Guidelines**. Use scrap paper to plan your response. Then write your response to Part A. After you finish your response for Part A, complete Part B.

PART B

Directions: Read the text and study the graphic on the following pages, answer the multiple-choice questions, and write a response based on the situation described below. You may use the margins to take notes as you read and scrap paper to plan your response.

> **The Situation:** As part of a social studies unit on contemporary issues, your class is preparing a panel discussion on the topic "Forest fires: What are the best ways to deal with them?" In preparing for the panel discussion, your teacher has asked you to write an essay in which you discuss the practices that lead to forest fires and recommend ways to deal with forest fires.

Your Task: Using relevant information from **both** documents, write an essay in which you discuss the practices that lead to forest fires and recommend ways to deal with forest fires.

Guidelines:

Be sure to

- Tell your audience what they need to know about forest fires and the practices that lead to forest fires

- Recommend ways to deal with forest fires

- Use specific, accurate, and relevant information from the text **and** the graphic to develop your discussion

- Use a tone and level of language appropriate for an essay for your social studies class

- Organize your ideas in a logical and coherent manner

- Indicate any words taken directly from the text by using quotation marks or referring to the author

- Follow the conventions of standard written English

Text

Ninety years ago today, in the choking heat of a summer without rain in the northern Rockies, the sun disappeared from the sky and a sound not unlike cannon fire began rattling throughout Montana and Idaho. The Big Burn, as the three-million-acre firestorm of 1910 was called, eventually consumed entire
5 towns, killed 87 people and burned a lesson into the fledgling United States Forest Service.

Thereafter, the service vowed, it would snuff out every fire, at one point swearing to do so by 10 a.m. on the day after the fire started. The best-known forester of that time, Gifford Pinchot, equated wildfire with slavery as a historic
10 scourge of the nation. Another, Bernhard Fernow, blamed "bad habits and loose morals" for the fires.

Now, in the midst of the worst wildfire year in nearly half a century, a new round of finger-pointing is under way. Touring Montana last week, J. Dennis Hastert, the speaker of the House, blamed the Clinton administration for not
15 logging the tinder-dry forests. Environmentalists pointed at the timber industry and development for altering forest ecology and creating an artificial landscape ripe for catastrophe.

But the Forest Service remains focused on its own primary culprit: the symbol of fire eradication, Smokey Bear.

20 The era of prevention and suppression represented by Smokey and his shovel may have been good for safety, but it was not the best thing for forests. The agency had reached that conclusion even before the additional evidence foresters drew from the fires that tore through almost half of Yellowstone National Park in 1988.

25 Fire is as much a part of nature as creeks and wildflowers. Most forests have a natural cycle, in which a purging burn comes through every 10, 20, 50 or 100 years. The cycle may be suppressed, foresters say, but only at the cost of more powerful fires when it re-emerges.

"We have a problem when people say these fires are destroying all these areas,"
30 said Mr. Wiebe, the former Smokejumper. "It's just not correct to say a forest is destroyed by fire."

During the decades when fires were routinely suppressed, forests choked themselves with excess growth, creating better habitats for tree-killing insects. The dying trees became tinder.

35 "These forests are long overdue," said Mick Harrington, a research fire ecologist with the Forest Service in Montana, a state that has just been declared a disaster area. "They were just ready to go."

The fires that have already run through five million acres this year are hotter, faster-burning, more ferocious than any burns of modern times, the people
40 battling them say. And a number of reports say future fire seasons may be worse,

identifying about 40 million acres of public land as being at risk of catastrophic fire.

Fire suppression is only part of the problem. In some forests, experts say, logging has removed the biggest and most fire-resistant trees. Their replacements 45 — some planted, some natural — are crowded stands of young and disease-prone trees, with 500 or more to the acre, where there used to be 50. Foresters also point to other elements — excessive grazing by cattle and sheep, diversion of rivers to newly developing areas — that have contributed to what some call ghost forests, spectral stands of diseased and dying timber now baking, if not yet 50 burning, in the August sun.

In addition, there are many new areas demanding fire protection. Homes and vacation cottages that have sprung up at the edge of national forest boundaries have become firefighters' front lines.

"We've become so good at putting out fires because that's what the public 55 wants," said Lindon Wiebe, a fire ecology specialist with the Forest Service in Washington, and a former Smokejumper, as the service's firefighters are called. "But what we can do is pretty small compared to what Mother Nature wants to do."

Just as people have gradually learned not to build homes in areas prone to 60 flooding, they need to understand the danger of erecting structures in fire zones, says Dr. Phil Omi, a professor of forest fire science at Colorado State University and director of the Western Forest Fire Research Center.

"Somebody has got to get the message to these people that they are putting themselves at risk, whether it's the insurance industry or the government," Dr. 65 Omi said. But he said he could not blame the Forest Service, or homeowners, for being slow to understand the nature of wild fire in the West. "Our understanding of forest fire ecology is relatively new," he said.

Those trying to address the future fire threat are focusing on two solutions: taking out more trees by logging or thinning, and deliberately setting fires.

70 Under Mr. Clinton, logging in national forests has declined by nearly 75 percent, and some critics blame this decline for the explosive fires. A number of Western senators back the idea of allowing the timber industry to remove more trees.

However, environmental groups point out that the biggest fires in 75 Montana and Idaho are burning not in wilderness areas, but in land that has been developed or logged. Such areas also account for 90 percent of the acreage identified as most vulnerable to wildfire, the Forest Service says.

"Commercial logging is not a prescription for forest health — it is one of the major causes of unhealthy forest conditions," said Thomas Powers, chairman of 80 the economics department at the University of Montana, whose specialty is natural resource issues.

The other solution — planned fire — has become a public relations debacle. Last year, a record 1.4 million acres of Forest Service land was deliberately burned. Most prescribed burns go off without trouble. But it only takes one to
85 stir public ire. And this year, the one that got away, a 43,000-acre blaze set by the National Park Service near Los Alamos, N.M., destroyed more than 200 homes.

And no matter how convinced the experts are that Los Alamos was an exception, the fires now raging in every state of the West look horrific on television, blackening national treasures like Mesa Verde National Park and
90 raining embers on popular campgrounds.

— Timothy Egan
"Why Foresters Prefer to Fight Fire with Fire"
The New York Times, August 20, 2000

Common Practices Contributing to Forest Fires

Hazardous Homes

Building a home in or near the edge of forest land brings the risk of fire, but many homeowners and builders fail to take simple precautions that could reduce damage.

Logging and Clear-Cutting

In many areas, logging removed the oldest, most fire-resistant trees. The smaller, denser tree stands that grew in their absence burn more easily. Logging can also leave behind debris that acts as kindling for wildfires.

Water Diversion

Diverting the natural waterways to serve growing communities can also change the ecology of surrounding forests, leaving them dry and undernourished. Also, rivers that once served as natural barriers to fast-moving wildfires have been narrowed, enabling flames to leap to neighboring groups of trees easily.

Fire Suppression

Development in general led to a consistent policy of stifling fires, but this inhibited the natural process of burning and allowed stands of fire-prone trees to grow.

Grazing

The growth of cattle raising throughout the 19th and 20th centuries reduced grasslands, which fuel natural forest fires and keep the flames low to the ground.

Roofing

Metal, tile and fiberglass are best; common materials like asphalt shingles and tar paper are more flammable.

Outer Walls

Although it seems natural to build a forest home of wood, the danger is obvious. Stone, brick and metal are best.

Air Pockets

An open foundation and raised decks can stoke flames as they pass through. Storing fuel tanks in these areas is particularly dangerous.

Building on Slopes

Although a hillside may offer the best views, slopes create a natural chimney for advancing flames.

Sources: National Forest Service; Great Lakes Forest Fire Compact; and Tom Zeller and John Papasian / *The New York Times* (adapted and taken from a larger set of graphics that accompanied the article)

Multiple-Choice Questions

Directions (7–16): Select the best suggested answer to each question and write its number in the space provided on the answer sheet. The questions may help you think about ideas and information you might want to use in your writing. You may return to these questions anytime you wish.

7   According to the author, one result of the Big Burn in 1910 was that the Forest Service adopted a policy of
   (1) gradually removing dead trees from dry areas
   (2) quickly extinguishing all fires
   (3) routinely setting small, controlled fires
   (4) occasionally thinning out healthy trees

8   As used in line 26, "purging" most nearly means
   (1) cleansing   (3) alarming
   (2) damaging   (4) frightening

9   In saying that it is "not correct to say a forest is destroyed by fire" (lines 30 and 31), Mr. Wiebe implies that
   (1) most fires could be prevented
   (2) fire is less destructive than smoke
   (3) few forest animals are harmed by fire
   (4) some fires should be allowed to burn

10 The author implies that one result of the practice of suppressing forest fires is that, eventually,
   (1) trees become more resistant to fire
   (2) the public loses interest in fire prevention
   (3) forest fires do more damage
   (4) more fires occur outside of forests

11 Lindon Wiebe's comment that "what we can do is pretty small compared to what Mother Nature wants to do" (lines 57 and 58) emphasizes the capacity of nature to
   (1) inspire   (3) confuse
   (2) adapt   (4) destroy

12 What question is at the center of the disagreement about logging?
   (1) How can logging national forests be made less difficult?
   (2) How can data about logging and forests be made more reliable?
   (3) What is the effect of logging on the health of forests?
   (4) Who should pay for the logging of the national forests?

13 The author implies that the primary purpose of prescribed burns is to
   (1) remove excess growth
   (2) train firefighters
   (3) educate the public
   (4) research forest ecology

14 The irrigation system shown at the right of the graphic is an illustration of what practice?
    (1) removing the oldest trees
    (2) diverting natural waterways
    (3) stifling fires
    (4) raising cattle

15 According to the graphic, houses in forests can be made somewhat safer if builders
    (1) cover roofs with asphalt shingles
    (2) use small logs for outer walls
    (3) enclose areas under the houses
    (4) situate houses on slopes

16 All of the practices on the graphic are closely related to
    (1) slowing economy
    (2) changing climate
    (3) decreasing population
    (4) increasing development

After you have finished these questions, review **The Situation** and read **Your Task** and the **Guidelines**. Use scrap paper to plan your response. Then write your response in Part B.

The University of the State of New York

REGENTS HIGH SCHOOL EXAMINATION

COMPREHENSIVE EXAMINATION IN ENGLISH

SESSION ONE

June 2003

ANSWER SHEET

Session One – Essay A _____

Essay B _____

Session Two – Essay A _____

Essay B _____

Total Essay Score ☐

Session One –

A–Multiple Choice _____

B–Multiple Choice _____

Session Two –

A–Multiple Choice _____

Total Multiple Choice ☐

Final Score ☐

Student . . . . Sex: ☐ Male ☐ Female

School . . . . Grade . . . . . . Teacher . . . .

Write your answers to the multiple-choice questions for Part A and Part B on this answer sheet.

Part A

1 _____
2 _____
3 _____
4 _____
5 _____
6 _____

Part B

7 _____
8 _____
9 _____
10 _____
11 _____

12 _____
13 _____
14 _____
15 _____
16 _____

HAND IN THIS ANSWER SHEET WITH YOUR ESSAY BOOKLET, SCRAP PAPER, AND EXAMINATION BOOKLET.

Your essay responses for Part A and Part B should be written in the essay booklet.

I do hereby affirm, at the close of this examination, that I had no unlawful knowledge of the questions or answers prior to the examination and that I have neither given nor received assistance in answering any of the questions during the examination.

_____

Signature

SESSION TWO – PART A

Directions: Read the passages on the following pages (a poem and an essay). Write the number of the answer to each multiple-choice question on your answer sheet. Then write the essay in your essay booklet as described in **Your Task**. You may use the margins to take notes as you read and scrap paper to plan your response.

Your Task:

> After you have read the passages and answered the multiple-choice questions, write a unified essay about lessons from childhood as revealed in the passages. In your essay, use ideas from *both* passages to establish a controlling idea about lessons from childhood. Using evidence from *each* passage, develop your controlling idea and show how the author uses specific literary elements or techniques to convey that idea.

Guidelines:

Be sure to
- Use ideas from *both* passages to establish a controlling idea about lessons from childhood
- Use specific and relevant evidence from *each* passage to develop your controlling idea
- Show how each author uses specific literary elements (for example: theme, characterization, structure, point of view) or techniques (for example: symbolism, irony, figurative language) to convey the controlling idea
- Organize your ideas in a logical and coherent manner
- Use language that communicates ideas effectively
- Follow the conventions of standard written English

Passage I
The Thing You Must Remember

The thing you must remember is how, as a child,
you worked hours in the art room, the teacher's
hands over yours, molding the little clay dog.
You must remember, how nothing mattered
5   but the imagined dog's fur, the shape of his ears
and his paws. The gray clay felt dangerous,
your small hands were pressing what you couldn't
say with your limited words. When the dog's back
stiffened, then cracked to white shards
10   in the kiln, you learned how the beautiful
suffers from too much attention, how clumsy
a single vision can grow, and fragile
with trying too hard. The thing you must
remember is the art teacher's capable
15   hands: large, rough and grainy,
over yours, holding on.

—Maggie Anderson from Windfall, 2000
University of Pittsburgh Press

Passage II

She was only about five feet tall and probably never weighed more than 110 pounds, but Miss Bessie was a towering presence in the classroom. She was the only woman tough enough to make me read *Beowulf* and think for a few foolish days that I liked it. From 1938 to 1942, when I attended Bernard High School in
5 McMinnville, Tenn., she taught me English, history, civics—and a lot more than I realized.

I shall never forget the day she scolded me into reading *Beowulf*.

"But Miss Bessie," I complained, "I ain't much interested in it."

Her large brown eyes became daggerish slits. "Boy," she said, "how dare you
10 say 'ain't' to me! I've taught you better than that."

"Miss Bessie," I pleaded, "I'm trying to make first-string end on the football team, and if I go around saying 'it isn't' and 'they aren't,' the guys are gonna laugh me off the squad."

"Boy," she responded, "you'll play football because you have guts. But do you
15 know what *really* takes guts? Refusing to lower your standards to those of the crowd. It takes guts to say you've got to live and be somebody fifty years after all the football games are over."

I started saying "it isn't" and "they aren't," and I still made first-string end— and class valedictorian—without losing my buddies' respect.

20 During her remarkable 44-year career, Mrs. Bessie Taylor Gwynn taught hundreds of economically deprived black youngsters—including my mother, my brother, my sisters and me. I remember her now with gratitude and affection— especially in this era when Americans are so wrought-up about a "rising tide of mediocrity" in public education and the problems of finding competent, caring
25 teachers. Miss Bessie was an example of an informed, dedicated teacher, a blessing to children and an asset to the nation.

Born in 1895, in poverty, she grew up in Athens, Ala., where there was no public school for blacks. She attended Trinity School, a private institution for blacks run by the American Missionary Association, and in 1911 graduated from
30 the Normal School (a "super" high school) at Fisk University in Nashville. Mrs. Gwynn, the essence of pride and privacy, never talked about her years in Athens; only in the months before her death did she reveal that she had never attended Fisk University itself because she could not afford the four-year course.

At Normal School she learned a lot about Shakespeare, but most of all about
35 the profound importance of education—especially, for a people trying to move up from slavery. "What you put in your head, boy," she once said, "can never be pulled out by the Ku Klux Klan, the Congress or anybody."

Miss Bessie's bearing of dignity told anyone who met her that she was "educated" in the best sense of the word. There was never a discipline problem
40 in her classes. We didn't dare mess with a woman who knew about the Battle of Hastings, the Magna Charta and the Bill of Rights—and who could also play the piano.

This frail-looking woman could make sense of Shakespeare, Milton, Voltaire, and bring to life Booker T. Washington and W. E. B. DuBois. Believing that it was important to know who the officials were that spent taxpayers' money and made public policy, she made us memorize the names of everyone on the Supreme Court and in the President's Cabinet. It could be embarrassing to be unprepared when Miss Bessie said, "Get up and tell the class who Frances Perkins is and what you think about her."

Miss Bessie knew that my family, like so many others during the Depression, couldn't afford to subscribe to a newspaper. She knew we didn't even own a radio. Still, she prodded me to "look out for your future and find some way to keep up with what's going on in the world." So I became a delivery boy for the Chattanooga *Times*. I rarely made a dollar a week, but I got to read a newspaper every day.

Miss Bessie noticed things that had nothing to do with schoolwork, but were vital to a youngster's development. Once a few classmates made fun of my frayed, hand-me-down overcoat, calling me "Strings." As I was leaving school, Miss Bessie patted me on the back of that old overcoat and said, "Carl, never fret about what you *don't* have. Just make the most of what you *do* have—a brain."

Among the things that I did not have was electricity in the little frame house that my father had built for $400 with his World War I bonus. But because of her inspiration, I spent many hours squinting beside a kerosene lamp reading Shakespeare and Thoreau, Samuel Pepys and William Cullen Bryant.

No one in my family had ever graduated from high school, so there was no tradition of commitment to learning for me to lean on. Like millions of youngsters in today's ghettos and barrios, I needed the push and stimulation of a teacher who truly cared. Miss Bessie gave plenty of both, as she immersed me in a wonderful world of similes, metaphors and even onomatopoeia. She led me to believe that I could write sonnets as well as Shakespeare, or iambic-pentameter verse to put Alexander Pope to shame.

In those days the McMinnville school system was rigidly "Jim Crow," and poor black children had to struggle to put anything in their heads. Our high school was only slightly larger than the once-typical little red schoolhouse, and its library was outrageously inadequate—so small, I like to say, that if two students were in it and one wanted to turn a page, the other one had to step outside.

Negroes, as we were called then, were not allowed in the town library, except to mop floors or dust tables. But through one of those secret Old South arrangements between whites of conscience and blacks of stature, Miss Bessie kept getting books smuggled out of the white library. That is how she introduced me to the Brontës, Byron, Coleridge, Keats and Tennyson. "If you don't read, you can't write, and if you can't write, you might as well stop dreaming," Miss Bessie once told me.

So I read whatever Miss Bessie told me to, and tried to remember the things she insisted that I store away. Forty-five years later, I can still recite her "truths to live by," such as Henry Wadsworth Longfellow's lines from "The Ladder of St.

Augustine":

> The heights by great men reached and kept
> Were not attained by sudden flight,
90   But they, while their companions slept,
> Were toiling upward in the night.

Years later, her inspiration, prodding, anger, cajoling and almost osmotic infusion of learning finally led to that lovely day when Miss Bessie dropped me a note saying, "I'm so proud to read your column in the Nashville *Tennessean.*"

95   Miss Bessie was a spry 80 when I went back to McMinnville and visited her in a senior citizens' apartment building. Pointing out proudly that her building was racially integrated, she reached for two glasses and a pint of bourbon. I was momentarily shocked, because it would have been scandalous in the 1930s and '40s for word to get out that a teacher drank, and nobody had ever raised a rumor 100 that Miss Bessie did.

I felt a new sense of equality as she lifted her glass to mine. Then she revealed a softness and compassion that I had never known as a student.

"I've never forgotten that examination day," she said, "when Buster Martin held up seven fingers, obviously asking you for help with question number seven, 105 'Name a common carrier.' I can still picture you looking at your exam paper and humming a few bars of 'Chattanooga Choo Choo.' I was so tickled, I couldn't punish either of you."

Miss Bessie was telling me, with bourbon-laced grace, that I never fooled her for a moment.

110   When Miss Bessie died in 1980, at age 85, hundreds of her former students mourned. They knew the measure of a great teacher: love and motivation. Her wisdom and influence had rippled out across generations.

Some of her students who might normally have been doomed to poverty went on to become doctors, dentists and college professors. Many, guided by 115 Miss Bessie's example, became public-school teachers.

"The memory of Miss Bessie and how she conducted her classroom did more for me than anything I learned in college," recalls Gladys Wood of Knoxville, Tenn., a highly respected English teacher who spent 43 years in the state's school system. "So many times, when I faced a difficult classroom problem, I asked 120 myself, *How would Miss Bessie deal with this*? And I'd remember that she would handle it with laughter and love."

No child can get all the necessary support at home, and millions of poor children get *no* support at all. That is what makes a wise, educated, warm-hearted teacher like Miss Bessie so vital to the minds, hearts and souls of this country's 125 children.

> — Carl T. Rowan
> "Unforgettable Miss Bessie"
> from *Reader's Digest*, March 1985

Multiple-Choice Questions

Directions (1–10): Select the best suggested answer to each question and write its number in the space provided on the answer sheet. The questions may help you think about the ideas and information you might want to use in your essay. You may return to these questions anytime you wish.

Passage I (the poem) — Questions 1–5 refer to Passage I.

1   In line 4, the words "how nothing mattered" help to emphasize the child's
   (1) fear   (3) indifference
   (2) memory   (4) concentration

2   The description in lines 6 through 8 conveys the child's feeling of
   (1) anxiety   (3) importance
   (2) control   (4) resentment

3   According to the poem, what is most likely the "thing you must remember"?
   (1) the broken dog
   (2) the hard work
   (3) the teacher's support
   (4) the clay's texture

4   The tone of the poem is best described as
   (1) bitter   (3) ironic
   (2) reflective   (4) lively

5   What aspect of the poet's craft suggests that the child and the speaker are the same person?
   (1) the narrative point of view
   (2) the simple words
   (3) the blank verse
   (4) the irregular line lengths

Passage II (the essay) — Questions 6–10 refer to Passage II.

6   Miss Bessie's remarks about learning correct grammar (lines 7 through 17) stress the importance of
   (1) participating in sports
   (2) avoiding peer pressure
   (3) reading classical literature
   (4) enforcing team spirit

7   In lines 44 through 55, the author's references to memorization and reading the newspaper serve to emphasize Miss Bessie's desire that her students be
   (1) financially independent
   (2) socially adept
   (3) emotionally stable
   (4) politically aware

8   The author's references to the world of poetry (lines 66 through 71) have the effect of stressing Miss Bessie's power to
     (1) instill confidence
     (2) encourage dependence
     (3) predict events
     (4) discourage imitation

9   Miss Bessie most likely recommended that her students remember Longfellow's verse to illustrate the value of
     (1) spiritual discipline   (3) hard work
     (2) regular rest   (4) heroic behavior

10   The author most likely includes the quotation from Gladys Wood (lines 119 through 121) to emphasize the extent of
     (1) the author's grief
     (2) Miss Bessie's influence
     (3) the student's disobedience
     (4) Gladys Wood's success

After you have finished these questions, review **Your Task** and the **Guidelines**. Use scrap paper to plan your response. Then write your response to Part A. After you finish your response for Part A, complete Part B.

PART B

Your Task:

Write a critical essay in which you discuss *two* works of literature you have read from the particular perspective of the statement that is provided for you in the **Critical Lens**. In your essay, provide a valid interpretation of the statement, agree *or* disagree with the statement as you have interpreted it, and support your opinion using specific references to appropriate literary elements from the two works. You may use scrap paper to plan your response. Write your essay in Part B.

Critical Lens:

> "Good people ... are good because they've come to wisdom through failure."
>
> —William Saroyan as quoted in
> "Room for Hate—and Hope"
> from *New York Journal-American*,
> August 23, 1961

Guidelines:

Be sure to

- Provide a valid interpretation of the critical lens that clearly establishes the criteria for analysis

- Indicate whether you agree *or* disagree with the statement as you have interpreted it

- Choose *two* works you have read that you believe best support your opinion

- Use the criteria suggested by the critical lens to analyze the works you have chosen

- Avoid plot summary. Instead, use specific references to appropriate literary elements (for example: theme, characterization, setting, point of view) to develop your analysis

- Organize your ideas in a unified and coherent manner

- Specify the titles and authors of the literature you choose

- Follow the conventions of standard written English

REGENTS HIGH SCHOOL EXAMINATION

COMPREHENSIVE EXAMINATION IN ENGLISH

SESSION TWO

June 2003

ANSWER SHEET

Student . . . . Sex: Male   Female

School . . . . Grade . . . . . . Teacher . . . .

Write your answers to the multiple-choice questions for Part A and Part B on this answer sheet.

Part A

1 _____		6 _____
2 _____		7 _____
3 _____		8 _____
4 _____		9 _____
5 _____		10 _____

HAND IN THIS ANSWER SHEET WITH YOUR ESSAY BOOKLET, SCRAP PAPER, AND EXAMINATION BOOKLET.

Your essay responses for Part A and Part B should be written in the essay booklet.

I do hereby affirm, at the close of this examination, that I had no unlawful knowledge of the questions or answers prior to the examination and that I have neither given nor received assistance in answering any of the questions during the examination.

_____

Signature